NEW PROCLAMATION
COMMENTARY ON FEASTS,
HOLY DAYS, AND OTHER CELEBRATIONS

NEW PROCLAMATION COMMENTARY ON FEASTS,

HOLY DAYS, AND OTHER CELEBRATIONS

WILLIAM F. BROSEND II
BILL DOGGETT
GORDON W. LATHROP
JENNIFER L. LORD
RUTH A. MEYERS
GAIL RAMSHAW
CRAIG A. SATTERLEE
GERARD S. SLOYAN

DAVID B. LOTT, EDITOR

FORTRESS PRESS
MINNEAPOLIS

NEW PROCLAMATION COMMENTARY ON FEASTS, HOLY DAYS,
AND OTHER CELEBRATIONS

Library of Congress Cataloging-in-Publication Data
New proclamation commentary on feasts : Holy Days and other celebrations / William F. Brosend II, ... [et al.] ; David B. Lott, editor.
        p. cm. -- (New proclamation)
    ISBN 978-0-8006-6228-8 (alk. paper)
    1. Fasts and feasts. I. Brosend, William F. (William Frank), 1954– II. Lott, David B.
    BV30.N49 2007
    263'.9--dc22   2007036674

Manufactured in the U.S.A.
    11   10   09   08   07   1   2   3   4   5   6   7   8   9   10

CONTENTS

PART TWO
NATIONAL DAYS AND
OTHER CELEBRATIONS
Jennifer L. Lord

PREFACE

New Proclamation Commentary on Feasts: Holy Days and Other Celebrations represents the first volume of lectionary aids on the lesser festivals of the church year that Fortress Press has offered in over twenty years. When Fortress first introduced the *Proclamation* lectionary aids series in the mid-1970s, a set of volumes focused on these so-called lesser festivals was included into each three-year cycle, a practice discontinued in the late 1980s. Since that time, *Proclamation* has been succeeded by *New Proclamation*, the major lectionary traditions have gone through some significant alterations, and most of the mainline Protestant traditions—including most recently the Episcopal Church—have adopted the Revised Common Lectionary. Given these factors, as well as other changes in the church scene in the past couple of decades, including the 2006 launch of our related lectionary preaching Web site www.NewProclamation.com, the time seemed right to renew this old practice. Thus we are proud to issue this all-new volume of lectionary commentary aids on the lesser festivals and other church celebrations.

New *Proclamation Commentary on Feasts* continues the tradition of excellent biblical commentary that users of the seasonal *New Proclamation* volumes have come to expect. Yet because of the nature of the lesser festivals and how they are celebrated in the life of the church, this volume also differs in significant ways from those seasonal volumes. First, each saint's day or festival provides some essential background about what or who is being celebrated and places the day into the context of the church year. Second, quotes related to the festival day from prayers, liturgies, and other sources have been included to help enliven the sermon and enhance worship. Third, since the biblical commentary is necessarily brief in order to accommodate this essential information, each chapter includes information as to where one might find additional textual commentary from the Revised Common Lectionary in the seasonal volumes of *New Proclamation*. Fourth, even as the Sunday lectionary holds priority over the assigned lessons for the festival, this volume's contributors provide insights into how the saints and occasions being commemorated might be incorporated into that larger context. Yet users should also note that the Revised Common Lectionary holds that a handful of festivals may supercede the Sunday observance, including these that are included in the present volume: Presentation of the Lord; Nativity of John; St. Peter and St. Paul; Transfiguration (August 6); Mary, Mother of the Lord; Holy Cross; and St. Michael and All Angels.

Like the seasonal volumes of *New Proclamation*, this volume is designed for users of the primary lectionary traditions: the Revised Common Lectionary (RCL), the Episcopal (*Book of Common Prayer*) lectionary (BCP), and the Roman Catholic *Lectionary for the Mass* (LFM). It must be noted, however, that the RCL assigns lessons for almost none of these lesser festivals; only the Presentation of the Lord (February 2) and Holy Cross Day are included in that lectionary's listings. For most of the saints' and festival days, therefore, the assigned readings from *Evangelical Lutheran Worship* (ELW) are included as suggested primary readings for most mainline Protestant users; the names of the days as listed in the ELW are also given priority. Moreover, even though the Episcopal Church is in transition to the RCL, the assigned readings from the BCP lectionary are included as well.

The festivals in part 1 of the book, "Saints' Days, Solemnities, and Other Feast Days in the Church," are ordered according to their appearance in the church year (with those days with floating dates listed according to their earliest possible occurrence). Readers will also note that the various traditions occasionally celebrate the same feast on different days—for instance, the saint days of Philip and James, Matthias, and Thomas, as well as the Confession of St. Peter. In those cases, the date as it appears in the ELW is given priority. Exclusively Roman Catholic feasts are included in this primary listing as well.

Major festivals of the church year that occur in all three lectionary traditions, including the Nativity of Our Lord, The Name of Christ (January 1), Epiphany, The Baptism of Our Lord, Ash Wednesday, Palm Sunday, the Triduum, Easter, Ascension, Pentecost, The Holy Trinity, and Reign of Christ, continue to be included in the regular seasonal volumes of *New Proclamation*, as does the national holiday of Thanksgiving. However, the August 6 feast of the Transfiguration (from the Episcopal and Roman Catholic traditions) and Reformation Day (celebrated mostly in Lutheran churches), previously included in the seasonal volumes, have been moved to this book. The feast of St. James of Jerusalem (October 23), celebrated only in the Episcopal Church, is not included here, nor is the Roman Catholic feast commemorating the Dedication of the Lateran Basilica (November 9).

Part 2 of this book, "National Days and Other Celebrations," provides suggested lessons and preaching strategies for incorporating these nonliturgical days and commemorations into the life of the church. Here Presbyterian homiletician and liturgist Jennifer L. Lord provides wise counsel on how preachers may address these occasions in ways that place priority on the gospel rather than straying over the church/state divide. These days are listed in order of their occurrence in the Roman calendar, beginning with January 1. Two celebrations, Harvest and Peace, go dateless and may be celebrated according to the congregation's preference.

Users of this volume will want to spend time first with liturgist Gordon Lathrop's marvelous introduction, which begins by helping us to contemplate the very nature of festival, and closes with a helpful list of ideas on how these festivals may be faithfully and powerfully incorporated into the life of the church. Since Protestant and Roman Catholic traditions have differing theological understandings of the role of Mary, those traditions that celebrate the feast days that focus on her (especially the Annunciation, the Visitation, the Assumption, and the Nativity of Mary) may do so in strikingly different ways. For that reason, in addition to the commentaries on those feast days by Catholic biblical scholar Gerard Sloyan and Episcopal homiletician Bill Brosend, Father Sloyan has written a brief, thoughtful essay outlining the emergence of the Mary feasts and their special significance in both traditions.

Those four writers, along with our other contributors, Lutherans Gail Ramshaw and Craig A. Satterlee and Episcopalians Ruth A. Meyers and Bill Doggett, represent some of the best thinkers in preaching and liturgy today. Each one brings her or his unique voice and talents to their assigned festivals, yet readers will undoubtedly notice a real unity of quality and perspective to their contributions as well. I began to create this project in early 2006 out of the conviction that it needed to be done, but admittedly with little real background in these lesser festivals. Thus, even as they had to give me periodic gentle correction and good-humored admonishment as we proceeded with the work, each one also rose magnificently to the occasion despite very short deadlines. Each of these writers has much to teach us about the saints and celebrations of the church that deserve our attention. So it is with deep gratitude to them—and to God for their marvelous gifts—that we offer this new-generation volume on the lesser festivals to both newly minted and experienced preachers.

David B. Lott

PART ONE
SAINTS' DAYS, SOLEMNITIES, AND OTHER FEASTS OF THE CHURCH

William F. Brosend II

Bill Doggett

Gordon W. Lathrop

Ruth A. Meyers

Gail Ramshaw

Craig A. Satterlee

Gerard S. Sloyan

INTRODUCTION
CHRISTIAN FESTIVALS IN CURRENT CONTEXT

GORDON W. LATHROP

All days are not the same. Sometimes, in current experience, it may seem as if they are. The same news reports about what seems the same state of the world reach us day after day. The same demands of work extend themselves into every day, now reaching us electronically in places that used to be immune from the ringing telephone, the demanding boss, the inquiring client. The same television shows—or does it just seem like they are the same?—surround our leisure hours. The same anxieties—about security, self-realization, death—dog our sleeping as well as our waking hours, day in, day out. Hour after hour, measured on our ever-present wristwatches, seems the same.

But even this familiar state of semi-depression, so characteristic of some current lives in Western societies, remains permeable at least to the *memory* of festival. Was there not a time when every day was not the same, when some days were high days, celebrative days, festivals?

This book is about a specific set of Christian festivals and about the ways in which pastors and preachers may assist communities to understand and to keep them. Still, in order begin such a book, we need to think about the nature of *festival* itself.

3

INTRODUCTION
───────────
GORDON W.
LATHROP

In fact, all days have not been the same in human experience. Humankind, since long before the dawn of history, since the earliest communities of hominids ran upright upon the savannahs of Africa and as they spread into the wider world, has noted the difference in days. Some days were marked by success in the hunt, by food to share. Some days were not so marked, depending instead upon stored food or simply enduring hunger. The shared food—and with it, the shared story of the tribe on the land—was one beginning of festival. In the museum at Altamira, in northern Spain, there is a small piece of bone, thousands of years old, on which is inscribed an image of a slain aurochs or bison, with a group of human figures gathered around it as at a great table: *festival*. The precious bone engraving kept alive the memory and the anticipation of the event.

It seems as if such memories and hopes for festival-time are inscribed upon our own bones.

Indeed, as human beings began to notice, some nights are marked by the full moon. Such a moon enabled the community to see a little better in the dark, giving light to the communal feast, helping ensure greater safety, even enabling travel at night. The hunters could come back. The community could safely eat, then safely move. The regular return of that light-filled night was also noticed, the beginning of the idea of the *month*. We do not know for sure, but perhaps along with that observation, there came the observation of the changing sky, the movement of the planets, the growing and the waning light of the sun, the solstices and the equinoxes, the beginning of the sense of the *year*. Then, in relationship to that year, the communities of humans spreading throughout the earth knew times of small-group dispersal in the surrounding wilderness and times of large-group reunion, times of summer wandering and times of winter storytelling, dry-time need and wet-time abundance. With agriculture and with cities, there came work time, planting time, germinating time, harvest time. And there were market days, a new version of the old times of joyful reunion. New cycles arose: the regular recurrence of those market days, for example, the agricultural importance of the year, or, under the influence of planetary observance, the division of the month into quarters and the birth of the *week*. Thus woven through all of these cycles was the festival: the meal-sharing time, gathering time, storytelling time, harvest time, rest time, remembering time, reunion time. By means of the festival, human beings knew themselves in the context of their communities, knew their stories and their identities, hoped again that they would survive—even thrive. Sometimes that very hope, encouraged by the stories, could then be acted out in festival reversals, the least for the moment

> By means of the festival, human beings knew themselves in the context of their communities, knew their stories and their identities, hoped again that they would survive–even thrive.

being the greatest, the hungriest the soonest fed, either to release the tensions of daily life or genuinely to propose again another way of human order. In any case, those festival gifts, that knowledge of the stories, sharing of food, and genesis of hope, belonged to being human.

But the differences in days are not only ecological, not only found in the relationships between human communities and the surrounding cycles of the earth. They are also interior to human life. Today a child is born. Today an old person dies. Today a woman begins to get her period. Today she knows she is pregnant. Today we make someone our leader. Today members of our community return from a dangerous journey. I have been sick and my whole community has been burdened by my illness, but today I am well. And we keep festival. More: even the morning itself can be an echo of festival. Last night I slept well. This morning I awake refreshed, restored to the people with whom I live. More yet: today I see you, look into your eyes, and am amazed to recognize another and to be recognized. We experience some times as *thicker* with meaning, other times as *thinner*. Festivals can also mark the small group, the family, and even—though more rarely—the individual life.

We ignore such thick time at our peril. Human life is much impoverished if we think of ourselves only as workers or if we seek only the well-being of our individual selves. We belong to communities, inserted in an ecology. We know what we are and how we fit in the world at least partly through stories, shared meals, communal encounters, shared memories, communally marked time—through festival. So, even if we do not do it very well, we do try to keep alive something of this primal marker of human life. We have birthday parties. We keep Christmas. And we remember that there are traditions that have come down to us, however meagerly we may have kept them: a weekly day of rest and reunion; a few annual days that mark the movement of the year; days associated with important communal stories; days that are dear to our families; and times when we remember our beloved dead.

Of course, festival exists by contrast. Not every day can be a high day. The shared meal is especially important if we have also shared in hunger, the communal story if we realize that we do not have much identity by ourselves. So human communities have found their various intense observances at a few very special times—at the harvest, at the annual reunion, at the full moon, at the new moon, at the turning points of the year, at communally remembered dates. Perhaps part of our trouble with festival may be that many of us are hardly ever hungry, many of us think we are unaffected by the changes in the year, and most of us have come to think that we do indeed exist by ourselves. Still, we also sense that we are wrong. The dark and the light, the springtime and the fall, affect us more than we articulate. If nothing else, we are hungry for meaning, hungry for authentic stories, stories that matter—perhaps stories that matter for a world where we know widespread hunger does exist. Now *that* might draw our attention: real festivals, festivals that tell the truth and not pretense, amid deep, bone-rejoicing, hope-producing celebration.

For there are also significant problems with festivals. They can be only about us, about our survival, our abundance, our stories, conveniently forgetting or even demonizing everybody else. Probably the aurochs pictured on the bone was intended only for that tribe, not for anybody else. We eat. They starve—though they will probably do so out of sight of our own boundaried feast. For about such narrow focus, festivals can also lie. The stories of the American Thanksgiving, for example, born amidst the Civil War when the country needed hope, too often simply made the native peoples of the continent to be glad helpers at the arrival of the English colonists, guests who brought the turkey and the corn. Those peoples then disappeared from the story, which gave no further reflection to the history of genocidal disease and violence that pushed them out of the story. Abraham Lincoln himself, one of the founders of the feast, deeply knew that a nation cannot have thanksgiving without repentance. But that complexity—which would make the festival so much more interesting and real to us today—is too often missing from the conventional narrative. Certainly a festival dreams impossible dreams of peace, abundance and sharing, but those dreams need to be more nuanced and complex than lies. The biblical festival at the return of the people from exile, according to the narration of Nehemiah 8 and 9, was marked by both weeping and gladness, feasting and sending to those who have none, repentance and thanksgiving. Such is the sort of festival we need.

> If nothing else, we are hungry for meaning, hungry for authentic stories, stories that matter—perhaps stories that matter for a world where we know widespread hunger does exist.

CHRISTIANITY AND FESTIVAL

One of the vocations of the Christian churches in the present time has been to help human beings with festivals. It is actually a double task. First, Christians have needed simply to keep the idea of festival alive. There are of course other groups than Christians and other places than churches where festivals are celebrated. Communal religious practice of any kind usually comes to expression in time-keeping, day-keeping ways. But Christians have also tried to nurture the idea that a group of people can come together, do the needed festive preparations, and then share the meal, the stories, the songs, the reversals, and the sense of thick, meaningful time. Christians have done that, at least partly, out of a largely unspoken sense that human beings need festivals. The church year can be kept, not simply as an obscure discipline for clergy as they figure out what to do on the next Sunday, but as a pattern of festivals and ordinary days for us all, illuminating our identity and our ecological location in world. Congregations can become the festival group itself, especially in a time when people live in smaller and smaller groups and are not very good at festival practice anyway. Or the congregation can become a locus of teaching: here is what you might do at Easter or at Christmas or in preparation for these feasts.

But the second part of the task is even more characteristically Christian. Christians have wanted to use festivals to tell the gospel story of Jesus Christ and to celebrate an identity deeper and wider than human festivals have ordinarily carried. Indeed, there is a certain Christian criticism of festivals if they are only about us, our food, our identity. The deep Christian intention is to keep festival—as all humanity longs to do—but to insist that the story we most have to tell is the story of God's gift, not our achievement; that whatever food we have ought to be shared as widely as possible, in celebration of that gift; and that the identity celebrated is the identity of humankind itself, on the redeemed, beloved earth, before the face of God. Christian festivals focus on Jesus Christ and, through that very particularity, yearn toward hospitable, open—not tribal—meaning.

> The church year can be kept, not simply as an obscure discipline for clergy as they figure out what to do on the next Sunday, but as a pattern of festivals and ordinary days for us all, illuminating our identity and our ecological location in world.

The history of Christian festivals demonstrates this double task. All of the major Christian festivals are transformed versions of earlier human observances. Festivals were received—and turned to new purpose. Christians learned this transformation of human festivals from the biblical pattern in Jewish life. Sabbath itself was probably the old Babylonian observance of an "unlucky day" turned into the commemoration of God's actions in creation and redemption. Passover was likely an old springtime agricultural and herders' rite turned to similar purpose. The Jewish Sabbath and the Jewish Passover stand behind the Christian Sunday and the Christian Easter. But the sources for Christian observance are wider yet. The ancient Mediterranean winter solstice observance stands behind Christmas. The Roman (and Hellenistic Jewish) commemorations of the death-days of a family's beloved dead stand behind the days of saints and martyrs.

But the transformations are extensive. Sunday is a day of meeting on the first day of the week, not a day of rest on the last. If Sabbath indicated that the gift of this day marked the Jews as God's own people, then Sunday, while honoring that story, intends to proclaim that Christ is risen for all of humanity, including us who are so lately come into God's mercy. Easter is a night in which the whole community keeps vigil and then keeps fifty days of rejoicing, not a small family festival followed by fifty days of mourning. If Passover celebrates the story of God's acting to deliver a slave-people and give them an identity, then Easter, while deeply depending upon that story, proclaims that there is an exodus for all humanity and a renewal for all creation in the death and resurrection of Jesus. More: the Christmas cycle has come to be four weeks of quiet acknowledgment of the truth of the darkness followed by twelve days of communal rejoicing, not weeks and weeks of Saturnalia. If solstice intended to assure the community that there would be abundance for them, in spite of it being winter, and that the sun would return, Christmas means to say that Jesus Christ is the sun of justice and that God's abundance is meant for all. And while the commemorations of the dead were for a particular family, the saints are meant as heroes and models for all people, especially as they mirror something of the openness to sinners and the trust in the mercy of God we have known in Jesus.

> Christian festivals focus on Jesus Christ and, through that very particularity, yearn toward hospitable, open—not tribal—meaning.

Those four building blocks—Sunday, Easter, Christmas, martyr's days—came to make up the Christian year. One—the most important one—is a *weekly* feast, the foundational festival of Christianity, Sunday. Two are *annual* feasts, Easter and Christmas—one, the second most important, near the springtime equinox, at a date determined by the full moon and its following Sunday, and one at the winter solstice. And one, any day of a saint, is more like those personal, familial festivals, marking familial thick time: a *death-day* anniversary, now become a wider, communal remembrance. Those four festivals certainly represent the state of *festival* in the ancient Near Eastern world at the time of the origin of Christianity, the first two or three centuries. But, in a certain sense, they also recapitulate the whole human history of festival: shared food and story, survival-giving food and identity-giving story, at occasions that mark both familial history and the intersection of the fate of the tribe with the seasons of the earth.

Recover festival and its importance for human life. Criticize festival and turn it toward celebrating the mercy of God, identifying the community with the well-being of all of needy humanity and with the care of the earth. These goals remain a lively Christian concern. If we are to consider festivals in this present volume, we will need to keep these goals in mind.

THE PRIORITY OF SUNDAY

But, for Christians, the first and basic festival is Sunday. It is, of course, the only Christian festival mentioned in the New Testament, the only festival shared by virtually all Christians. Its origin predates the second-century Easter, the second-century martyrs' days, and the fourth-century Christmas. It stands at the very origin of the Christian movement, identified with the basic Christian narrative. In all of its primary stories, Sunday was the day after the Sabbath on which the community gathered in fear and need, holding a shared meal, and yet the day on which the community came to know that the Crucified One is risen and his Spirit is poured out for forgiveness and life. Since then, this assembly, repeated every week, gathered around word and prayers and meal, is itself an appearance of the risen Christ and an outpouring of the Spirit for the life of the needy world. Every Sunday is Easter, every Sunday Pentecost. The paschal mystery, the passover of Jesus from death to life, and with him the passover of all things, lives at the heart of every Sunday. So, Sunday is the day of truth telling about our need and of authentic joy about God's mercy, the day to read all the old stories in the light of Christ and to pray for all the needs of the world, the day of the meal and of sending to the poor, the day of a particular local assembly and yet, always, of the open door for everyone to come in. Metaphorically, it is the Day of Light or the Day of the Lord or—impossibly, in a seven-day system—the Eighth Day. But it is that "day" by being a *meeting*, a reunion, a festival together.

This festival carries and reinforces the identity of Christians. Paradoxically, that reinforced identity is "being with Christ" and "being enlivened by the Spirit," while this Christ is the One who identifies with those who are outside of every circle and the Spirit of God blows where it will. Christian identity, as it is established on Sunday and imaged in the biblical stories, is thus a criticism of any tribal identity, a longing for fruitful peace among the whole of humanity as it stands on the earth before God.

And this festival grounds the week. The Eighth Day, the day of the resurrection and of the defeat of the fear of death, the day that cannot be and yet is, is also the first day of the week. The Christian community moves into the week in the light of the assembly in the life-giving Spirit, around the risen Crucified One, before the face of God the source of all. While Sunday is the festival, every day is holy in this light, every day an occasion for mercy, forgiveness, and the sharing of life in the face of death. Sunday speaks the identity and mission of the community while it also speaks the identity and mission of God. Every Sunday is Trinity Sunday.

> Sunday speaks the identity and mission of the community while it also speaks the identity and mission of God.

And every Sunday is Earth Day. The stories used here in assembly are earth-loving, earthy stories. The prayers here are rightly prayers for all creatures. The all-important meal-of-Christ, celebrated here, uses a little local food, calling that an abundance, and so sets out a feast for everyone in a model of sustainable consumption. Meanwhile, we have newly learned again what ancient Christians knew: to send portions of this meal to the absent and to take a collection for the hungry and the poor.

Therefore, if Christians have a double agenda of helping communities recover festival and, yet, critically turning festival toward larger need, they are already given the basic tool of that agenda: Sunday. In all of the churches, liturgical renewal has aimed at the recovery of the centrality of Sunday. The lectionary so widely used in the churches—in whatever variations—is focused on Sunday. Talk about the "participatory assembly" and about the regular "parish Eucharist" is talk about Sunday.

It may not seem so right away in your place. There is a lot of Sunday assembly that hardly seems like what we have been calling festival, hardly seems like thick time. There are a lot of Sunday services that are boring, untruthful, and disconnected from the earth. But it is worth the effort to clear out this ancient spring so that the water can once again run clear, in thirsty times. The gifts and resources of Sunday really are gifts and resources for authentic festival. Here is a day we cannot keep alone, by ourselves in our houses. We need each other for this assembly.

> The gifts and resources of Sunday really are gifts and resources for authentic festival. Here is a day we cannot keep alone, by ourselves in our houses. We need each other for this assembly.

Here are nuanced and complex stories that can tell the truth about us and our world, inviting us out of lies. Here is room for both gladness and mourning, both repentance and thanksgiving, as we have needed in contemporary festivals. Here is a little meal—food shared so that we may not die—lifting our heads up to see and not to hide from the hunger of the world. Here is a celebration of reversals in Christ. Here is the possibility of recovering a really interesting identity. Here is a community that can be reflecting on life and death and our place in the local ecology. And, most fascinatingly, here is a genuine festival close to daily life. Held every week and thereby marking one quarter of the month, one repeated count of the planetary seven, these gatherings remain far enough apart to seem really festive, yet close enough together actually to illuminate—and not just be an exception to—our days.

Recover the Sunday assembly as festival, assembly, Eucharist, day of honesty, resurrection appearance, outpouring of the Spirit, Trinity Sunday, Earth Day. This remains a central item on our agenda for reform in the churches.

But then what of the *other* festivals? What is this book for anyway?

In fact, all of the other, later Christian uses of festival always are echoing Sunday. Easter—or Pascha, as it was called in the ancient church and is still named in the Romance languages—is a kind of Sunday for the year, a fifty-day-long Eighth Day to the somewhat more than seven times fifty days of the solar round, a proclamation of the resurrection and the outpoured Spirit for the transfiguration of our year. And Christmas is a kind of Pascha in winter, the solstice made into another annual Sunday. Partly because of their love of the number eight, Christians have long played with the ways in which feasts echo feasts, eight days later. Each Sunday is an octave of the last Sunday. Easter has eight Sundays. New Year's Day—or the Feast of the Name of Jesus—is the octave of Christmas. And, Easter is Sunday for the year, Christmas Sunday at solstice.

If it is true that every time a human being loses someone in death, the mourning calls up and intensifies any earlier loss, all of the mourning becoming one sorrow, this evocative character is also true of authentic festival. Sunday, recovered in its brilliance, will also illuminate Easter and Christmas. And it will also illuminate and be recalled by the so-called lesser festivals.

WHAT SHALL WE DO WITH THE LESSER FESTIVALS?

The lesser festivals also are echoes of Sunday and of the Sunday-to-the-year that is Pascha and the Pascha-in-winter that is Christmas. So, Holy Cross, Corpus Christi, and All Saints echo something of Pascha. Trinity Sunday is the octave of Pentecost, itself the eighth Sunday of Easter. So, Presentation is the fortieth day of Christmas, and Annunciation, Visitation, and the feasts of Mary and of Joseph all circle at greater distance around Christmas as well. In fact, Annunciation may be among the oldest of Christian feasts, echoing the Pascha, celebrating the incarnation at the very time of Jesus' death and resurrection, the time of the vernal equinox. And the feasts of the saints, the commemorations of witnesses to the gospel of Jesus Christ, were at their origin Sunday-like assemblies in memory of the paschal mystery of this one witness, in honor of the transparency of this passover to the greater passover, the transparency of this witness to the greater Witness who is Jesus Christ. The Christians at Smyrna, in the mid-second century, began to gather annually, on Polycarp's death day, because his was a death "according to the gospel," reflecting and bearing witness to the death and witness of Jesus. They told their story (in the still remarkable *Martyrdom of Polycarp*), and other Christians in other places were moved to remember Polycarp's witness as well, year after year, in a death-day festival larger than that of a local family, in a kind of Sunday-echo.

Of course, all of this can seem like impossible complication and endless number games to the contemporary mind. But built up carefully, used wisely, this economy of festivals can be genuinely helpful to the current life of the churches and the current lives of human beings. There really is only one multifaceted festival story that Christians have, and it is repeated and intensified in all of these various ways. The gospel can be seen as marking the week and the major turning points of the year and as illuminating a few important lives of witness. Festival can be recovered in strength.

> Built up carefully, used wisely, this economy of festivals can be genuinely helpful to the current life of the churches and the current lives of human beings.

With care. The cautionary tale of medieval festival life is important to remember. The calendar of the saints became so overloaded that there really was no day that was not a festival, and festival lost it purpose altogether. The Reformation churches, first, and then the Roman Catholic church itself, in its calendar reform, dumped many of these "festivals," the Reformation churches arguing that we should keep only Sundays, a few annual festivals, and only the days of those saints mentioned in the Bible. These latter should be seen not as intercessors but as witnesses to faith, the original intention of such commemorations. That multiplying of saints days is not our problem, but neither is it possible to argue for recovered festival and especially the recovery of Sunday as festival, and at the same time work again to overload our present calendar. These ancient lists of feasts lie tantalizingly at our fingertips. Here, in this book, many of them (though by no means all!) are listed. What shall we do with them?

What follows is a series of suggestions for parish life. If they are useful in your place, consider them. If they are not, discard them. The most important is the first:

• Work on the recovery of Sunday. Keep the day as the most important festival, the day of the truth-telling, open assembly. Use the lectionary in the light of the crucifixion and resurrection of Jesus and the outpouring of the Spirit. Pray for the needs of the world. Hold the holy meal. Keep the day always as both Trinity Sunday and Earth Day. Teach the meaning of Sunday.

• Then work on the recovery of Pascha and Pascha-in-winter. Hold the great Vigil of Easter. Make that vigil the primary time of baptism in your place. Use Lent as baptismal preparation and baptismal remembrance time. Celebrate the resurrection for all fifty days. Let Advent be honest about the darkness and the need of all humanity right now. Keep Christmas for all twelve days.

• Then honestly assess what days through the year that are not Sundays can be added as assembly days, festival days, in your place. You will probably begin with days that directly prepare for or echo Pascha and Christmas: Ash Wednesday, Maundy Thursday, Good Friday, Epiphany, then perhaps Annunciation, Presentation, Holy Cross, Ascension Day, perhaps more. Some of these days are included here, in this volume, and the reflections on the celebration itself and on its lectionary texts may be helpful to you. If you keep these days, keep them with an eye to their recalling and anticipating the central feast to which they are related and thus being transparent to the single mystery of all Christian festivity: the gospel of Jesus Christ for the life of the world.

• If you exercise leadership in an assembly that gathers for daily prayer—for example, a cathedral or a large parish, a college or seminary or church-office chapel—consider using all of the days available to you. Do not overshadow the Sunday Eucharist, the foundational Christian festival, but if there is a midweek Eucharist, consider moving it to a festival day, if one occurs in any given week. If there is a daily Eucharist, use all these observances with joy. In any case, let daily prayer on all the days observe these feasts as they occur. While the new ecumenical daily lectionary with its echoes and anticipations of Sunday may provide the best regular flow of readings for daily prayer, one or more of the readings for any festival presented and discussed in this book might be used at morning or evening prayer on that day. (For more on the daily lectionary, see *Evangelical Lutheran Worship* [Minneapolis: Augsburg Fortress, 2006], 1121–53.)

• While you work on the renewal of Sunday, Pascha, Christmas and their echoes, do not forget that fourth building block of the ancient Christian festival calendar: the witnesses, the martyrs, the saints. Perhaps—especially, again, if your assembly meets daily—you will keep the entire list of biblical saints included here. Perhaps you will especially keep the Confession of Peter and the Conversion of Paul and the octave that stretches between them as the Week of Prayer for Christian Unity. Perhaps you will keep the feasts that immediately follow Christmas—Stephen, John, the Holy Innocents, called sometimes the "companions of Christ"—since these very feasts will help to give full scope to the meaning of Christmas: the incarnation occurs amid our death-dealing ways. Perhaps you will keep the feasts of the four evangelists, using these celebrations to deepen your assembly in the diversity of the Gospels. The texts discussed here can assist with those observances. In fact, the biblical texts help to make clear that the point of such a celebration is not so much to tell the story of the saint as to move through the saint to the One to whom he or she points.

• Perhaps more: the worship books of many churches today include a yet longer list of commemorations, including a rich variety of people through the ages. Consider that list. In fact, if we take the intention of the Reformation seriously, many of the so-called biblical saints carry with them a variety of dubious legends that are not necessarily helpful—we do not know much, really, about Bartholomew!—while some nonbiblical figures—Polycarp, Perpetua, George Herbert, Julian of Norwich, Chief Seattle, Sojourner Truth—have accessible and fascinating stories that do not have to be made into legends. It might be wise to consider your community and the figures that might best be remembered there. All of the names on the list might be recalled in the intercessions on the preceding Sunday, as the community gives thanks for their witness. Similarly, if you meet for daily prayer, all of these names can be recalled, each in a collect on their day or in the thanksgiving at the end of the litany in Evening Prayer. But a genuine festival of a saint in our congregations will be seldom held and will need to have some local resonance. Perhaps the name-day of the parish will suggest such an observance. Perhaps a local interest or a local need will do the same. The point is not that these people are all wonderful or that they are our saviors. On the contrary. In all of their oddness, they are simply models of the saved, examples of people who trusted in God and whose deaths can be seen as transparent to the one death that saves us all.

• Even if you do not use this list of lesser festivals and commemorations to plan actual services, of Eucharist or of daily prayer or of the Word, consider teaching the availability of the list to the people of your assembly. Put it in their hands. Knowing about this list and following something of the lives that it includes can be a way that anybody may find our present days to be accompanied, surrounded by a cloud of witnesses, transparent to the continuing Christian story. The present volume may be one help in making some of this material available to your congregation.

• If one of these lesser festivals or commemorations happens to fall on a Sunday, remember the priority of Sunday. Do not replace the lectionary readings of the Sunday or make this primary Sunday festival into a festival of the saint. But do consider welcoming the witness of the saint, in some way, into the preaching of the day and the name of the saint into the final thanksgiving of the intercessions.

• Finally, if your assembly meets on any of the national days, look at the material included on those days here. It remains so that the Christian vocation in regard to such festivals includes the need to introduce nuance and critique: repentance with thanksgiving, truth telling with myth, human identity before God more important than tribal or national identity.

But the deep task remains an old Christian agenda. Knowledge of the lesser festivals can once again stir up that task, echoing and supporting it: recover festival and its importance for human life. Criticize festival and turn it toward celebrating the mercy of God. May this book help you to those ends.

For Further Reading

Johnson, Maxwell. *Between Memory and Hope: Readings on the Liturgical Year.* Collegeville, Minn.: Liturgical Press, 2000.

Lathrop, Gordon W. *Holy People: A Liturgical Ecclesiology.* Minneapolis: Fortress Press, 1999.

Nelson, Gertrud Mueller. *To Dance with God.* New York: Paulist, 1986.

Pfatteicher, Philip H. *The New Book of Festivals and Commemorations: Toward a Common Calendar of Saints.* Minneapolis: Fortress Press, 2008 (forthcoming).

Portaro, Sam. *Brightest and Best: A Companion to the Lesser Feasts and Fasts.* Cambridge, Mass.: Cowley, 1998.

Pryce, Mark. *Literary Companion to the Festivals.* Minneapolis: Fortress Press, 2003.

Stookey, Laurence Hull. *Calendar: Christ's Time for the Church.* Nashville: Abingdon, 1996.

Vogel, Dwight W. "Liturgy: The *Ordo* of Time." In Dirk G. Lange and Dwight W. Vogel, eds., *Ordo: Bath, Word, Prayer, and Table.* Akron: OSL, 2005.

THE MARY FEASTS
DEVOTION TO MARY IN EAST AND WEST

GERARD S. SLOYAN

Christian devotion to Mary originated even before the Gospels according to Luke and John were received into the canon of Scripture in the mid-second century. So, too, with Paul's letter to the Gentile Christians in Galatia, which was composed before both. In that epistle Paul maintains Jesus' Jewishness and his status as a human being in a single phrase: "When the fullness of time had come, God sent his Son, born of a woman, born under the law" (Gal. 4:4). The latter part was perhaps intended to underscore Paul's insistence in that letter on his own Jewishness. The mention of Jesus' human birth may, as a matter of hypothesis, have been to refute early Gnostic claims that the earthly Christ was spirit only. That strange departure from the apostolic tradition viewed him as nothing so gross as a human born *inter feces et urinam*, in the words of a pagan poet descriptive of all human birth.

The earliest extant reference to Mary after the New Testament, where she is known simply as a virgin and a wife and mother, occurs in the anonymous epistle to Diognetus whose probable author was a certain Quadratus, writing in 124 or 129. His way of finding a new Eve in Mary was: "Eve is not seduced but a Virgin is found trustworthy." Justin Martyr takes up that presentation of prototype to type in his *Dialogue with Trypho*, 100 (written after 155). Tertullian does the same in his treatise *On the Flesh of Christ*, 17.211–12. The first mention that we have of Mary or indeed any of the saints in a Christian liturgy occurs in Hippoly-tus's early-third-century *Apostolic Tradition*.[1] There, in the rite of ordination of a bishop, we come upon a prayer that speaks of Jesus Christ Savior, Redeemer, and Word as "having been sent by God into the womb of the Virgin who, dwelling within her, was made flesh and was manifested as your Son, being born of the Holy Spirit and the Virgin" (4.6). The same phrase occurs in that document in the second of three questions addressed by the bishop to an adult candidate for baptism, the first having been, "Do you believe in God, the Father Almighty?" The second was, "Do you believe in Jesus Christ, the Son of God, whom the Virgin Mary bore of the Holy Spirit . . . ?" The third was, "Do you believe in the Holy Spirit?," followed by what came to be called the Spirit's goods of salva-tion, "the holy church and the resurrection of the flesh?" A pouring of water or immersion—it is impossible to tell which—came after each affirmative response. There is, however, no mention of Mary in the Hippolytan canon of the Lord's Supper of the year 215 or so.

The title *Godbearer*, favored by the Alexandrian party led by its bishop Cyril at the Council of Ephesus in 431, won out over the more comprehensive, God-anointed *Christbearer* of Nestorius and the Syrians. The title had long encompassed the divinity and the humanity of Christ. The other, *theotokos,* came to be in ver-nacular languages like ours *Mother of God.* Finally, the creed that was approved at Chalcedon in 451 consolidated two previous creedal statements, one at a council in Nicaea in 325 and another held at Constantinople in 381, and contained the affirmation in faith that "the Lord Jesus Christ . . . for us humans and for our salvation came down from the heavens, and was made flesh of the Holy Spirit and the Virgin Mary, and became man."

Something of longstanding consequence as regards Mary came of the two chris-tological councils cited above, which spanned the years 325–431. Beginning with Nicaea and culminating in Chalcedon twenty years after Ephesus, Jesus Christ's possession of the fullness of deity was spelled out against any who would deny it and just as forcefully his humanity in its fullness, body, soul, and spirit. But St. Cyr-il's theological position, encapsulated in the philosophical phrase "in accord with his subsistence," to describe the union of two natures in one undivided person, led to the conclusion that Jesus Christ is a divine person who has a human nature (the so-called hypostatic union). Chalcedon said nothing of this but contented itself with condemning Nestorius for holding that Jesus was a human person intimately conjoined to a divine person, a position he did not hold. What had been build-ing since Nicaea was the conviction that Jesus, as divinity in human flesh, was less apt than before to be venerated as humanity's intercessor with the Father. Even though calling on him as Lord and Christ to be our mediator with God in virtue of his sacrificial death and resurrection continued in the form of a lengthy litanic prayer ("Lord, have mercy . . . Christ have mercy"), the view of him as priestly intercessor on our behalf began to be diminished although it was never to fade.

Into this partial vacuum in piety and prayer the Mother of God (now *deipara* in the Latin-speaking West) began to be placed. A purely human creature as her Son was not, Mary was increasingly called on to intercede with him to exercise his mediatorial office on our behalf. Needless to say, she never took his place in that regard. The movement of late nineteenth-century Western piety to have Mary declared co-redemptrix with her Son or mediatrix of all graces was obviously wrongly conceived. But as derived from her unique position as mother of her Son the Redeemer, it could at least be understood. He had no coming to be as a member of the human race but from her. More than that, there had developed the cult of the martyrs who were considered to be already enjoying the blessed vision of God, a cult (in Latin *dulia,* namely of servants of God) that went back to the late 100s. They were being called on to intercede with Jesus the great intercessor with God for the gift of courage in refusing to worship nonexistent gods and the emperor. If these men and women could be thought of in that role, why not the person from whose flesh and blood his whole human being was fashioned? And so it continued in the second half of the first millennium.

The heightened veneration of Mary in the West after the year 1000 is a matter of record. Between 1250 and 1350 some one hundred cathedral churches and shrines of pilgrimage were dedicated to Mary in France alone. In imitation of knighthood, many men of violence committed themselves to her as their liege Lady in defense of her honor against the Albigenses or Cathari who were slandering her motherhood.

The Eastern observance of the *Falling Asleep of Mary* in Jerusalem, found in certain apocryphal Gospels from the fourth century onward, developed gradually into the Western feast of her bodily *Assumption* into heaven. It had long been in the Roman calendar of feasts but was defined as a dogma of faith as late as November 1, 1950. It is celebrated in some Protestant traditions as Mary's "saint" day. Commentary on it, and on the biblical lections of the feasts of Gabriel's *Annunciation* to Mary (March 25) and her *Visitation* to her kinswoman Elizabeth (May 31), occur elsewhere in this volume on feasts and solemnities.

The reformers wished to have a Bible-based scheme of mediation rather than one supplemented by appeal to a communion of saints. As a consequence of failure to trust the voice of a living Church, the Virgin Mother of Jesus ceased to be part of the piety of half of Western Christendom. Martin Luther's devotion to Mary to his last breath was a casualty of what has been called seventeenth-century Lutheran orthodoxy. Calvin and Zwingli repudiated "saint worship" rather harshly. The stigmatization of any Marian pieties under this watchword flourished in the Church of England in the forty-five-years reign of Elizabeth I and was intensified among dissidents from the Anglican settlement, the so-called Puritans, Baptists, and Quakers. Meantime in the Christian East, Orthodox and Catholic devotion to Mary as a corollary to calling on Christ as sole mediator went undiminished. It had a place in all the prayer forms of the Holy Liturgy and was nourished through icons in churches, in family homes, and in shrines along the highways and byways. Mary was found everywhere and loved everywhere in the cultures that took their rise in Constantinople, Rome, Syria, Persia, Armenia, Ethiopia, and Upper Egypt.

From Egypt there comes what is in all likelihood the earliest prayer to Mary, known as *Sub tuum praesidium*. A Greek papyrus containing it was discovered in 1907. It is dated in the third century by certain experts in paleography, and reads: "We fly to your patronage, O holy Mother of God; despise not our petitions in our necessities, but deliver us from all dangers always, you who are all-pure and glorious." Before the discovery of this papyrus, now in the John Rylands Library of the University of Manchester, no documentary evidence of devotion to Mary before Nicaea had been found. The history and careful examination of the phrases of this prayer are to be found in an essay of the present writer[2] as the history also of the *Ave, Maria* and of the four prayers proposed for song or private recitation seasonally at the conclusion of the daily Divine Office—*Salve Regina* ("Hail, holy Queen"); *Alma Redemptoris Mater* ("Nourishing Mother of the Redeemer"); *Regina Caeli, laetare, Alleluia* ("Rejoice, O Queen of heaven, to see")—and *Ave, Regina caelorum* ("Hail, holy Queen enthroned above"). Also discussed there is the *Memorare,* first recorded by a Strasbourg Cistercian in 1489 but popularized by the "Poor Priest" Claude Bernard two centuries later the Angelus and the Litany of Loreto.

> By the prayers of your mother who brought you forth
> and that of all the saints:
> I will adore you O King, my Lord, the only begotten
> Son, the word of the heavenly Father, who is immortal,
> who by your grace came for the life of all humanity,
> and did become incarnate of the holy and glorious
> Virgin Mary, Mother of God, who did become man,
> being God without change, and who was crucified for us.
> O Christ, our Lord, who by your death
> did trample our death and destroy it,
> who is one among the Holy Trinity
> and is worshipped and glorified.
> In the unity of your Father and your living
> Holy Spirit, have mercy upon us.[3]

Notes

1. Burton Scott Easton, trans., *The Apostolic Tradition of Hippolytus* (Cambridge: Cambridge University Press, 1934), 35.

2. Gerard S. Sloyan, "Marian Prayers," in *Mariology, Volume 3,* ed. J. B. Carol, O.F.M., (Milwaukee: Bruce 1961), 64–87.

3. From the Sixth Hour of Prayer, written by Mar Severus, Patriarch of Antioch (512–38).

ANDREW, APOSTLE

NOVEMBER 30

BILL DOGGETT

LUTHERAN (ELW)	EPISCOPAL (BCP)	ROMAN CATHOLIC (LFM)
Ezek. 3:16-21	Deut. 30:11-14	Rom. 10:9-18
Ps. 19:1-6	Psalm 19 or 19:1-6	Ps. 19:2-3, 4-5
Rom. 10:10-18	Rom. 10:10b-18	
John 1:35-42	Matt. 4:18-22	Matt. 4:18-22

KEY THEMES

- Evangelism in action: Hearing, telling, feeding.
- Little-known saints in your community.
- First things first: Does being first matter?

Although the Fourth Gospel tells us that Andrew was one of two disciples of John the Baptist who left to follow Jesus when John identified Jesus as the Lamb of God, of the two, it is Andrew whom tradition has identified as the "First Apostle," because he is the one who immediately brings the news about Jesus to his brother, Simon Peter. Scripture doesn't offer a very detailed picture of Andrew. The Fourth Gospel has the most detail—it tells us that Andrew was born in Bethsaida, describes Andrew bringing Simon Peter to Jesus after John's declaration, and shows Andrew as a leader among the Twelve at the miraculous feeding of the five thousand (John 6:8-9) and as the one to whom Philip defers when he is approached by those who want to see Jesus (John 12:20-22). Matthew and Mark tell the story of Jesus' call to Andrew and Simon Peter to put down their fishing nets and follow him, but Luke's Gospel doesn't mention Andrew as being present on that occasion. Mark says that Jesus stayed in Andrew and Simon's house in Capernaum, healing Simon's mother-in-law and many others who came to the door. Other than that, Andrew shows up in lists of the Twelve in the Synoptics and Acts, always among the first four named.

Tradition and legend fill out Andrew's story. He is variously reported by early church writers as having done missionary work in Scythia, Epirus, Achaia, Hellas,

Cappadocia, Galatia, Bithynia, Byzantium, Thrace, Macedonia, and Thessaly. It is generally agreed that he was martyred at Patrae in Achaia on November 30, 60 C.E., and a fourth-century tradition has it that he was executed on an X-shaped cross—bound, not nailed, in order to prolong his suffering.

After his death, his bones were equally peripatetic. The relics were moved from Patrae to Constantinople in 357 C.E. In the eighth century some of the bones were removed to Scotland, with several competing stories accounting for the motive and means of transportation, while the remaining bones were moved to Amalfi, Italy, in the thirteenth century. Andrew's head was placed in St. Peter's Basilica in Rome in the fifteenth century, and some relics were returned to Patrae in 1964 as a gesture of goodwill toward the Orthodox Church by Pope Paul VI. Andrew is the symbolic head of the Byzantine Church, and is claimed as Patron by Russia and Scotland.

The Feast

The idea of "first things" is central to the commemoration of St. Andrew. In addition to being one of the two first called by Jesus, his declaration to his brother Peter that "We have found the Messiah" (John 1:41) makes Andrew the first evangelist among the disciples in that Gospel. There is even an air of "first things" about the feast day itself, since the First Sunday of Advent, the beginning of the church year, is traditionally identified as the Sunday closest to St. Andrew's day. Andrew may also be the first subject of Jesus' wordplay: in Matthew and Mark, Jesus' declaration that he will make his followers fishers of men (*halieis anthrōpōn*, Mark 1:17; Matt. 4:19) might be punning on *anthrōpōn*, "men," and Andrew's name, *Andreas*, "manly."[1]

But if "first things" is the theme of the day, evangelism is certainly the subject. All of the lectionary texts are about proclamation, and the traditions about Andrew's life paint him as an evangelist of great scope. He is reported to have founded the See of Byzantium, which became the Patriarchate of Constantinople, and accounts that his missionary work carried him along the Black Sea and as far as Kiev caused him to become the patron saint of both Romania and Russia. As noted, after his martyrdom, his bones traveled even farther. The X-shaped cross, called a saltire, which is Andrew's symbol, has ranged farther still, and may be found on the flags of Scotland, Great Britain, Nova Scotia, and Tenerife. Quite a reach for a missionary whose only recorded missionary words are "We have found the Messiah"! Still, those words, taken together with the two other actions of Andrew in the Gospels—bringing the Greek-speaking outsiders

> The firstborn of the apostolical choir, the first settled pillar of the church, the Peter before Peter, the foundation of the foundation, the firstfruits of the beginning.
> —Hesychius of Jerusalem[2]

to Jesus (John 12:20-22) and bringing the boy with the loaves and fishes to Jesus (John 6:8-10)—might make a blueprint for Christian mission: acknowledge Jesus, bring outsiders to him, and feed his flock.

Politics has played a role in the broad reach of this apostle about whom so little is known. Over the centuries, the title "First Apostle" has made Andrew's patronage attractive to churches and nations that saw themselves as competing for prestige and power with those who claimed Andrew's younger brother Peter as patron. In preaching on St. Andrew's day, it might be worth noting how the argument the disciples had about who was the greatest among them (Mark 9:33-37; Luke 9:46-48) has continued to be carried out in their names, despite Jesus' admonition against such striving.

THE READINGS

The Gospel readings in the various lectionaries give us Matthew and John's accounts of the calling of Andrew. Matthew's account (along with the other Synoptics) puts the focus on the story of following Jesus, immediately and without counting the cost of leaving their livelihood behind. The story of Andrew's responding to Jesus' call by going to tell others the news is found in John's Gospel, as are all the stories we have in Scripture of Andrew in an active role.

Much more than the discipleship emphasis in Matthew, it is the evangelical thrust in the passage from John's Gospel that is reinforced by all of the other readings. The reading from Deuteronomy in the Episcopal lectionary is about the accessibility of God's word—"The word is very near to you; it is in your mouth and in your heart for you to observe" (Deut. 30:14)—while the RCL's Ezekiel reading speaks of the responsibility of one entrusted with the word of God. God will hold Ezekiel accountable if the prophet fails to speak the warning that God has given him, but if he warns them and they keep away from sin, "they shall surely live, because they took warning; and you will have saved your life" (Ezek. 3:21).

The evangelical imperative is expressed in cosmic terms in the psalm. Not just humankind but the whole cosmos is compelled to convey God's glory:

After Andrew had stayed with Jesus and had learned much from him, he did not keep this treasure to himself, but hastened to share it with his brother Peter. Notice what Andrew said to him: "We have found the Messiah, that is to say, the Christ." Notice how his words reveal what he has learned in so short a time. They show the power of the master who has convinced them of this truth. Andrew's words reveal a soul waiting with the utmost longing for the coming of the Messiah, looking forward to his appearing from heaven, rejoicing when he does appear, and hastening to announce so great an event to others. To support one another in the things of the spirit is the true sign of good will between brothers, loving kinship and sincere affection. —St. John Chrysostom[3]

The heavens are telling the glory of God;
    and the firmament proclaims his handiwork.
Day to day pours forth speech,
    and night to night declares knowledge.
There is no speech, nor are there words;
    their voice is not heard;
yet their voice goes out through all the earth,
    and their words to the end of the world. (Ps. 19:1-4)

This is the other side of Ezekiel's message. On the one hand, God holds accountable those who fail to speak; on the other hand, to speak the word of God is to join joyfully in the chorus of the earth and heavens that declares God's glory echoing back and forth through all creation. And notice how skillfully the psalmist brings the images down to earth, moving from the rising sun emerging like a bridegroom from the wedding tent, to the earthly treasure of gold, to the simple pleasure of honey, and finally landing the glory of God in the words of the mouth and the meditations of the heart of the psalmist.

In the passage from Romans, Paul quotes Psalm 19 to make a point about how God has continually reached out to Israel, even when the chosen people persisted in unrighteousness. But the universal reach of the heavenly proclamation in the psalm speaks to Paul's larger point, which is that God's message has always reached beyond Israel, and indeed has been heard and heeded by Gentiles at times when the Israelites weren't paying attention. The Christian mission to the Gentiles, therefore, is not a radical new idea, but the continuation of what God has been doing all along. To claim, as Paul does, that there is no distinction between Jew and Greek either in sin's power (Rom. 3:22) or in salvation's reach is, he argues, an old truth, well supported by Hebrew Scripture. Salvation, then, comes to all who confess Jesus as Lord with their lips and believe in his resurrection in their hearts (Rom. 10:9). This, then, points us back to the example of Andrew in the passage from John's Gospel, where Andrew's two exemplary actions are to believe in Jesus and then to confess him as the Messiah.

God, our loving Father, St. Andrew introduced Peter, the Greek visitors, and the little boy with loaves and fishes, to your Son, Jesus Christ. May we be like him in sharing friendship and hospitality, and in faithfulness to Jesus and his Kingdom of justice, love and peace. May our country be a community in which everyone matters, everyone has an honoured place, and the dignity of each is assured by our faith in you as Father of us all. We ask this through Christ our Lord. Amen.—A Prayer for St. Andrew's Day[4]

For Further Comment

Additional comments on these Scripture texts, in part or in full, may be found in the seasonal volumes of *New Proclamation* as follows:

- Deuteronomy 30:11-14—Year C, Proper 10
- Psalm 19:1-6—Year A, Proper 22; Year B, Lent 3, Proper 19; Year C, Epiphany 3
- Romans 10:9-18—Year A, Proper 14; Year C, Lent 1
- Matthew 4:18-22—Year A, Epiphany 3
- John 1:35-42—Year A, Epiphany 2

Notes

1. Luke's account uses similar language but places Peter, rather than Andrew, in the story (Luke 5:5-11).

2. Hesychius of Jerusalem, *Eulogy of St. Andrew,* quoted in *Biblioteca Photius,* Codex 269, trans. Isaac Barrow in "A Treatise on the Pope's Supremacy" in *The Theological Works of Isaac Barrow* (Oxford: Oxford University Press, 1830), 7:155.

3. St. John Chrysostom, from *Homily 19 on the Gospel of St. John,* http://www.catholic-forum.com/saints/sainta12.htm (accessed July 9, 2007).

4. A Prayer for St. Andrew's Day, from Glasgow Churches Together, http://www.stmungomusic.org.uk/standrewspage.html (accessed July 9, 2007).

IMMACULATE CONCEPTION OF THE BLESSED VIRGIN MARY

DECEMBER 8

GERARD S. SLOYAN

ROMAN CATHOLIC (LFM)
Gen. 3:9–15, 20
Ps. 98:1, 2–3, 3–4
Eph. 1:3–6, 11–12
Luke 1:26–38

KEY THEMES

• The reason for today's feast is the fullness of divine favor an angel attributed to the virgin of Nazareth.
• Whatever may be said of the baptized with respect to divine election can be said preeminently of Mary.
• Mary's motherhood is reason enough for the Church to see her as first in faith.

NEW TESTAMENT READINGS
LUKE 1:26–38
EPHESIANS 1:3–6, 11–12

Since Mary's holiness from the moment she came to be in her mother's womb is the reason for this feast, it is fitting that the subject of the day's Gospel portion be how and why God so sanctified her. It was, of course, her having conceived in her womb the holiest of humans, Jesus fashioned of her flesh and blood. In Luke's narrative she is not immediately ready for motherhood. She is "espoused to a man," meaning that the first stage of an arranged marriage has taken place but not the second. This commitment would have been made for her in early girlhood. Now at perhaps age fifteen she can challenge the mysterious visitor from heaven: "How can this be since I am a virgin?," a modern rendering of the starker Semitic phrase, "I know not man." She is declaring a fact, namely that the second stage of an arranged marriage, consummation, has not taken place. Gabriel's reply is the biblical "Fear not!" found some fifty-eight times in the two testaments. Often it is a challenge to a person to proceed unintimidated by circumstance or human hostility. Here, however, the fear is rather awe at the proximity of the Holy One of Israel (see v. 49 of Mary's hymn of praise). The assurance Gabriel gives is based on the fact that the young woman who has been "most highly favored" of God has nothing to fear. The angel's one-word salutation descriptive of Mary is an intensive form of a verb for God's gracious act; hence the Latin Bible's rendering "full of grace," familiar to any who have sung an *Ave, Maria* or said a *Hail, Mary,* is on the mark. The fullness of divine favor attributed to the virgin of Nazareth by an angel is the reason for today's feast. There was not a moment of her existence when she was not the subject of God's gift of holiness. Her motherhood of Jesus lay well in the future of her having been conceived, but it was the reason for the gift (*charis*). Luke writes from the vantage point, which was that of the entire early church, of one who knew the Son to be born as the now-ascended Risen One. Consequently, he assigns the naming of Jesus to Mary (Matthew at 1:2 will make it Joseph). Luke also draws from the future his title "Son of the Most High" and role as the Davidic descendant "who will reign forever over the house of Jacob." Jacob, the father of twelve sons, was the father of Judah by Leah. Explaining further how this young virgin will bear a child in the near future, the angel attributes the marvel to the Holy Spirit acting as the power of the Most High. This entire Lukan phrase is, among other things, an early witness to the church's trinitarian belief.

Mother! whose virgin bosom was uncrost
With the least shade of thought to sin allied;
Woman! above all women glorified,
Our tainted nature's solitary boast; . . .
Yet some . . . the supplicant knee might bend
As to visible Power, in which did blend
All that was mixed and reconciled in thee
Of mother's love with maiden purity,
Of high with low, celestial with terreen.
—William Wordsworth[1]

The mystery in the Catholic and Eastern Orthodox traditions of Mary's having been conceived sinless has often been mistaken for the mystery of her conceiving the child Jesus without a man. In this erroneous view the term *immaculate conception* has been the subject of much ribald humor. This is ignorance compounded by coarse vulgarity. The sorry jests are not likely to be silenced by the reminder that Matthew's account of Jesus' virginal conception derives from the same tradition as Luke's, making it a belief of the apostolic age. While the Matthew narrative is centered on Joseph's legal fatherhood, it does not speak of him as all-holy as a result of his intimate relation with the Child as Luke does Mary. The first reading on this feast in the Roman Missal of 1570 (which means that it was in use going back several centuries) was from the book of Wisdom [of Solomon] at 8:22-35. The wisdom that the Lord possessed from the beginning and that provided him daily delight was there made a type of Mary. Perhaps because Paul says that "Christ Jesus became for us wisdom from God" (1 Cor. 1:30)—hence Constantinople's magnificent basilica Holy Wisdom, which bears a Christ title, not a Mary title—the framers of

Lectionary for Mass deserted that reading in favor of another typological one from the first chapter of Ephesians. In a sustained panegyric of the God and Father of our Lord Jesus Christ, blessed be He, God is praised for having destined us for "adoption as his children," "a glorious grace bestowed on us in the Beloved" (1:5-6). The passage was chosen on the principle that whatever may be said of the baptized with respect to divine election can be said preeminently of Mary. It had a special recommendation in the phrase "we who were the first to set our hope on Christ" (v. 12). The Ephesians' author is speaking of the providential "will and good pleasure" (v. 9) that made early choice of the Gentiles of the province of Asia. As to firstness, however, the church traditionally considered Mary the first believer, regardless of the candidates whom three of the Gospels propose for having seen the Risen Lord shortly after his resurrection. Jesus' commendation of his mother from the cross to a well-loved disciple he called "son" is the scriptural reason for this if one were needed. But her motherhood is reason enough for the Church to see her as first in faith.

Because John's Gospel has Jesus address his mother as "Woman" both at Cana and from the cross, a usage for which there is no parallel in any Semitic writing of the time, it must be concluded that this evangelist whose prose is rich in symbolism is making Mary a type of woman among all who believe in her Son.

Another reason for the choice of this reading is the Eve-Mary contrast spelled out by Irenaeus in his *Five Books against the Gnosis Falsely So-called*. There he writes: "The Lord . . . by his obedience on a tree did in a new [and different] way (literally, recapitulated) what was done by disobedience in [connection with] a tree; and that seduction by which the virgin Eve, already betrothed to a man, had been wickedly seduced was negated when the angel brought good tidings to Mary, who already belonged to a man. . . . The former was seduced to disobey God but the latter was persuaded to obey Him so that the Virgin Mary might become the advocate of the virgin Eve. . . . Then indeed . . . was the wisdom of the serpent conquered by the simplicity of the dove" (V.19.1).[2] Clearly, the late second-century missionary to Gaul who, finding Gnostic Christianity widely adopted by the intelligentsia in Rome, had the Adam-Christ balance in mind when he set about his refutation of the dangerous trend. Then, indeed, "the sin of the first-formed man was amended by the chastisement of the First-begotten [Son] . . . the serpent conquered by the dove and the chains broken by which we were in bondage to death."[3]

OLD TESTAMENT READINGS
GENESIS 3:9–15, 20
PSALM 98:1, 2–3, 3–4

The Genesis author needs the snake for his three-character play in one act. The LORD God does not require being borne from above on a machine like the deities in Greek drama. He walks in the garden in the breezes of late afternoon after the day's punishing heat and deals calmly with the rebellious pair. They had been given only one *mitzvah*, one commandment, and they broke it. Punishments that fit the crime had to be meted out by a God who is all-just. They are these: shame at their nakedness, the author's explanation of why the human race goes clothed; for women, the pain of childbearing; for men, the hard labor of tilling the resistant soil; for all, universal mortality as the fitting punishment for universal sin. The snake is a deceiver by nature, lying low in the grass to strike lethally at the unwary. He has been declared the enemy of the offspring of the woman who is the mother of all the living, forever after crushing the serpent's head who strikes at the human heel. This is the victory celebrated in the psalm in response to that cryptic reading: "The LORD has made known his victory. . . . All the ends of the earth have seen the victory of our God" (Ps. 98:2a, 3b).

The ultimate punishment for the sin of disobeying the divine command is, of course, the necessity of dying (vv. 2–3). In the tale, the snake is not the devil of the piece. He was thought to be Satan only later in the mentality testified to in Wisdom at 2:24, just as the sin of the first pair was much later considered a heritage of guilt imposed on all who would come after them.

Andrew of Crete in the eighth century was the first to record a Feast of the Conception of Anna, the mother of Mary, at a time when another feast titled The Conception of Mary was also being celebrated. Photius, patriarch of Constantinople, seems to have made it a feast of Eastern churchwide observance a century later. It appears in the Western calendar of feasts of Leofric in eleventh-century England, then in Canterbury at the time of Eadmer and a different Anselm than the Saint. The feast was being kept in several other regions of England, only to meet with theological resistance because of the conviction that Mary would have to be born a sinner in need of redemption like everyone else. By the year 1200 the feast was being observed almost universally in France and in parts Germany and Belgium. The Italian Dominican friar, St. Tomasso d'Aquino, opposed the possibility of a sinlessly conceived Mary for that reason as

Father, You prepared the Virgin Mary to be the worthy Mother of Your Son. You let her share beforehand in the salvation Christ would bring by His death, and kept her sinless from the first moment of her conception. Help us by her prayers to live in Your presence without sin. We ask this through our Lord Jesus Christ, Your Son, Who lives and reigns with You in the community of the Holy Spirit, one God, for ever and ever. Amen.
—Collect for the Feast[4]

St. Bernard had already done. But a number of English Franciscans persisted in making the claim, notably Blessed John of Duns in Scotland who was born shortly before Aquinas's death. Scotus was the first well-known theologian to defend the doctrine. A late fifteenth-century pope went on to approve the text of a Mass and Office of the feast, while two seventeenth-century popes gave the feast strong approbation. It was left to the vigorous Pius IX, who entertained few doubts, to declare as a dogma of faith what had long been Catholic teaching in the West. His promulgation of the mystery was marked by a resurgence of all the doubt and denial that had marked its slow development. He consequently wrote in his *bulla* (the lead seal on a document) of promulgation of 1854: "We declare, pronounce, and define the teaching which holds that the most blessed virgin Mary was, in the first moment of her conception, by a singular grace and privilege of God, in view [*intuitu*] of the merits of Jesus Christ, savior of the human race, preserved immune from all taint of original sin, a teaching revealed by God and for that reason to be firmly and constantly believed by all the faithful." The Latin wording is frequently Englished as "in virtue of the foreseen merits of Jesus Christ . . . from all stain [*lábe*] of original fault [*culpae*, or guilt]."

For Further Comment

Additional comments on these Scripture texts, in part or in full, may be found in the seasonal volumes of *New Proclamation* as follows:

- Genesis 3:9-15, 20—Year B, Proper 5
- Psalm 98:1-4—Year B, Easter 6; Year C, Proper 27, Proper 28; Years ABC, Christmas Day 3, Easter Vigil
- Ephesians 1:3-6, 11-12—Year B, Proper 10; Year C, All Saints; Years ABC, Christmas 2
- Luke 1:26-38—Year B, Advent 4

Notes

1. William Wordsworth, "The Virgin," in *The Complete Poetical Works* (London: Macmillan, 1988), http://www.bartleby.com/145/ww626.html (accessed June 29, 2007).

2. Irenaeus, *Five Books against the Gnosis Falsely So-called,* in Cyril C. Richardson, ed., *Early Christian Fathers* (Philadelphia: Westminster Press, 1953), 389f. Author trans. from the Latin (Greek is extant).

3. Ibid.

4. http://www.catholic.org/prayers/prayer.php?p=324 (accessed June 29, 2007).

STEPHEN, DEACON AND MARTYR

DECEMBER 26

RUTH A. MEYERS

LUTHERAN (ELW)	EPISCOPAL (BCP)	ROMAN CATHOLIC (LFM)
2 Chron. 24:17-22	Jer. 26:1-9, 12-15	Acts 6:8-10; 7:54-59
Ps. 17:1-9, 15	Psalm 31 or 31:1-5	Ps. 31:3cd-4, 6, 8ab, 16bc, 17
Acts 6:8—7:2a, 51-60	Acts 6:8—7:2a, 51c-60	
Matt. 23:34-39	Matt. 23:34-39	Matt. 10:17-22

KEY THEMES

• Stephen, the first Christian martyr, bears witness to Christ as he dies.

• God stands with those who are persecuted for their faith.

• In what ways have you borne witness to your faith in Jesus Christ? Have you ever found yourself rejected or ridiculed or persecuted for your faith? How was God present to you in that experience?

• How do you understand the relation between Christianity and Judaism?

THE SAINT

All that is known of Stephen is found in chapters 6 and 7 of the book of Acts. He is likely to have been a Hellenist, that is, a Jewish Christian of Greek origin. When the Hellenists complained that the Hebrew Christians were neglecting their widows in the daily distribution of food, the apostles responded by setting apart men for this responsibility. Stephen is listed first among this group of seven, and the narrative further distinguishes him as "a man full of faith and the Holy Spirit" (Acts 6:5). Traditionally, these seven are understood as the first deacons, ordained by the apostles through prayer and laying on of hands to wait on tables, that is, to serve those in need. The text does not name them as "deacons," however, and Stephen's ministry was not limited to service; Acts goes on to relate that he "did great wonders and signs among the people" (Acts 6:8).

Stephen's actions stirred up hostility among some of the Jews. They denounced him to the Jewish council (the Sanhedrin), accusing him—falsely, according to Acts—of blasphemy against Moses, against the law and the Temple, and against God. Stephen defended himself with a lengthy speech (Acts 7:2-53) that recapitulated the history of Israel, turning each of the charges of blasphemy against his accusers. God had sent Moses "as both ruler and liberator" (Acts 7:35), but the Israelites rejected him. God had given the law to Moses on Mount Sinai, but the Israelites turned away to worship false gods. The Israelites had worshiped without a temple from the time of Moses until the time of David; even though eventually Solomon built the Temple, the prophet Isaiah attests that God "does not dwell in houses made with human hands" (Acts 7:48; cf. Isa. 66:1-2). At the climax of his defense before the Sanhedrin, Stephen accused them of betraying and murdering Jesus, the "Righteous One" (Acts 7:52) who was the prophet that Moses had promised.

The response to Stephen's speech is unsurprising. Who would not be enraged at being described as "stiff-necked people, uncircumcised in heart and ears . . . forever opposing the Holy Spirit" (Acts 7:51)? While Stephen was filled with the Spirit and saw a vision of Jesus enthroned in heaven, the members of the council dragged him away, outside the city, to stone him. This scene should

> If Stephen had not prayed, the Church would not have Paul.—St. Augustine[1]

not be interpreted as raw mob violence. Rather, it is likely that the Sanhedrin imposed the death penalty. Stoning outside the gates of the city was the Jewish penalty for blasphemy, and the witnesses against the blasphemer were to cast the first stones (Deut. 17:2-7; Lev. 24:13-16).

Stephen thus became the first Christian martyr. His example was remembered and often imitated in the early centuries when Christians were frequently persecuted. However, the earliest record of a liturgical commemoration of Stephen dates from the fourth century. (The veneration of Polycarp, the Bishop of Smyrna who was martyred *circa* 155, began within a few years of his death and marks the beginning of Christian liturgical celebration of the death of martyrs.)

Although the date of Stephen's death is not recorded, December 26 has traditionally been his feast day. The commemoration originated in Jerusalem in the fourth century and quickly spread throughout Christendom. Its appearance on the calendar may have predated the earliest celebration of Christmas. However, commentators since the late fourth century have noted how appropriate it is that Stephen should be remembered on the day immediately following the celebration of the Nativity, since Stephen is so closely related to Jesus through the act of martyrdom. During the Middle Ages, Stephen, together with John the Evangelist (December 27) and the Holy Innocents (December 28), was given the title "Companions of Christ." In the Christian East, beginning in the seventh century, the commemoration of the parents of Jesus on December 26 shifted the feast of Stephen to the following day.

Acts reports Stephen's burial but gives no indication of the place. Nonetheless, in 415 a priest named Lucian discovered Stephen's bones in Jerusalem, providing a strong impetus for the spread of the feast. His remains were entombed in a church built by the Empress Eudoxia outside the Damascus Gate in Jerusalem; the Dominicans discovered the ruins of this church in 1882, and a new church dedicated to Stephen was rebuilt on the site. Other shrines dedicated to Stephen, many having a portion of his relics, were built around the Mediterranean world during the Middle Ages. A feast celebrating the finding of the body was introduced in the Western church in the ninth or tenth century on August 3, which may have been the date of the dedication of a church to Stephen. The Greek church commemorates the translation of Stephen's relics to Constantinople on August 2.

THE GOSPEL
MATTHEW 10:17–22 (LFM)
MATTHEW 23:34–39 (ELW, BCP)

Jesus' proclamations about the persecution that disciples will face address the situation of the early church, including the martyrdom of Stephen. Matthew 10 includes this warning as part of Jesus' instructions to the twelve apostles, whom he sends out to proclaim the good news. "Councils" refers to the Jewish authorities, while "governors and kings" are Roman officials; the disciples can expect persecution from both religious and government leaders. Moreover, the members of their own families will participate in their persecution. Jesus encourages the disciples to persevere no matter what they face. He assures them that God will remain with them and give them the words with which to respond to their accusers. Furthermore, Jesus promises salvation for those who "endure to the end," that is, who remain steadfast in their faith even to the point of death.

Troparion

O Protomartyr and mighty warrior of
  Christ our God,
  You are victorious in battle and crowned
  with glory, O holy Stephen!
  You confounded the council of your
  persecutors,
  Beholding your Savior enthroned at the
  right hand of the Father.
  Never cease to intercede for the
  salvation of our souls![2]

The passage from Matthew 23 is the conclusion of seven "woes" in which Jesus denounces the scribes and Pharisees. The inference is that the contemporary Jewish leaders are implicated in the murder of prophets throughout the history of Israel. The murder of Abel (Gen. 4:8) extends this guilt to the beginning of human history. Zechariah is probably wrongly identified as the prophet who was the son of Berechiah (Zech. 1:1). Instead, Zechariah, son of Jehoiada, who was stoned to death in the Temple (2 Chron. 24:20-21), was more likely originally intended. The murder of the latter Zechariah would be the last reported in the Hebrew Bible, in which 2 Chronicles is the final book. While there are actually very few instances of prophets killed by the people of Israel, rejection of the prophets is a more common occurrence in the Hebrew Scriptures.

Matthew adds Jesus' lament over Jerusalem at the conclusion of his woe sayings. The use of a feminine image of divine activity, that of a mother hen gathering her brood, is striking. "Blessed is the one who comes in the name of the Lord" was proclaimed earlier in Matthew's Gospel at Jesus' triumphal entrance into the city (21:9); here the reference is eschatological and leads to Jesus' teaching on the end of the age (Matthew 24).

THE READINGS
ACTS 6:8—7:2A, 51-60 (ELW, BCP)
ACTS 6:8-10; 7:54-59 (LFM)

The selection from Acts provides the key story for today's commemoration. Stephen's accusation incorporates descriptions of the Israelites in their stubbornness (Exod. 33:3, 5; Jer. 9:26; Ezek. 447; 2 Chron. 30:7-8; Isa. 63:10) and echoes Jesus' charges against the scribes and Pharisees in Matthew 23 (cf. Luke 11:49-51). Now Stephen names Jesus among those who were persecuted, and Stephen's audience is implicated in his murder.

Kontakion
Yesterday the Master assumed our flesh
    and became our guest;
Today His servant is stoned to death
    and departs in the flesh,
The glorious Protomartyr Stephen.[3]

His words stir up the council, leading them to enact against him the violence they (or their ancestors) have perpetrated against others. Stephen's apparent calm is a stark contrast against the frenzy of the mob. His martyrdom mirrors Jesus' passion: he commends his spirit to God (cf. Luke 23:46), and his final words are a prayer of forgiveness for his persecutors (cf. Luke 23:34).

The episode is a key turning point in the narrative of Acts. Stephen's death results in a severe persecution against the church in Jerusalem, scattering the apostles throughout the surrounding countryside (Acts 8:1). Yet this dispersion enables the spread of the gospel as it is carried beyond Jerusalem to Judea and Samaria, helping to fulfill Jesus' command for the apostles to carry the gospel to the ends of the earth (Acts 1:8). In addition, the story of Stephen's martyrdom introduces Saul, who will become a key figure.

The shorter version appointed in the Roman lectionary omits all detail of Stephen's dispute with the members of the synagogue. A preacher may need to explain why they became so enraged that they killed him.

2 CHRONICLES 24:17-22 (ELW)
JEREMIAH 26:1-9, 12-15 (BCP)

The Lutheran lectionary appoints the passage about the death of Zechariah that is probably the reference originally intended in Matthew 23. The books of Chronicles tell of the history of Israel. The period of the Davidic dynasty is characterized by movement between obedience and disobedience to God. Zechariah and his father Jehoiada served at the time of King Joash. While Jehoiada was alive, Joash restored the Temple to the worship of the God of Israel. But after Jehoiada died, the king allowed the abandonment of the Temple and a return to idolatry. Zechariah spoke against this and as a result was stoned to death in the Temple. While Stephen's last words were a prayer of forgiveness, Zechariah asks vengeance. Joash and his large army were then defeated by a small Syrian army, and Joash's own servants conspired to kill him (2 Chron. 24:23-25).

The blood of the martyrs is the seed of the church.—Tertullian, *Apologeticus*

The Episcopal lectionary appoints a different account of a persecuted prophet: Jeremiah. His offense is a sermon he preaches in the Temple, prophesying the destruction of the Temple if the people did not change their ways and obey God (Jer. 26:1-6; cf. Jer. 7:1-15). The Temple priests and prophets accuse Jeremiah of speaking words that did not come from God, an offense punishable by death (Deut. 18:20). The addition of "all the people" at several points in the narrative emphasizes that Jeremiah stands alone among the people. In his defense, Jeremiah reiterates his prophecy as a word spoken by God and warns of dire consequences if the officials put him to death. Nonetheless, he is willing to accept death rather than refuse to speak the words God has commanded. While Stephen's accusations resulted in his death, the officials of Judah relent, having determined that Jeremiah had actually spoken in the name of God.

PSALM 31:1-5 (BCP)
PSALM 31:3-4, 6, 8, 16-17 (LFM)

Stephen's prayer at his death, "Lord Jesus, receive my spirit" (Acts 7:59), echoes the psalmist's plea, "Into your hands I commend my spirit."

An Adult Christ at Christmas,[3] the title of a book by New Testament scholar Raymond Brown, captures the significance of the commemoration of Stephen on the day after Christmas. With a focus on the baby Jesus, Christmas can all too easily become sentimentalized. The feast of Stephen reminds us that the incarnation cannot be understood apart from the reality of Jesus' passion, death, and resurrection.

Stephen's diatribe against the leaders of the synagogue, taken with the Gospel passages, confronts us with the problem of Christian anti-Semitism. For centuries, Christians persecuted Jews, holding them responsible for the rejection and crucifixion of the Messiah. Our experience might more closely parallel that of the religious leaders accused of having blood on their hands, rather than Stephen's innocent suffering. Particularly in light of the Holocaust, some Christians have begun to acknowledge the history of Christian anti-Semitism and seek a more respectful understanding of our Jewish roots. Whether a preacher deals directly with the matter, it is worth considering how to preach on this feast and these texts in a manner that does not blame "the Jews" for the crucifixion.

FOR FURTHER COMMENT

Additional comments on these Scripture texts, in part or in full, may be found in the seasonal volumes of *New Proclamation* as follows:

- Psalm 17—Year A, Proper 13; Year C, Proper 27
- Psalm 31—Year A, Easter 5, Epiphany 9/Proper 4; Years ABC, Holy Saturday, Passion/Palm Sunday
- Acts 6:8—7:2a, 51-60—Year A, Easter 5
- Matthew 10:17-22—Year A, Proper 6

Notes

1. St. Augustine, Sermon 94, s.v., "Stephen (Protomartyr), St.," *New Catholic Encyclopedia* (Detroit: Thomson/Gale; Washington, DC: Catholic University of America, 2003).

2. http://orthodoxwiki.org/Apostle_Stephen_the_Protomartyr#Hymns (accessed June 21, 2007).

3. Raymond Brown, *An Adult Christ at Christmas: Essays on the Three Biblical Christmas Stories* (Collegeville, Minn.: Liturgical Press, 1977).

JOHN, APOSTLE AND EVANGELIST

DECEMBER 27

CRAIG A. SATTERLEE

LUTHERAN (ELW)	EPISCOPAL (BCP)	ROMAN CATHOLIC (LFM)
Gen. 1:1-5, 26-31	Exod. 33:18-23	
Ps. 116:12-19	Psalm 92 or 92:1-4, 11-14	Ps. 97:1-2, 5-6, 11-12
1 John 1:1—2:2	1 John 1:1-9	1 John 1:1-4
John 21:20-25	John 21:19b-24	John 20:2-8

KEY THEMES

- John provides an ideal of discipleship for all believers.
- This feast day is an occasion to proclaim Johannine theology, particularly a theology of the incarnation.
- Christ frees us to confess our sin.

ST. JOHN

The Gospels portray John, son of Zebedee, as one of Jesus' closest disciples, along with John's brother James and Simon Peter. The Gospels recount how Jesus called John from fishing. The Synoptic Gospels provide clues to how much Jesus trusted him. John is among the small group of disciples who accompany Jesus to Jairus's house, where Jesus raises Jairus's daughter, as well as to the Mount of the Transfiguration, and, in Mark, the Garden of Gethsemane. John is so familiar with Jesus that he requests special status among the disciples. In Mark, the Zebedee brothers ask Jesus to sit at his right and left hands; in Matthew, their mother asks Jesus for them.

Tradition holds that John is "that disciple whom Jesus loved" mentioned in the Fourth Gospel, who reclined with Jesus at the last supper, and who asked Jesus who would betray him. This disciple also stood with Jesus' mother at the foot of the cross (the only disciple not to flee), where Jesus commended his mother to this disciple's care. The beloved disciple reached the empty tomb ahead of Peter, and recognized the risen Lord on the lakeshore before Peter, enabling Peter to act on this disciple's recognition. This disciple embodies the love and intimacy with Jesus that, in John's Gospel, is the goal of discipleship.[1]

John is traditionally considered to be the author of the Gospel and three epistles that bear his name, as well as the book of Revelation. Legend says that, after being exiled to the island of Patmos, where John is said to have written Revelation, this son of Zebedee lived in Ephesus. Tradition says that John died there about the year 100 C.E. at an advanced age. John is considered the only one of the twelve apostles who was not martyred. In the fourth century, a church building in Constantinople was named for St. John. It is conceivable that the date of his feast day, December 27, marks the anniversary of the dedication of that church building. The symbol for John is a chalice with a serpent on it, reflecting that John is said to have drunk poison wine and was unharmed.

Coming just two days after Christmas, John's feast day is frequently (and rightfully) overshadowed by the church's celebration of the birth of Christ. Yet, as the Prayer of the Day suggests, the commemoration of St. John provides a fitting occasion to contemplate the mysteries of the Word made flesh, so that we may be instructed in the holy gospel, walk in the light of God's truth, and attain eternal life. The preacher might help the congregation to consider the incarnation in a way that leads them to glimpse and be awed by the presence of God in Jesus Christ. The preacher might also make an explicit tie to Revelation and emphasize that the church continues to look for Christ to come, bringing life and light. Regardless of the message, the homiletic challenge on this saint's day is to allow the power of Johannine metaphors and images to speak for themselves, and not to explain that power away.

The Gospel
JOHN 21:20-25 (ELW, BCP)
JOHN 20:2-8 (LFM)

On this festival day, John's resurrection narrative (20:2-8), which LFM appoints as the Gospel reading, is not so much about the empty tomb as the race to get there, and the relationship between Peter and the beloved disciple, whom the church traditionally assumes is John. This other disciple ran faster than Peter and reached the tomb first. While Peter enters the tomb, sees the linen wrappings lying there, and is confused, the beloved disciple enters the tomb, sees the same evidence, and believes. In contrast to Peter, the beloved disciple believes that Jesus has been raised, that the tomb's emptiness bears witness that Jesus conquered death and judged the ruler of this world. More than the first to believe in the resurrection, the beloved disciple's faith is exemplary in that it is immediate and is not the result of seeing Jesus. As Jesus will later say to Thomas, "Blessed are those who have not seen and yet have come to believe" (20:29). The beloved disciple exhibits this kind of faith.

In the narrative of the postresurrection appearance (John 21:19-25) appointed by the ELW and BCP, the contrast between the beloved disciple and Peter continues. Jesus says to Simon Peter, "Follow me." Looking over his shoulder, Peter sees "the disciple whom Jesus loved" already following Jesus. This unnamed disciple not only beats Simon Peter to the empty tomb and to believe in the resurrection. He is also the first to grasp what it means to be Jesus' disciple. That "the disciple whom Jesus loved" is the "follower *par excellence*"[2] is certainly the message of John 21. Perhaps this passage was chosen because this is the message of this feast day as well.

"Lord, what about this man?" Peter asks. On this day commemorating John, Peter's question about the beloved disciple is our question as well, should we attempt to preach about the beloved disciple as an example of discipleship for us. Peter's question, and that of the Johannine community, is about the future. They want to know what will happen to this disciple. What is God's plan for his life? If Peter will stretch out his hands and be crucified (v. 19), how will this disciple meet his end? If Peter's question is about the future, our question is about the past. What did this disciple do that makes him beloved and ideal? If we do not know the facts of the life of John, the son of Zebedee, what do we know about John that will help *us* to be beloved disciples? In other words, what do we celebrate on this day? Jesus' cryptic answer does not help. "Jesus said to Peter, "If it is my will that he remain until I come, what is that to you?" (21:22). Notice the word *if*. Jesus does not give much away. Perhaps this is precisely the point. Ideal discipleship does not consist in the details of John's life or of anyone's, but that one's life and ultimate outcome are entrusted to God. One does not have to be crucified like Peter or martyred like the rest of the apostles to be a beloved, ideal disciple. One can grow old peacefully, like John is said to have done. Discipleship is not the exclusive concern of the Christian elite and heroic, but of every believer.

> The other Evangelists instruct us in their Gospels on the active life; but John in his Gospel instructs us also on the contemplative life.—Augustine[3]

The author of John's Gospel then tells us what the beloved disciple did that makes him a faithful follower of Jesus and example for us. The beloved disciple believed without seeing, then faithfully and truthfully witnessed to Jesus. This disciple authentically testified with his life to who Jesus is and what Jesus does. Though he may not have authored the words of the Gospel According to John, or of anything else for that matter, the beloved disciple "stood behind" and "vouched for" what is written.[4] Like this beloved disciple, every Christian's life can faithfully and authentically bear witness to the gospel. We might think of John as the ideal disciple not because of the great things he accomplished but because, like "the disciple whom Jesus loved," John offers a model of what every Christian can do and be.

SECOND READING

1 JOHN 1:1—2:2 (ELW)
1 JOHN 1:1-9 (BCP)
1 JOHN 1:1-4 (LFM)

Despite scholarly uncertainty about the relationship of the Gospel and epistles that bear John's name, the second reading (1 John 1:1—2:2) is appointed to echo John's Gospel and provide a summary of Johannine theology. The preface of 1 John clearly recalls the prologue of John's Gospel. 1 John starts "from the beginning." John's Gospel opens with the words, "In the beginning." The epistle writer's claim that "the eternal life that was with the Father and was revealed to us" (v. 2) is synonymous with the Gospel prologue's claim that the creative Word, who was with God from the beginning and in whom is life and light, dwelt among us (John 1:9-13). The "word of life" is Jesus, the preexistent *Logos*. The "we" of 1 John, representing the church in solidarity with eyewitnesses, heard, saw with their eyes, looked at, and touched the incarnate Word, the Jesus of history. Seeing and touching Jesus is especially reminiscent of postresurrection appearances and coming to faith.

> It is the Son of Thunder, the Beloved of Christ, the pillar of all the churches in the world, who now comes to us. It is he who possesses the keys of heaven, who has drunk the chalice of Christ, and has been baptized with His baptism, and who so confidently reclined on the breast of the Lord.
> —St. John Chrysostom[5]

The introductions of both books also speak of "life revealed." The life that is God's gift to humanity is historically revealed in Jesus. God's life is concretely and completely visible to us in Christ. Moreover, Jesus not only reveals God's life. Jesus makes fellowship with and participation in the life of the Father possible (v. 3). This life is eternal. Rather than life prolonged to infinity, "eternal life" is a spiritual quality that Jesus gives to every believer. It is the sharing of living fellowship with the Father in which time loses importance.[6] This fellowship is available in the present (v. 2). Eternal life is characterized by complete joy (v. 4).

The incarnation is an experience that demands acceptance and response. The verbs in verse 2 (seeing, testifying, and declaring) suggest that the fitting response is experience, testimony, and evangelization. A personal encounter with and experience of the incarnate Word leads believers to testify to that Word. This testimony may lead to explicit proclamation and evangelization as believers reflect upon their testimony and experience. Separating the verbs *testify* and *declare* may suggest that what a Christian *is* takes precedence over what a Christian *says*.

So what is a Christian to be? Verse 5 suggests that God is absolute in glory, truth, and holiness. We cannot claim to be in right relationship with God and behave unrighteously, because beholding God's righteousness in Christ makes our sin undeniable. Followers of Christ are to walk in God's glory, truth, and holiness. Yet, Jesus Christ, our advocate and atoning sacrifice, forgives us of all sin and cleanses us from all unrighteousness. With this assurance, we can freely confess our sins and strive to walk in the way of God.

FIRST READING

GENESIS 1:1-5, 26-31 (RCL)
EXODUS 13:18-23 (BCP)

The texts appointed as the first reading for this day provide fruitful illustrative material for the theology summarized in the epistle reading. The ELW choice of Gen. 1:1-5, 26-31 is a second, more vivid illusion to the prologue of John's Gospel. God, through the Word in whom there is light and life, creates light and separates day and night, makes humankind in the divine image, and brings forth every plant and animal. God speaks a word of blessing on humankind and declares creation good. On this day, Exod. 13:18-23, appointed by the BCP, contrasts the limited vision of glory that God granted to Moses with the complete vision of God's glory granted to us in Jesus Christ. Whereas Moses was only permitted to see God's back, we see, hear, and touch God in Jesus Christ.

What does it mean for your congregation to entrust its ultimate outcome to God?

FOR FURTHER COMMENT

Additional comments on these Scripture texts, in part or in full, may be found in the seasonal volumes of *New Proclamation* as follows:

- Genesis 1:1-5, 26-31—Year B, Baptism; Year A, Trinity
- Exodus 33:18-23—Year A, Proper 24
- Psalm 92—Year B, Proper 6; Year C, Epiphany 8/Proper 3
- Psalm 97—Year C, Easter 7; Years ABC, Christmas Day 3
- Psalm 116—Year A, Easter 3, Proper 6; Years ABC, Holy Thursday
- 1 John 1:1—2:2—Year A, Easter 2
- John 20:2-8—Years ABC, Easter Sunday

Notes

1. Gail R. O'Day, *New Interpreter's Bible*, vol. 9 (Nashville: Abingdon, 2004), 840.

2. Gerard S. Sloyan, *John*, Interpretation: A Bible Commentary for Teaching and Preaching (Atlanta: John Knox, 1988), 231.

3. St. Augustine, "On the Agreement of the Evangelists," quoted by St. Thomas Aquinas, "Prologue," in *Commentary on the Gospel of St. John*, trans. James A. Weisheipl, O.P. (Albany, N.Y.: Magi Books, 1998), http://www.diafrica. org/nigeriaop/kenny/CDtexts/SSJohn.htm (accessed June 28, 2007).

4. Sloyan; John, 232.

5. St. John Chrysostom, *Commentary on St. John the Apostle and Evangelist,* trans. Sister Thomas Aquinas Goggin, S.C.H. (New York: Fathers of the Church, 1957), 4.

6. Stephen S. Smalley, *1, 2, 3 John*, Word Biblical Commentary, vol. 51 (Waco: Word, 1984), 10.

THE HOLY INNOCENTS, MARTYRS

DECEMBER 28

GAIL RAMSHAW

LUTHERAN (ELW)	EPISCOPAL (BCP)	ROMAN CATHOLIC (LFM)
Jer. 31:15–17	Jer. 31:15–17	1 John 1:5—2:2
Psalm 124	Psalm 124	Ps. 124:2-3, 4-5, 7b-8
1 Peter 4:12–19	Rev. 21:1-7	
Matt. 2:13–18	Matt. 2:13–18	Matt. 2:13–18

KEY THEMES

- The Christian liturgical calendar, by setting martyrs' days directly after the Nativity, means to balance the manger with the cross.
- Holy Innocents has recently focused less on the children as martyrs and more on them as representatives of all innocent sufferers.
- Matthew's Gospel harks back to the stories of Pharaoh, Moses, and Rachel.

THE DAY

The placement of the feast of the Holy Innocents only three days after Christmas surprises many contemporary people, in large part because the celebration of Christmas in much of our culture reflects more its origin as a communal festival at winter solstice than its Christian focus on the incarnation. An anthropologist would see our Christmas—a blow-out, over-the-top, month-long party marked by festive meals and lavish gift giving—as the way that an affluent society keeps a time of year at which in ancient societies the people in the Northern Hemisphere welcomed with gratitude the lengthening of daylight that arrives around December 21. It is not surprising that humans will delight in the return of warmth and light to their world. Of course they will light candles and give presents; of course they will laugh in the face of the barren fields by piling up food and drink on their tables. Perhaps some ancient peoples even imagined that their partying was the impetus for the sun to shine a little longer each day, that it was thanks to their ritual that the world turned in the other direction.

Yet some of the depth of the Christian proclamation of the incarnation is lost in all this partying, and the Christian liturgical calendar, by setting martyrs' days directly afterward, means to balance the manger with the tomb. Christ is born not mainly so I can get lots of Christmas presents. Only when we face the sorrows, the suffering, the hatred, the violence, the death all around us can we begin to contemplate why Christianity posits the necessity of the incarnation. Only surrounded by dark do we long for light. And so December 26 is kept as the day of the first martyr, Stephen; December 27 is for St. John, a witness to the incarnation; and at December 28 we come to what was often termed "The Slaughter of the Innocents." Many Christians keep also December 29 in this same vein as the martyrdom of Thomas Becket.

First mentioned as a feast day in Carthage in 505, Holy Innocents was observed as a martyrs' day, as if the dead children, although not Christian, had indeed died for Christ. In the thirteenth century, this post-Christmas lineup of martyrs and witnesses was called "the companions of Christ," accompanying Jesus in life and death. The liturgical color of the day is red, for the blood of martyrs. In recent times, the observance has focused less on the children as martyrs and more on them as representatives of all innocent sufferers. These observances mean to bring into our celebrations of the twelve days of Christmas attention on all those for whom Christ was born, all those who are killed for their faith, all those who are exiled from the community, and all the innocent who suffer violence for which they are not responsible. We might see the day of the Holy Innocents as calling into our living rooms the millions who did not feast, who received no gifts, all the innocent people suffering violence at the hands of others, all the infants who did not grow into adulthood.

The day is based on the story in Matthew 2. There is no corroboration from outside Matthew's Gospel of this event. Most likely the tale combines several facts about the sociopolitical situation during the life of Jesus with biblical memories of God's intervention in Israel's history of suffering. The sociopolitical background to the story includes the historical figure Herod, who was indeed responsible for the murder of members of his own family, including two of his sons, and who ordered that at the hour of his death various prominent citizens would be executed so that there would be grief in the land. Raymond Brown's magisterial study *The Birth of the Messiah* computes that had Herod ordered some such systematic executions, no more than twenty boys would have been killed.[1] Yet with or without the historicity of this Bethlehem story, Herod stands as a symbol of all the tyrants of history who kill others to enhance their own survival. Such Herods are as real today as he was twenty centuries ago. The narrative proclaims that Jesus was born, not merely to bring personal salvation, but to confront the greatest powers of evil in society. The baby in the manger is such that the heads of government fear for their future. No "Precious Moments™" manger scenes belong here.

The Eastern church elaborated on this story from Matthew, eventually claiming that 14,000 infants were killed. The Syrian calendar set the figure at 64,000. Many medieval churches in Europe display this story in graphic detail. Painted on the church walls or inlaid into the flooring are life-sized depictions of soldiers flinging bleeding babies into the sky and sobbing women in poses of agony. We are reminded that, if not ours, then other societies and past times recognized that death was powerful and ever-present, that violence caused the suffering of many people each day, that children no less than adults were victims. We seem always shocked by the death of a child, somewhat disoriented when witnessing the suffering of innocent people. Many United States citizens are taking year after year after year to deal with the violence of 9/11, as if such death simply cannot fit into our worldview. Today we can visit Siena, Italy, a city that saw half its population dead by the Black Plague, and marvel at the cathedral with its immense depiction of the slaughter of the innocents. Such medieval worship spaces show us that the violent death of innocent people was recognized as part of life, and we would be better able to deal with it if the church—its buildings, its observances, its prayers—faced that violence head on. It is easy to have faith in God as we gaze at the pile of gifts under the Christmas tree. It is more to the purpose of religion if we can have such faith in God when standing at the pit of the Twin Towers.

> In heaven the saints are most high, having made themselves most low, seeing themselves not as we see them, but in the light of the Godhead from which they draw their being.—T. S. Eliot[2]

The day of Holy Innocents can be seen as superb liturgical metaphor. Herod murders the babies. By saying less, we cover more. Let Herod stand for all powers of violence and the baby boys for all the innocent people who suffer. Matthew writes that Jesus was brought to safety; let this inspire our trust that in God we also are saved. Yet just like Jesus, we finally too submit to death. Jesus lives for a while more, and perhaps we who worship this year will live for a while more, but finally we too die. Physicians tell us that "a good death" is largely a fantasy. The death of most people, even if in their own bed, is far from "good," and many people, much reduced in their personhood, suffer far more than they should. In this light, Holy Innocents is about the future of each one of us. Our worship together can strengthen our faith in the salvation God offers, despite whatever violence or suffering comes our way.

MATTHEW 2:13-18 (ELW, BCP, LFM)
JEREMIAH 31:15-17 (ELW, BCP)

The evangelist Matthew, writing for a Jewish readership, wants to connect the mission of Christ in every way he can with familiar religious imagery. Thus we hear in the Gospel for Holy Innocents a narrative that ties Jesus to three different Israelite stories. Jesus, who will be crucified as King of the Jews, must even as an infant be confronted by the current and puppet king of the Jews. Herod, whose reign until 4 B.C.E. establishes for scholars a possible birth year for Jesus, sees the kingdom of God approaching, and he sets out to destroy it. Herod is then like the Pharaoh of Egypt, killing the boy babies of the Israelite slaves. Herod is like all other wicked kings who throughout Jewish history worked to conquer the people. But like all those whose stories are narrated in the Tanakh, Herod too will fail, for God will protect the chosen people and keep them in safety.

A second story that becomes backdrop for today's narrative is the exodus itself. Just as the people of Israel lived as strangers in Egypt, so too Jesus, now the new Chosen One, lives for a while as a stranger in Egypt. Just as Moses escaped the murderous plans of the Pharaoh, so Jesus comes out of Egypt. "When Israel was a child, I loved him, and out of Egypt I called my son," says the poem in Hosea, giving words to God that express the prophet's faith that in spite of appearances to the contrary, God will care for all whom God loves. God will bring back those who are exiled.

> The echo of those who weep for the young children
> Makes a crash like thunder on the earth . . .
> Herod snatched the children from their
>   mother's arms,
> And he slaughtered them, not understanding, the wicked fellow,
> That in spite of doing these things,
> His power will soon be destroyed.
> —A *Kontakion* of Romanos[3]

Matthew applies the Hosea quote even more precisely, since he can literalize the reference to "the son" by connecting the quote with Christ.

The third story that stands behind the Holy Innocents story is that of Rachel, the most beloved wife of Jacob, who died in the childbirth of the most beloved son Benjamin. Honored as one of the four matriarchs of the people, Rachel comes to represent the mother of the northern tribes. She, whom we assume should be a most blessed woman, most happy with her husband and her children, must instead weep at the death of her descendents. She stands with all the weeping mothers of all time and place, seeing the death of her children's children, helpless before the violence of advancing armies. Yet, says the citation from Jeremiah 31, God promises hope for the future: the children will return to their homeland. Matthew uses the old story to unite with Rachel all the weeping mothers of Bethlehem, and we use these layered stories to bring into our assemblies all the weeping mothers of the world. But the faithful are called to trust that God will at the end bring a blessing.

The Gospel appointed for Holy Innocents is a primary example of how the New Testament narratives of the life of Jesus rely on Old Testament stories. Perhaps even when the evangelist wrote the Gospel of Matthew, people alive would have remembered whether or not Herod had in fact murdered boys in Bethlehem. But one senses that facticity was never Matthew's point. (Note that the "two years" mentioned by Matthew does not jibe with Luke's tale of a short trip to Bethlehem for census registration.) Matthew means to tell his readers that Jesus is like Moses, going to and coming from Egypt; Jesus, the King of the Jews, is quite other than the other king of the Jews; and the reality of radical evil and the sorrow it brings are set next to the promises of a benevolent God. Of course, contemporary Christian hermeneutics must reject the anti-Semitism that so much marked church history. But in our search for a new way, we cannot now suggest that the New Testament stands independent of the Hebrew Scriptures. This narrative makes sense only when all the Old Testament stories are remembered and revered. The New Testament tells the story of Jesus Christ by using the imagery from the Old.

> Faith would be, in short, that God has any willful connection with time whatsoever, and with us. I take it as given that whatever he touches has meaning. The question is, then, whether God touches anything . . . .
> —Annie Dillard, *Holy the Firm*[4]

THE READINGS

PSALM 124 (ELW, BCP, LFM)
1 PETER 4:12-19 (ELW)
REVELATION 21:1-7 (BCP)
1 JOHN 1:5—2:2 (LFM)

The response to the reading from Jeremiah 31 is *Psalm 124*, a poetic song of thanksgiving for divine deliverance. Like the Israelites escaping from slavery in Egypt, the enemies are behind us, the raging waters in front of us. Added to the historical reference is another image of capture and escape, we the bird and evil the snare. This psalm has provided the opening versicle and response for centuries of Christians' praying morning prayer, since every day can bring to us the sorrow of death and the dangers of evil.

The reading from *1 Peter 4* urges believers to realize that violence may very well come to attack even the present assembly of Christians. The epistle sounds as if it is directed only to the insiders, who assume that their life as faithful ones will contain less suffering than that of "the ungodly and the sinners." Were our assemblies to face persecution for the faith, this passage could more easily find its meaning for us. The reading from *Revelation 21* is far more positive, being one of the most glorious biblical passages that describes the ecstasy of life together with God in the new holy city. We know what the old city Jerusalem was like, with Herod as its ruler. But our hope is in God and in a city when Rachel's children will be once again home, when the mothers and fathers of Bethlehem will have nothing to cry about, when God will parent all who have suffered. The reading from *1 John 1–2* asks us to be "little children" of God, committed to a life without sin, yet trusting that Christ is the sacrifice we know we need. We need not sacrifice ourselves, or—we will think on Holy Innocents Day—our children. And when we know ourselves to be a kind of Herod, then Christ's sacrifice will forgive even these sins, along with all the sins of the whole world.

So if you are ready, when you hear the sound of the readings for Holy Innocents, hold in one hand the blessed baby in Luke's manger, and in the other the slain children of Matthew's Bethlehem. May that juxtaposition deepen your gratitude for the incarnation. Be sure that the intercessions for the day are heartfelt petitions, worthy of human agony, bringing before God all the suffering ones of the world and begging God for safety for all and a home at the last.

FOR FURTHER COMMENTARY

Additional comments on these Scripture texts, in part or in full, may be found in the seasonal volumes of New Proclamation as follows:

- Psalm 124—Year A, Proper 16; Year B, Proper 21
- 1 John 1:5—2:2—Year B, Easter 2
- 1 Peter 4:12-19—Year A, Easter 7
- Revelation 21:1-7—Year B, All Saints; Year C, Easter 5; Years ABC, New Year's Day
- Matthew 2:13-18—Year A, Christmas 1

Notes

1. Raymond E. Brown, *The Birth of the Messiah* (New York: Doubleday, 1993), 204.
2. A speech by Thomas Becket in T. S. Eliot, "Murder in the Cathedral," in *The Complete Poems and Plays 1909–1950* (New York: Harcourt Brace, 1958), 200.
3. *Kontakia of Romanos, Byzantine Melodist*, vol. 1, trans. Marjorie Carpenter (Columbia: University of Missouri Press, 1970), 30.
4. Annie Dillard, *Holy the Firm* (New York: Harper Perennial, 1988), 47.

CONFESSION OF PETER (ELW/BCP) / THE CHAIR OF ST. PETER, APOSTLE (LFM)

JANUARY 18 (ELW/BCP) / FEBRUARY 22 (LFM)

BILL DOGGETT

LUTHERAN (ELW)	EPISCOPAL (BCP)	ROMAN CATHOLIC (LFM)
Acts 4:8–13	Acts 4:8–13	1 Peter 5:1–4
Ps. 18:1–6, 16–19	Psalm 23	Ps. 23: 1–3a, 3b–4, 5, 6
1 Cor. 10:1–5	1 Peter 5:1–4	
Matt. 16:13–19	Matthew 16:13–19	Matt. 16:13–19

KEY THEMES

• "You are the Messiah": How do we come to know this?
• Perfection not required: God loves and needs us even in our failings.
• Peter, Jesus, and ourselves—who are the rocks?

The primary feast of Peter, shared with Paul, is June 29. A secondary celebration of Peter has been celebrated variously as the Chains of Peter, the Chair of Peter, and the Confession of Peter since the fourth century on either January 18 or February 22. Most medieval calendars use the January date, probably because this puts the feast outside of Lent. The celebration of this day provides an opportunity to reflect on the life of Peter independent of Paul.

Peter is the apostle about whom we know the most from Scripture. Among the first called, many of his interactions with Jesus are recorded in the Gospels, and these interactions reveal him to be impulsive, not always clear thinking, and all-too-human in his fears and failings. It is because of this that he offers a unique entry into the Gospel stories for later readers. His sometimes humorous conversations, such as the dispute over the foot washing (John 13:6–10); his fearfulness, as when he attempts to join Jesus walking on water (Matt. 14:24–34); his sudden insights, as in the confession remembered today (Matt. 16:13–20; Mark 8:27–30; Luke 9:18–20); and his denial of Jesus at the crucifixion (Matt. 26:69–75; Mark 14:66–72; Luke 22:54–62; John 18:25–27) paint a picture of a person of faith and failings, who makes it possible to imagine our fallible selves being welcomed and loved by Jesus. In the Acts of the Apostles and in his epistles we see a Peter much changed by his experience and his faith, able to be steadfast in a perilous world in a way that he could not in the Gospels. The latter part of Acts abandons Peter's story for Paul's. Tradition going back to the second-century *Acts of Peter* holds that Peter ended his days in Rome, crucified upside down at his own request and preaching from the cross as he died. Another memorable story in the *Acts of Peter* has Jesus appearing to Peter as he flees Rome. Peter asks Jesus where he is going and Jesus says that he is going to Rome to be crucified again. Peter is persuaded by this vision to return to Rome and face his own crucifixion.

This festival offers an opportunity to hold up rocky faith journeys as part of our common human experience, and to live in hope in the certainty that human failings will not separate us from the love of God in Christ.

THE FESTIVAL

This day begins the Week of Prayer for Christian Unity, observed since 1918. It is ironic, perhaps, that this week of prayer should begin with a celebration, the interpretation of which outlines so clearly the divisions between churches. For the understanding of the passage that follows Peter's confession in Matthew's Gospel (Matt. 16:17-19)—what Jesus means by "rock" and "keys," "binding" and "loosing"—has been at the heart of arguments about Christian polity for many centuries. This is not the place to settle, or even rehearse, these debates, but there is something hearteningly Peter-like in beginning our prayers for unity with the Scripture passage that divides us. Peter's traditional patronages are generally drawn from scriptural stories about Peter. His patronages include fishers, netmakers, and shipwrights (because of his first career), clockmakers (because of the cock-crows), and cobblers and those with foot problems (because of the footwashing story). If a congregation wished to introduce the use of "Confession Stones" as described in *Children at Worship, Congregations in Bloom,*[1] the Confession of Peter might be a thematically apt time to do it.

And as they considered these things, Xanthippe took knowledge of the counsel of her husband with Agrippa, and sent and showed Peter, that he might depart from Rome. And the rest of the brethren, together with Marcellus, besought him to depart. But Peter said unto them: Shall we be runaways, brethren? and they said to him: Nay, but that thou mayest yet be able to serve the Lord. And he obeyed the brethren's voice and went forth alone, saying: Let none of you come forth with me, but I will go forth alone, having changed the fashion of mine apparel. And as he went forth of the city, he saw the Lord entering into Rome. And when he saw him, he said: Lord, whither goest thou thus (or here)? And the Lord said unto him: I go into Rome to be crucified. And Peter said unto him: Lord, art thou (being) crucified again? He said unto him: Yea, Peter, I am (being) crucified again. And Peter came to himself: and having beheld the Lord ascending up into heaven, he returned to Rome, rejoicing, and glorifying the Lord, for that he said: I am being crucified: the which was about to befall Peter.—*The Acts of Peter*[2]

All the lectionaries choose the account of Peter's confession found in Matthew. Each tradition's understanding of Jesus' response will be well known to the preachers of that tradition, but it is worth remembering that the focus of the passage, and indeed the focus of the day, is not on what Jesus says, but what Peter says. The identification of Jesus as Messiah is a not just a turning point for Peter, but for all the followers of Jesus. The responses to Jesus' question about what others say about him shows that the Jews of his day identified Jesus' actions of preaching, teaching, and healing with the role of prophet, but not with the role of God's Anointed One as described in the Hebrew Bible. Peter's epiphany—recognizing that the one whom God had sent was not a mighty warrior, but the man of peace who stood before him—is critical in shaping the work of Jesus' followers ever after. Absent this realization, the followers of Jesus could well have remained a Jewish sect. Even with it, some Christians continue to try to militarize the Christian mission, reshaping the image of Jesus as a military Messiah.

Last came, and last did go, The Pilot of the
   Galilean lake;
Two massy keys he bore of metals twain
(The golden opes, the Iron shuts amain).
He shook his mitred locks, and stern bespake:
"How well could I have spar'd for thee
   young swain,
Enow of such as for their bellies' sake
Creep and intrude, and climb into the fold?"
–John Milton[3]

Scholars disagree on the origins of the two epistles of Peter in the New Testament. The first uses Greek thought to be too refined for an Aramaic-speaking fisherman, but the letter clearly states that its author used the services of a scribe (1 Pet. 5:12). Stylistic and theological differences suggest a different and later author for 2 Peter. First Peter, whether written by Peter or not, is a problematic text, since a major theme is the submission to authority by slaves to masters, wives to husbands, and the young to their elders as conforming to Christ's obedience to God. While Christians have rejected the validity of that claim with regard to slaves, and are debating its validity with regard to women and children, the other side of that claim, as expressed in 1 Peter 5, is a strong one: that those in authority should exercise their oversight humbly, not lording it over their flock, but leading by example.

Saint Peter sat by the celestial gate:
   His keys were rusty, and the lock was dull,
So little trouble had been given of late;
   Not that the place by any means was full,
But since the Gallic era "eighty-eight"
   The Devils had ta'en a longer, stronger pull,
And "a pull altogether," as they say
   At sea–which drew most souls another way.
–George Gordon, Lord Byron[4]

The reading from Acts, which is common to the Episcopal and Lutheran lectionaries, and the Roman lectionary reading from 1 Corinthians provide an interesting counterpoint to the Gospel lesson, because in these two readings it is Jesus, and not Peter, who is called the rock. In 1 Corinthians, Christ is asserted to be the rock from which the thirsty Israelites drank in the desert, and in Acts, Peter himself calls Jesus the rejected stone, the cornerstone of salvation. Either of these readings, taken together with the Gospel passage, suggests a complimentarity between divine and human action on behalf of humankind. There is something rocklike—strong, unshakeable, unbreakable—about the foundations of both our faith and our community. Jesus and Peter both provide examples for present-day Christians to be equally strong and firmly rooted. Consider who are cornerstones and anchors of your own community.

For Further Comment

Additional comments on these Scripture texts, in part or in full, may be found in the seasonal volumes of *New Proclamation* as follows:

- Acts 4:8-13—Year B, Easter 4
- Psalm 23—Year A, Lent 4, Proper 23; Year B, Proper 11; Years ABC, Easter 4
- 1 Corinthians 10:1-5—Year C, Lent 3
- Matthew 16:13-19—Year A, Proper 16

Notes

1. Caroline Fairless, *Children at Worship, Congregations in Bloom* (New York: Church Publishing, 2000), 85–92.

2. From "The Acts of Peter," in *The Apocryphal New Testament*, trans. M. R. James (Oxford: Clarendon, 1924), p. 333.

3. John Milton, "Lycidas," in *Poems 1645*, facs. ed. (Menston, UK: Scholar Press, 1970), ll. 108–15.

4. George Gordon, Lord Byron, "The Vision of Judgment," Canto I, in *The Complete Poetical Works of Lord Byron,* ed. Paul Elmer More (New York: Houghton Mifflin, 1905), 285.

CONVERSION OF PAUL

JANUARY 25

BILL DOGGETT

LUTHERAN (ELW)	EPISCOPAL (BCP)	ROMAN CATHOLIC (LFM)
Acts 9:1-22	Acts 26:9-21	Acts 22:3-16 or 9:1-22
Psalm 67	Psalm 67	Ps. 116:1, 2
Gal. 1:11-24	Gal. 1:11-24	
Luke 21:10-19	Matt. 10:16-22	Mark 16:15-18

KEY THEMES

• Conversion: What road were you on when Jesus found you?
• Evangelism: Telling your own story.
• The extent of God's grace: Turning enemies into friends.

The celebration of the Conversion of Paul began in the eighth century. It commemorates a remarkable event in Scripture; remarkable in and of itself, for its meaning, and for its consequences. Saul of Tarsus, Roman citizen, tentmaker by trade, and faithful member of the Jewish sect of the Pharisees, had been diligent in pursuing and persecuting the newly forming communities of followers of Jesus in Jerusalem. By his own account, he had watched over the robes of those who stoned Stephen, the first Christian martyr (Acts 7:57—8:3) and was well known and feared by the Christians of Jerusalem. In the year 36 C.E., Saul was sent by the high priest in Jerusalem to arrest Christians in Damascus and return them to Jerusalem in chains.

As he neared Damascus, Saul saw a brilliant light, was thrown from his horse, and heard the voice of the Lord asking, "Saul, Saul, why do you persecute me?" In later tellings, he says that he saw Jesus at this time and received the gospel from him. As then instructed, Saul arose, now blind, and was led into the city by his companions. There he fasted for three days until Ananais, who had been sent by a vision of the Lord, restored his sight. He was baptized, and subsequently began preaching the good news to the Gentiles. Although it is common to associate his name change with this conversion event, in fact, he began to use the Greek Paul instead of the Hebrew Saul somewhat later, when he lived among the Greek-speaking Gentiles.

The story is dramatic in and of itself, but at its heart it demonstrates that even the most fervent enemy of Jesus is not beyond the reach of his love and redemption. Paul, of course, went on to be the greatest evangelist of his or any day, and his letters continue to feed and challenge Christians two thousand years later. The story has such resonance that the phrase "the road to Damascus" is a metaphor for any dramatic positive change of direction in life.

THE FESTIVAL

The Feast of the Conversion of Paul first shows up in calendars in the eighth century, a time when celebrations of biblical events, in addition to saints' days, begin to crowd the calendar. In the Roman calendar, from the sixth to the mid-twentieth century, Paul's principal feast day was June 30, having been separated from Peter's celebration on June 29 for practical reasons. The Vatican II calendar reforms restored the Feast of Sts. Peter and Paul on June 29, leaving the Feast of the Conversion of Paul as the only festival to focus solely on Paul. Since 1918, the feast of the Conversion of Paul has marked the end of the Week of Prayer for Christian Unity, which begins on the Feast of the Confession of Peter on January 18.

As a minor celebration, there aren't many traditions associated with the day, but one medieval practice is interesting. Peter and Paul came to be associated in Northern Europe with the weather, with Paul being called upon to restrain violent weather, which was believed to be caused by Peter's temperamental nature. A medieval superstition holds that this was one of several days in the year when the weather could be predicted:

> If St. Paul's day be fair and clear,
> It does betide a happy year;
> But if it chance to snow or rain,
> Then will be dear all kind of grain.
> If clouds or miste do dark the sky,
> Great store of birds and beasts shall die;
> And if the winds do flie aloft,
> Then war shall vexe the kingdom oft.[1]

This is Paul's only unshared festival, so his entire biography and the corpus of his writings could be considered in preparing a sermon. In particular, placing the grace of his conversion in the context of his subsequent actions and theological reflection gives a depth of meaning to this extraordinary event that, without what followed, would have been merely an eerie tale. Of particular note is the way the rest of Paul's life after his conversion illustrates a zeal for the gospel tempered by grace, which contrasts with his prior relentless zeal for persecution. The reading from Galatians gives Paul's own summary of his life and work; this might be a good beginning point for preaching on Paul's ministry.

As to thy last Apostle's heart
Thy lightning glance did then impart
Zeal's never-dying fire,
So teach us on thy shrine to lay
Our hearts, and let them day by day
Intenser blaze and higher.
–John Keble[2]

Paul's conversion experience was transformative for him, and the retelling of it became a "talking point" in his preaching. The book of Acts contains three versions of the story: a narrative account and two retellings by Paul. The three lectionaries have each chosen a different one of these accounts. Taken together, they illustrate what Paul says in 1 Cor. 9.22: "To the weak I became weak, so that I might win the weak. I have become all things to all people, so that I might by all means save some."

The narrative version in Acts 9 relates the events of the conversion without much interpretation, but with personal details such as what it felt like to have his sight restored (v. 18). In the subsequent retellings, though, Paul makes every effort to identify himself with his audience. In Acts 22, where Paul is speaking to the angry mob of Jews in Jerusalem, he emphasizes his Jewishness, both in describing his persecution of Christians before his conversion (vv. 3–5) and in relating that Ananais uses the phrase "the God of our ancestors" in explaining Paul's new vocation. In Acts 26, Paul is speaking to King Agrippa, and tells the story in a way that emphasizes not only his Roman citizenship and Greek culture, but his role as an enforcer of the law, similar to Agrippa's (vv. 9–12). After the famous words "Saul, Saul, why are you persecuting me?" in this telling Paul reports that Jesus says, "It hurts you to kick against the goads," a quotation from Euripides that had by the first century C.E. become a common Hellenic saying. The three versions of Paul's conversion in Acts

There are Saints in whom grace supersedes nature; so was it not with this great Apostle; in him grace did but sanctify and elevate nature. It left him in the full possession, in the full exercise, of all that was human, which was not sinful. He who had the constant contemplation of his Lord and Saviour, as if he saw Him with his bodily eyes, was nevertheless as susceptible of the affections of human nature and the influences of the external world, as if he were a stranger to that contemplation. . . . His mind was like some instrument of music, harp or viol, the strings of which vibrate, though untouched, by the notes which other instruments give forth, and he was ever, according to his own precept, "rejoicing with them that rejoice, and weeping with them that wept"; and thus he was the least magisterial of all teachers, and the gentlest and most amiable of all rulers.
–John Henry Newman[3]

illustrate the importance of personal witness in spreading the Good News. Paul's own experience is a sign of the truth of his message.

The three lectionaries choose different Gospel readings with a common theme: evangelism. The parallel passages from Matthew and Luke in the Episcopal and Lutheran lectionaries seem to predict Paul's experiences directly: "they will hand you over to councils and flog you in their synagogues; and you will be dragged before governors and kings because of me, as a testimony to them and the Gentiles" (Matt. 10:17-18; Luke 21:12 is similar). What follows, the instruction not to worry about what to say in advance, would seem to contradict the purpose of this series, but Jesus is, after all, not talking about preaching to an assembly of the faithful, but about testifying before violent persecutors. Both passages end with encouraging words for the persecuted, that by endurance they will attain salvation.

The Gospel lesson from the Roman Lectionary is more problematic: it includes the verses about handling snakes and drinking poison unharmed (Mark 16:18). If understood literally, this passage must be juxtaposed with the stricture against putting God to the test (Matt. 4:7; Luke 4:12), but Matt. 23:28-36 suggests a metaphorical interpretation: the faithful will be able to handle the vipers of the hypocritical generation and swallow their poisonous words unharmed. Note the parallel between Matt. 23:33-34—"You snakes, you brood of vipers! How can you escape being sentenced to hell? Therefore I send you prophets, sages, and scribes, some of whom you will kill and crucify, and some you will flog in your synagogues and pursue from town to town"—and Matt. 10:17-18 and Luke 21:12 cited above.

> Praise for the light from heaven
>   And for the voice of awe,
> Praise for the glorious vision
>   The persecutor saw.
> O Lord, for Paul's conversion,
>   We bless your name today.
> Come shine within our darkness
>   And guide us in the Way.
> —Horatio Bolton Nelson[4]

FOR FURTHER COMMENT

Additional comments on these texts, in full or in part, may be found in the seasonal volumes of *New Proclamation* as follows:

- Acts 9:1-22—Year C, Easter 3
- Psalm 67—Year A, Proper 15; Year C, Easter 6
- Psalm 116:1-2—Year A, Proper 6, Easter 3; Year B, Proper 19; Years ABC, Holy Thursday
- Galatians 1:11-24—Year C, Proper 5
- Matthew 10:16-22—Year A, Proper 6; see also Stephen [LFM]
- Mark 16:15-18—Year A, Proper 16; see also Mark [LFM]
- Luke 21:10-19—Year C, Proper 28

Notes

1. Quoted in Thomas Willsford, *Nature's Secrets, Or, The Admirable and Wonderfull Historie of the Generation of Meteors* (Cornhill, Eng.: Nathaniel Brook, Angel Press, 1658).

2. John Keble, "LXXIX, The Conversion of St. Paul," in *The Christian Year; Thoughts in Verse for the Sundays and Holy Days Throughout the Year* (Oxford, 1827), stanza 13.

3. John Henry Newman, "St. Paul's Gift of Sympathy" (1857), from *Sermons Preached on Various Occasions,* Sermon 8 (London: Burns & Oates, 1857), 113–14.

4. Horatio Bolton Nelson (1823–1913), "From all thy saints in warfare," in *Hymns for Saints Days and Other Hymns* (London, 1864). In many contemporary hymnals it is known as "By all your saints still striving" (*The Hymnal 1982,* nos. 231 & 232; *Lutheran Book of Worship,* no. 177).

PRESENTATION OF OUR LORD

FEBRUARY 2

WILLIAM F. BROSEND II

REVISED COMMON	EPISCOPAL (BCP)	ROMAN CATHOLIC (LFM)
Mal. 3:1–4	Mal. 3:1–4	Mal. 3:1–4
Psalm 84 or 24:7–10	Psalm 84 or 84:1–6	Ps. 24:7, 8, 9, 10
Heb. 2:14–18	Heb. 2:14–18	Heb. 2:14–18
Luke 2:22–40	Luke 2:22–40	Luke 2:22–40 or 2:22–32

KEY THEMES

• Celebration of the Presentation dates from at least the mid-fourth century, spreading east and west and ebbing and flowing in popularity and observance.
• Anna and Simeon embody the "hopes of Israel" and depict the fulfillment of those hopes to anticipate through their prophetic words the arc of the story soon to unfold.
• The Presentation is about an act of stewardship.

If ever the liturgical and secular calendar clash about the meaning of a certain day, February 2 is it. Is today "Groundhog's Day," a midpoint between the winter solstice and the spring equinox, or the "Feast of the Presentation," forty days after Christmas, a midpoint between our celebration of Christ's birth and our preparation for his passion? And if ever there was an occasion to ignore such clash, today is also it. At least I can think of no smooth way to segue between Punxsutawney Phil and Simeon and Anna, except perhaps by way of the tradition of "Candlemas" in many communities (or at least their historical traditions). So the possibilities for confusion are significant.

We are helped by the lectionary's separation of Luke 2:21, the circumcision, from 2:22–40. We are not helped by Luke's own confusion about what exactly took place in the Temple, and why, a confusion evidenced by the use of the third-personal "their purification." Torah calls only for the ritual purification of the mother (Lev. 12:4), so whether Luke meant Jesus or Joseph to be included he was mistaken. Instead, the firstborn child is to be "redeemed," something Luke does not mention because he is more interested in Jesus' "presentation" in the Temple after the fashion of Samuel (1 Sam. 1:22—2:10). My strategy is to unpack as much of the important background as possible, both biblical and traditional, and suggest at least one (possibly) unconventional homiletical focus.

PURIFICATION, PRESENTATION, AND PROCESSION

"When the time came for their purification according to the law of Moses, they brought him up to Jerusalem to present him to the Lord (as it is written in the law of the Lord, 'Every firstborn male shall be designated as holy to the Lord'), and they offered a sacrifice according to what is stated in the law of the Lord, 'a pair of turtledoves or two young pigeons'" (Luke 2:22-24). As was and will be discussed there is considerable ground to think Luke was not entirely clear in his understanding of Torah as it applied to the tradition of Joseph and Mary bringing Jesus to the Temple. According to Lev. 12:1-8 a woman was required to make an offering for *her* "purification" forty days following the birth of a male child. According to Exod. 13:1-2 every firstborn was to be consecrated to the Lord, and according to Num. 3:47 and 18:15-16 the cost to "redeem" the firstborn from/for this consecration was five shekels.

When the days of her purification are completed, whether for a son or for a daughter, she shall bring to the priest at the entrance of the tent of meeting a lamb in its first year for a burnt offering, and a pigeon or a turtledove for a sin offering. He shall offer it before the Lord, and make atonement on her behalf; then she shall be clean. . . . This is the law for her who bears a child, male or female.—Leviticus 12:6-7

Luke hints at (2:22-24, 39) but does not actually describe the offering for purification. He does not mention the payment for redemption. Instead he focuses on something not called for in Torah, the physical "presentation" of Jesus in the Temple. The guiding text here, as elsewhere in the birth and infancy narrative, is the story of Samuel and his mother Hannah. We are, of course, well familiar with the influence of "Hannah's Song" on Luke's theology, expressed most passionately and eloquently in the Magnificat. When did Hannah sing her song of joy and praise to God? When she "presented" Samuel "to the house of the LORD" (1 Sam. 1:24). This act of presentation is intentionally echoed by Luke, and although Jesus will not remain in the Temple as Samuel remained in Shiloh, he will return to it (2:41-50), judge/cleanse it (19:28-48), and teach in it, including the teaching of its destruction (chaps. 20 and 21).

How exactly the biblical traditions around the "Presentation" led to liturgical traditions of procession, and specifically to candlelit processions, and finally to the blessing of candles for the liturgical year (Candlemas) is far from clear. Again, what is clear is the key text guiding these developments. Just as the presentation of Samuel foreshadowed the presentation of Jesus, so the words of Simeon in the

Nunc Dimittis, "my eyes have seen your salvation, which you have prepared in the presence of all peoples, a light for revelation to the Gentiles and for glory to your people Israel" (Luke 2:30-32), undoubtedly fostered the traditions of Candlemas. Celebration of the Presentation dates from at least the mid-fourth century in Jerusalem, spreading east and west and, as with many other festivals, ebbing and flowing in popularity and observance. Pope Sergius I authorized a procession at the turn of the seventh century, but it was centuries later when the "light to the nations" and the blessing of candles evolved into Candlemas. Interestingly, we learn more about this combination from its suppression than from its practice. In *The Stripping of the Altars,* Eamon Duffy tells us first about the ritual practice, then describes the periodic attempts to abolish it before, during, and after the "English Reformations":

> The Purification was marked by one of the most elaborate processions of the liturgical year, when every parishioner was obliged to join in, carrying a blessed candle, which was offered, together with a penny, to the priest at Mass. . . . The blessing of candles and procession took place immediately before the parish Mass, and, in addition to the candles offered to the priest, many others were blessed. . . . The people then processed round the church carrying lighted candles, and the "Nunc Dimittis" was sung.[1]

What does this have to do with Groundhog's Day, you ask? A traditional English verse of uncertain origin reads:

> If Candlemas be fair and bright
> Come, Winter have another fight.
> If Candlemas brings cloud and rain,
> Go, Winter, and come not again.

The marking of seasons and the iteration of holy light is what, albeit loosely, connects the festivals. Our homiletical interests, however, will likely return us to Scripture, and not traditions or customs.

THE READINGS

Malachi 3:1-4 is an interesting text, the music-loving listeners apt to hear the booming basso from Handel's oratorio warning us that we cannot abide the day of God's coming. Purification is the theme of the text, but it is likely not the theme of our homily. The responsive readings, both *Psalm 84* and *Psalm 24,* are psalms of procession, focused on Jerusalem, and are ones pilgrims would sing on the way to the Temple for a feast, or an offering. *Hebrews 2:14-18* emphasizes Jesus' humanity, though not frailty, and despite the catchphrase mention of "children" in 2:14 and the echo of Simeon's hints about Jesus' "suffering" in 2:18, connects only tangentially to the focus of the day. That focus is *Luke 2:22-40*, and in particular, Simeon and Anna.

Question: Why did Luke bring the Holy Family to the Temple? Physical presence was not required to make the required offering and payment (at least not according to the rabbis). One answer we have already seen is that he wanted to "present" Jesus, in the manner of Samuel. There is another—he needed the family in the Temple precincts to link them to the traditions he wanted to tell about Simeon and Anna, the real point of the passage.

We tend to think of the two as a matched pair, older than Methuselah, patiently waiting for the fulfillment of the messianic promise. There are historical problems with this composite, which need not distract us. The more apparent narrative purposes suggest at least three reasons for their presence: (1) to embody the "hopes of Israel" and depict the fulfillment of those hopes; (2) to anticipate through their prophetic words the arc of the story soon to unfold; (3) to sing one last wonderful song.

Luke uses the word *law* (Gk. *nomos*) nine times in his Gospel and five of the uses are in this passage, a marked concentration. Why is he here so concerned with the law when he generally is not, and why, if Luke is so concerned about things being done "according to the law" (2:22, with similar meaning but varied phrasing at 2:23, 24, 27, and 39), did he not get the law right? Because his concern was not with precision but to show the law both kept and fulfilled, the latter in the sense of the fulfillment of the hopes of Israel. The keeping of the law is shown in the action ("they brought him up to Jerusalem"; v. 22) and narrative summary ("when they had finished everything required by the law of the Lord"; v. 39). Fulfillment was embodied and voiced by Simeon, who had been promised "by the Holy Spirit that he would not see death before he had seen the Lord's Messiah" (v. 26).

English translations of the Greek New Testament drop the rough breathing mark before the opening vowel, so we may miss it, but when transliterated the Greek text is rendered "Hanna" not Anna. Perhaps it is just as well, because this is not the parallel Luke is after, having already used Hannah's song (1 Sam. 2:1-10) as the model for Mary's song. Anna is not a model progenitor, but prophet, speaking God's truth about the child's future: "[she] and began to praise God and

> Almighty and everliving God, we humbly pray that, as your only-begotten Son was this day presented in the temple, so we may be presented to you with pure and clean hearts by Jesus Christ our Lord; who lives and reigns with you and the Holy Spirit, one God, now and for ever. Amen.
> —Collect for the Feast of the Presentation, *The Book of Common Prayer*

to speak about the child to all who were looking for the redemption of Jerusalem" (v. 38).

When it comes to the *Nunc Dimittis*, poetically we often are best off letting the Authorized Version alone. What shall we do with it, though?

> Lord, now lettest thou thy servant depart in peace,
>   according to thy word.
> For mine eyes have seen thy salvation,
>   which thou hast prepared before the face of all people;
> A light to lighten the Gentiles,
>   and the glory of thy people Israel.
> —Luke 2:30-32 (KJV)

PREACHING THE FEAST

When it is next my turn to bring all these themes and customs together I will move in one or more of the following directions. Two are not surprising, none spectacular.

In the Bill Murray classic *Groundhog Day* (you knew that reference was coming eventually!), the protagonist must live the day over and over again until he gets it "right." That, unfortunately, also describes common responses to the idea of "tradition" in the church. Over and over again. The responses to tradition in our texts are markedly different. Joseph and Mary respond to the requirements of tradition with faith, Anna and Simeon respond with lifetimes of patient waiting. All four respond with trust. The tradition of Candlemas, largely ignored except by the liturgically minded, may be a way of reconnecting congregations with their own (mostly forgotten) history. If recent sociological studies are correct, such reconnecting will appeal to generations X, Y, Z, and whatever comes next.

Anna and Simeon speak powerfully to the theme of fulfillment. But it is nascent fulfillment. They have been waiting a loooong time, we are told. And it is hard to believe that what they finally see matches exactly with their hopes and expectation. But it is enough. The hint of what is to come is enough. Would that we all could be blessed with eyes to see—not to mention words to praise—like theirs!

Tradition and fulfillment, big surprise. What about stewardship? Isn't that what the Presentation is really about, an act of stewardship? Mary and Joseph

Here the young friend of God called to a prophetic work, who has sung her Magnificat, given birth, and pondered the meaning of it all, carries out with her husband the law of the covenant in ceremonies imbued with their people's profound gratitude for the living God's gracious and liberating care. Depicting so clearly Mary's religious engagement in temple worship according to Torah, this text offers a strong antidote to a remembrance that would erase her Jewish identity and paint her as a Gentile Christian.
—Elizabeth A. Johnson[2]

symbolically "present" Jesus in the Temple and, though Luke does not mention it, presumably make the five-shekel offering required to "redeem" him back to their care. And while certainly this child is *the* exception of all exceptions, who ever truly "owns" their children, patriarchal society or not? We are stewards of our children, God entrusting them to our care and keeping for God's good and pleasure, not ours. As is true of the "child" of Mary and Joseph, and true of our children, so is true of all creation. All the firstborn, the first fruits, were to be consecrated to the Lord according to Torah (Exod. 23:19; Leviticus 23; and elsewhere). But that does not mean God cares less about what comes after. Our acts of presentation and dedication do not exempt us from care of the "middle child" or the rest of the fruits of the vineyard, but remind us that "the earth is the LORD's and all that is in it," as one of the psalms appointed for today boldly proclaims. They won't be expecting it, so today may be a perfect day for a "stewardship sermon"!

FOR FURTHER COMMENT

Additional comments on these Scripture texts, in part or in full, may be found in the seasonal volumes of *New Proclamation* as follows:

- Malachi 3:1-4—Year C, Advent 2
- Psalm 24—Year B, Proper 10, All Saints
- Psalm 84—Year B, Proper 16; Year C, Proper 25
- Hebrews 2:14-18—Year A, Christmas 1
- Luke 2:22-40—Year B, Christmas 1

Notes

1. Eamon Duffy, *The Stripping of the Altars* (New Haven: Yale University Press, 1992). The quotation is from p. 16, which also describes a local suppression. Later acts of suppression under Cranmer (pp. 434, 459) and the feast's persistence (p. 589) are also detailed. The phrase "English Reformations" is from the book of the same name by Christopher Haigh (Oxford: Clarendon, 1993).

2. Elizabeth A. Johnson, *Truly Our Sister* (New York: Continuum, 2003), 279–80.

CHRISM MASS

Holy Thursday: March 19 (earliest)
−April 22 (latest)

Gerard S. Sloyan

Roman Catholic (LFM)
Isa. 61:1–3ab, 6a, 8b–9
Ps. 89:21–22, 25, 27
Rev. 1:5–8
Luke 4:16–21

KEY THEMES

• The three chrisms are those of the sick, of the catechumens, and of priestly ordination.
• The bishop blesses all three oils in the cathedral church to be taken back to the local parishes.
• This is not a day for scolding or censure of a sinful presbyterate but for reminding them of the healing Christ.

An assistant pastor of my youth who was also an instructor in high school religion caused infinite mirth by pronouncing the English tongue in the manner of his native Northern Ireland. The ashes for Ash Wednesday were derived from the burned "pam" of the previous year's "Pam Sunday." Needless to say, he also made clear that one of the holy oils called chrism was olive oil mixed with "bam." How provincial we were on being exposed to another mode of spoken English! The man was, by the way, an excellent teacher. Ordained to the presbyteral order, he had had the chrism above described smeared on both "pams" in a twofold arc from each index finger to the heel of the opposite hand. We were not to know at the time that this was part of the rite of priestly ordination performed by a bishop. What was well known at an early age, however, was that there was a recessed cabinet in the sanctuary wall of the parish church with a locked metal door on which was inscribed *Olea Sancta*.

The holy oils are three, all of them called chrism, of perfumed olive oil, consecrated by the diocesan bishop in the cathedral church in a Chrism Mass on Holy or Maundy Thursday. The cabinet described above is called an ambry and the oils those of the sick, of catechumens, and holy chrism above described. The first of these is employed in the Sacrament of the Sick, formerly called the Last Anointing (of the various ones administered in Christian life). The epistle of James proposes summoning the church's presbyters whose prayers for the gravely ill are accompanied by the latter's being anointed with oil (5:14). Catechumens are those adults or adolescents preparing for baptism or, as already baptized, entry into the Catholic Church. The oil proper to that rite is applied to the crown of the head after the threefold immersion or infusion and to the chest and between the shoulders of candidates before the actual baptism if feasible. The head is anointed with chrism, usually on the forehead, in the rite of Confirmation. The crown of the head of a priest ordained to the order of bishop is anointed with chrism. It and the oil of catechumens are poured into the water to be blessed and used for baptism throughout the coming year, on the Great Night of Easter, its vigil service. Lastly, sacred vessels, church bells, and the walls and door of churches being dedicated are anointed with chrism, the last named application in the form of a cross.

God of all consolation, you chose and sent your Son to heal the world. Graciously listen to our prayer of faith: send the power of your Holy Spirit, the Consoler, into this precious oil, this soothing ointment, this rich gift, this fruit of the earth. Bless this oil and sanctify it for our use. Make this oil a remedy for all who are anointed with it; heal them in body, in soul, and in spirit, and deliver them from every affliction.
–Rite of Blessing of the Oil of the Sick[1]

All three oils are blessed by the bishop during the Chrism Mass in the cathedral church. This has been for centuries a eucharistic celebration earlier on Holy Thursday than the Mass of the Lord's Supper, which is normally in the evening. Large numbers of the presbyterate of a diocese and others assisting the diocesan clergy traditionally come to the cathedral to concelebrate with the bishop and bring the three types of oil to their parishes in small, cylindrical metal vessels called stocks. The demands on clergy in preparation for the upcoming *triduum sacrum* (the sacred three days), plus travel in dioceses very large in area, have made the Chrism Mass on Thursday morning infeasible. Pope Paul VI, moreover, had proposed the event of the gathered presbyterate as an optimum occasion for the public recommitment of priests to their pastoral office. All these circumstances have contributed in many dioceses to locating the Chrism Mass earlier in the week with the hope that many lay people may join their clergy in this liturgy.

The Old Testament Readings
ISAIAH 61:1–3AB, 6A, 8B–9
PSALM 89:21–22, 25, 27

The fittingness of the portion of Third Isaiah and its response in psalmody, once the Gospel passage had been chosen for this Eucharist, is immediately evident. With Luke's placing of this snatch of Isaiah on Jesus' lips in his home synagogue, the lectionary framers had the challenge of how much of the poem to propose as constituting the first reading. By not proceeding to verse 4 of Isaiah 61, the mystery remains for a congregation of hearers as to who the anointed one was in the poet's postexilic era on whom the spirit of the Lord descended. In that verse it is clearly the returned exiles: "They shall build up the ancient ruins . . . they shall repair the ruined cities, the devastations of many generations." To those exultant returning Judahites has fallen the multiple task of bringing good tidings to the oppressed, liberty to the captives, and on their shoulders a mantle of praise in place of a faint spirit. In verse 20 of Psalm 89 (88 in the LXX and Vulgate), which is most directly related to the day's episcopal blessing of the oils, the poet assures the mourners who will view the ruins of Solomon's temple upon their return to Zion (v. 3; see Ezra 3:12) that the oil of gladness rather than mourning will be theirs. This anointing will be of a people "called priests of the LORD" by Isaiah (v. 6a; see Exod. 19:6; 1 Peter 2:9) and a Davidic people in the echoing Psalm, whose descendants the Isaian poet would have seen as the returning people of Judah. The reference there to "priests of the LORD" and "ministers of our God" (61:6a)—although a description of a whole people (as it also is in 1 Peter's use of the Exodus text)—was not lost on the framers of the lectionary, as a bishop and his presbyterate are assembled.

THE GOSPEL
LUKE 4:16-21

The evangelist Luke's faith of the earliest church is that Jesus is uniquely the anointed of the Lord, hence the attribution of the title *Meshiah/Christos* to him. Well known to have been a layman and not of Aaronide or priestly stock, Jesus was nonetheless sprung from the royal line (Luke 2:4, of Joseph, his father at Law) and was both priest (Hebrews throughout) and prophet as well (Matt. 21:11; Luke 7:16) in an utterly transcendent sense. The Gospel portion from Luke stops short at the quoted portion from Isaiah that is made to describe Jesus' role, and not only that of his people half a millennium before. As anointed and Spirit-invested servant of the poor and of captives, of the blind and the oppressed, he will exercise a prophetic and priestly office outside and beyond his own people Israel as Elijah and Elisha had done. Since that is the whole point of the Lukan passage the homilist at this Mass, whether a bishop or presbyter, would do well to emulate the evangelist and speak of the body of Christ in the world as being in the service of that world.

Just as Jesus had no frontiered heart but put his gift of miracle at the service of Samaritan and Syrian, Phoenician and Roman legionary indiscriminately, so the local church has from an early date relieved the needs of those outside it as well as within as its resources allowed. Whenever the bishop and all the clergy of a diocese are gathered, you have a body large or small anxious about the people's resources and how to put them at the disposal of the less favored in society. Often these will be the ill favored: abandoned children, the aged, prostitutes, the infirm, the imprisoned. The list is long and the resources short relative to the need. While the clergy are assembled to witness the blessing of oils symbolic of healing in body and spirit, their designated homilist may not avoid mention of those of their own company among the wounded healers, not by name certainly: the addicted, whether to gambling, drink, or sex—the assembled clerics know who their brothers are—and those, once anointed in the sacrament of order, sound in mind and body, who have caused pain and hurt to parishioners by their thoughtless or conscious bad behavior in speech or act. This is not a day for scolding or censure but a day for reminder of the healing, and never the wounding, Christ.

SECOND READING
REVELATION 1:5-8

The brief lection from Revelation might alone suffice as the subject of homiletic exposition at the Chrism Mass. This biblical book generally is more suited than any other for a place in the liturgical prayer of praise. It proliferates titles of the risen and glorified Jesus, among them "the faithful witness," "the firstborn of the dead," and "the ruler of the kings of earth." Jesus the Anointed One has also been known to a believing church as prophet, priest, and king from apostolic times. For this reason, a homily centered on the oils and their ritual use in the various sacramental anointings is eminently fitting.

For Further Comment

Additional comments on these Scripture texts, in part or in full, may be found in the seasonal volumes of *New Proclamation* as follows:

- Isaiah 61:1–3ab, 6a, 8b–9—Year B, Advent 3; Years ABC, Easter Vigil
- Psalm 89:21-22, 25, 27—Year B, Advent 4, Proper 11
- Revelation 1:5-8—Year B, Reign of Christ; Year C, Easter 2
- Luke 4:16-21—Year C, Epiphany 3

Note

1. http://www.canticanova.com/planning/year-c/plncm_1.htm (accessed June 29, 2007).

JOSEPH, GUARDIAN OF JESUS (ELW/BCP) / ST. JOSEPH, HUSBAND OF THE BLESSED VIRGIN MARY (LFM)

MARCH 19

WILLIAM F. BROSEND II

LUTHERAN (ELW)	EPISCOPAL (BCP)	ROMAN CATHOLIC (LFM)
2 Sam. 7:4, 8–16	2 Sam. 7:4, 8–16	2 Sam. 7:4–5a, 12–14a, 16
Ps. 89:1–29	Ps. 89:1–29 or	Ps. 89:2–3, 4–5, 27, 29
	89:1–4, 26–29	
Rom. 4:13–18	Rom. 4:13–18	Rom. 4:13, 16–18, 22
Matt. 1:16, 18–21, 24a	Luke 2:41–52	Matt. 1:16, 18–21, 24a
		or Luke 2:41–52

KEY THEMES

• The homiletical fun to be had is in relating this down-to-earth everyman to the transcendent role he accepted in the divine drama.
• There is much we do not know about Joseph. It is best to preach from what we do know, not from what we do not.
• Matthew believes in Joseph, who trusted in his dreams.

Joseph of Nazareth, first century, dates uncertain," says seven-year-old Damian in the wonderful 2004 British film *Millions*. As a crucial figure in the unfolding drama, who guards and guides the young boy assigned to play "Joseph" in the school Christmas pageant, for the first and only time in cinematic and literary history Joseph gets his due. Entirely in character, however, for he barely says a word.

What shall we do with Joseph, silent throughout the Gospels, largely missing except in Matthew, a role player cast in a part already taken? Indeed, this last point seems the essential intent of the assigned lessons from 2 Samuel, Romans, and Luke, leaving the preacher the unenviable challenge of speaking from texts that all but dismiss the significance of the saint the community has gathered to celebrate. Fortunately the tradition has, as is its wont, been kind enough to fill in many of the gaps, and used with care these traditions to enlarge and enliven Joseph's reputation. (Or am I the only one to invoke Joseph's assistance in selling my house?) With a cue from young Damian, a favorite character from a favorite movie, I believe the preacher can have a marvelous time giving Joseph his due. To do that, though, we must start with the biblical and traditional material about Joseph, then turn to the lessons of his day.

JOSEPH OF NAZARETH IN SCRIPTURE

Our "Joseph" is met fifteen times in the New Testament, all in the Gospels—twice in John (1:45; 6:42, both times in the phrase, "son of Joseph"), three times in the Lukan birth and infancy narrative (1:27; 2:4, 16) and again in the genealogy (3:23), and, most significantly for our purposes, nine times in Matthew, first in the genealogy and then in the birth narrative. Matthew 13:55 is also important, though Joseph is not mentioned by name in the question, "Is not this the carpenter's son?" (*ho tou tektonos huios*). Much can be made of the apologetic basis for Joseph's brief appearance followed by his total disappearance from the Gospel stage, but this is not the day to do so. This is the day to celebrate Joseph's important presence and contribution.

We will look at the assigned verses from Matthew in more detail below, but to appreciate Matthew's narrative strategy, which has important implications for any preaching about Joseph, we need to recall Matthew 1 and 2 in its entirety.[1] Any fair reading of these two chapters concludes that Matthew's birth narrative is really *Joseph's* story. It is Joseph's dreams that propel the narrative, Joseph's faithful response in accepting Mary that creates the "holy family," Joseph's decisive action that saves the child from the slaughter of the innocents. Matthew tells us that Joseph was "a righteous man" (*dikaios*) in 1:19, and proceeds to show us exactly that in the rest of the birth narrative and flight to Egypt.

As noted, it is Matthew who tells us that Joseph was a carpenter. Precisely what this means socioculturally is disputed. My own position, based on the likelihood that the decision to settle in Nazareth after the sojourn in Egypt hints at leaving any

> O St. Joseph whose protection is so great, so strong, so prompt before the Throne of God, I place in you all my interests and desires. O St. Joseph do assist me by your powerful intercession and obtain for me from your Divine Son all spiritual blessings through Jesus Christ, Our Lord; so that having engaged here below your Heavenly power I may offer my Thanksgiving and Homage to the most Loving of Fathers. O St. Joseph, I never weary contemplating you and Jesus asleep in your arms. I dare not approach while He reposes near your heart. Press him in my name and kiss His fine Head for me, and ask Him to return the Kiss when I draw my dying breath. St. Joseph, Patron of departing souls, pray for us. Amen.
> —Traditional prayer

Judean patrimony behind, is that Joseph was not a landowner. Carpentry was a step below landowning but a step above day labor. Tools and skill were the primary asset, used to fashion doors, simple furnishings, and the like (and not, *please*, mangers and crosses).

Before moving to the tradition it is worth noting what we do not know from the biblical evidence: We do not know Joseph's age at the time of Jesus' birth. We do not know if Mary was Joseph's first wife. We do not know if Joseph was alive when Jesus began his ministry. As always, it is best to preach from what we do know, not from what we do not.

Joseph of Nazareth in Christian Tradition

It is the tradition that assigns Joseph advanced years, Mary as a second or third bride, and kills him off before Jesus' public ministry. There are apologetic, theological, and biblical bases for these traditions, but a basis is different from a citation, and when we forget that, we end up with the *Protoevangelium of James*.[2] Or quotations like this.

> Tucked away in the recesses of Lent, this day commemorates a man who was asked in advancing age to take a child bride. . . . We must peer into the shadows, where he seems nearly always to have stood, to see this man who provided for a family while others were resting in the ease of years, who took upon himself the rearing of a boy who must have been in many ways a trial to him.
>
> Joseph was not a sophisticated man . . . he was the kind of man who could take a pregnant, teenaged wife and a troublesome, temperamental boy and make a life with them . . .
>
> For his labors he is rewarded with anonymity. There is benediction in that; for the self-effacing and shy, the simple and unschooled, it is fitting heaven to be gently forgotten.[3]

There is plenty more where that came from, believe me, dating back to the New Testament Apocrypha and continuing to the statues suitable for burying next to the "for sale" sign. One task for this day is not to add to the legendary schmaltz surrounding St. Joe. Before considering how best to do that we must look at the texts for the day.

2 SAMUEL 7:4, 8-16 (ELW, BCP)
2 SAMUEL 7:4-5A, 12-14A, 16 (LFM)
ROMANS 4:13-18 (ELW, BCP)
ROMANS 4:13-18, 22 (LFM)

If there is a theme in the Old Testament, epistle, and Lukan readings it is displacement. David, the man after God's heart, is told in this lesson that his son, yet unborn, will be the one to build a house for God, not David himself. Both the connections and reversals with Joseph and Jesus are interesting. Solomon will be David's biological offspring, but God says, "I will be a father to him, and he shall be a son to me" (2 Sam. 7:14), anticipating Joseph's role with Jesus. The fulfillment is not in Joseph's action, as it is not in David's, but in the actions of the sons yet to be born. Paul, looking past David to father Abraham, lifts up another prolepsis, Abraham's trust in a promise whose fulfillment he would only see in the birth of a son. This was enough, and in an echo/anticipation of Matthew's assessment of Joseph, "Therefore his faith 'was reckoned to him as righteousness'" (Rom. 4:22). David does not build the house, nor does Abraham see even his grandson Jacob, through whom the promise would move toward fulfillment. According to tradition Joseph does not live to see the fulfillment of the promise made by the angel of the Lord. The births, it seems, are enough.

> O God, who from the family of your servant David raised up Joseph to be the guardian of your incarnate Son and the spouse of his virgin mother: Give us grace to imitate his uprightness of life and his obedience to your commands; through Jesus Christ our Lord, who lives and reigns with you and the Holy Spirit, one God, for ever and ever. Amen.
> —Collect for the Feast of Saint Joseph, *The Book of Common Prayer*

MATTHEW 1:16, 18-21, 24A (ELW, LFM)
LUKE 2:41-52 (BCP, LFM ALT.)

As an Episcopal priest I find preaching about St. Joseph with the Luke text as the Gospel more than a little problematic. Therefore I must declare my thanks that the lectionary from *Evangelical Lutheran Worship* has opted for the Matthew text. In Luke, Joseph is not mentioned by name, subsumed under "parents" (NRSV; the Greek uses only the pronoun "they"). Mary does the speaking, and "treasured all these things in her heart" (Luke 2:48, 51). To finish the displacement, mom's and dad's anguish at three days (!) (v. 46) of searching is met with, "Did you not know that I must be in *my Father's* house?" (v. 49). Ouch. This is for Joseph's feast day? If you can, go with Matthew. If you cannot, go with God, and segue to Matthew as soon as you can.

Matthew believes in Joseph. He believes in his forerunner, the dreamer of Genesis, and takes everything he believes about Jacob's son and applies it to Jesus' earthly "father." A visionary who trusts his dreams, a righteous man, a man of action, a man of virtue. Not schmaltz. Virtue. The verse that transcends the crèche is 1:24, "When Joseph awoke from sleep, he did as the angel of the Lord commanded him . . . ." Doing as the angel of the Lord commanded. That will preach.

PREACHING ST. JOSEPH

How do we best bridge the gap between the biblical Joseph of Nazareth (nè of Bethlehem?) and the figurine buried in the front yard of desperate home sellers? Not by way of the *Protevangelium of James,* that is for sure. In this case the tradition may do more harm than good. Matthew's veneration is adequate. Look at it again. A "righteous man" is how he is introduced *before* the first dream. As a righteous man he wants to do the right thing, not the legal thing. Not to overdo the legalities, but Deuteronomy can be understood to have given Joseph some rights we should all be thankful he did not exercise (Deut. 22:13-21; 24:1). Like his biblical namesake, he trusted in his dreams. Stop right there. He trusted in his dreams. He took Mary for his wife. He sped to Egypt with his family. He returned to his homeland only when his dream said it was safe.

He trusted in his dreams. That, I think, is where to start. Not with reckless abandon, as if every nocturnal voice is divine, but with conviction and trust. God speaks. God speaks today. In visions and dreams, in hopes and convictions. God speaks. Are we listening? Do we trust what we hear? One of the ways the biblical and traditional Joseph challenges us today is in his trust in his dreams, and in his obedience to God's will for his life ("When Joseph awoke from sleep, he did as the angel of the Lord commanded him"; Matt. 1:24). The second way is in his willingness to do this despite the fact that doing so required him to ignore Torah (Scripture) and ignore custom (tradition). He took Mary for his wife. Never mind the tradition's notion of a pretty extreme May–December issue. Point me out a male of any age, race, or nation who would welcome as his wife a woman who was pregnant and he *knew* he was not the father, and did so because his God asked him to in a dream. If that is not a depiction of faith and trust I don't know what is.

> Joseph is completely within the field of the New Covenant: physically he can seem merely the child's foster-father, but spiritually he has a very much more profound share in God's fatherliness by assenting silently to the renunciation demanded by the angel.
> –Hans Urs von Balthasar[4]

This attitude of faith, and the decisive actions Joseph takes because of his faith, are the foundation for a homily in his honor, and do not require hoary tales about his dotage, his children from a prior marriage, or his timeless respect for Mary's virginal honor. We may honor Joseph well without raising issues for which we have few answers, and which the creeds do not address. *Born of the Virgin Mary* neither looks back to her immaculate conception nor forward to her perpetual virginity, and unless either issue is of timely importance to your community, there is no real reason to raise it on this day. After all, today is about Joseph.

Joseph was a righteous man. Biblically this means he was clear in his relationship to God, and acted out of that clarity. Traditionally it means he was willing to do what few would do, and is rightly honored as guardian of home and hearth. As a carpenter he was a man of vigorous and slightly rewarded labor, but given the absence of craftsmen-related parables in the teaching of Jesus it is not clear how this had an impact on his "son." I like to think of Joseph as a union man who had paid his dues, not a blue-collar, shot-and-a-beer guy, but there was definitely dirt under his fingernails. The homiletical fun to be had is in relating this down-to-earth everyman to the transcendent role he accepted in the divine drama.

FOR FURTHER COMMENT

Additional comments on these Scripture texts, in part or in full, may be found in the seasonal volumes of *New Proclamation* as follows:

- 2 Samuel 7:4, 8-16—Year B, Advent 4, Proper 11
- Psalm 89—Year A, Proper 8; Year B, Advent 4, Proper 11
- Romans 4:13-18—Year A, Proper 5; Years A & B, Lent 2
- Matthew 1:16, 18-21, 24a—Year A, Advent 4
- Luke 2:41-52—Year C, Christmas 1

Notes

1. The place to do this remains the magisterial work of the late Raymond E. Brown, *The Birth of the Messiah,* updated ed., Anchor Bible (New York: Doubleday, 1999).

2. While versions are easily available online, the standard edition is found in vol. 1 of Wilhelm Schneemelcher, ed., *New Testament Apocrypha,* trans. Robert McL. Wilson (Louisville: Westminster John Knox, 1991).

3. Sam Portaro, *Brightest and Best: A Companion to the Lesser Feasts and Fasts* (Boston: Cowley, 1998), 60–61.

4. Hans Urs von Balthasar, *Mary for Today,* trans. Robert Lowell (San Francisco: Ignatius, 1988), 52–53.

ANNUNCIATION OF OUR LORD

MARCH 25

WILLIAM F. BROSEND II

LUTHERAN (ELW)	EPISCOPAL (BCP)	ROMAN CATHOLIC (LFM)
Isa. 7:10–14	Isa. 7:10–14	Isa. 7:10–14; 8:10
Psalm 45 or 40:5–10	Ps. 40:1–11 or 40:5–10	Ps. 40:7–8, 8–9, 10, 11
Heb. 10:4–10	Heb. 10:5–10	Heb. 10:4–10
Luke 1:26–38	Luke 1:26–38	Luke 1:26–38

KEY THEMES

- On the Feast of the Annunciation we emphasize Mary within tradition.
- Mary was a young woman, confronted within history with an unprecedented proclamation, who accepted her unique calling with faith and trust.
- We must keep Mary connected to her historical context as a peasant Jewish woman, under Roman authority, in a period of rebellion and dislocation.

This is a strange and wondrous feast, tucked away in an unlikely place—sometimes the middle of Lent, other times during Holy Week or even after Easter—surprisingly reminding us that incarnation and atonement are continuous. While the chronology is obvious, counting back nine months from December 25, the significance of the feast may be lost in the vagaries of the calendar. The preacher's challenge is to fit, theologically and spiritually, meanings that the faithful often keep apart but which on this day must be held together, however great the tension.

There is, of course, an added responsibility for the preacher, for the Feast of the Annunciation is one of many feast days devoted to Mary addressed in these pages. Beginning with this day, if not before, we must be intentional about our own Marian theology, so that we may faithfully shape the thoughts and aspirations of our audience. We will do this by first examining the biblical texts assigned for this feast, then laying the foundation for what might be called a "homiletical theology of Mary," and finally by considering how one proclaims the texts and one's Marian theology on this feast day.

The epistle ("the offering of the body of Jesus Christ once for all"; Heb. 10:10) and psalm for the day draw our attention to the corporeality of the annunciation and the incarnation, and the proclamation of God's love ("I proclaimed righteousness in the great congregation; behold, I did not restrain my lips"; Ps. 40:9, BCP), and need little attention. The Old Testament and Gospel readings are another matter altogether.

ISAIAH 7:10-14 (ELW, BCP)
ISAIAH 7:10-14; 8:10 (LFM)

If there are more contested verses in the prophetic corpus I am not aware of them. With George Handel-like precision we focus on verse 14, "therefore the Lord himself will give you a sign. Look, the young woman is with child and shall bear a son, and shall name him Immanuel," as if it had no context in the life, ministry, and message of the prophet of eighth century B.C.E. But it does, and knowing what that was, and how then to understand the influence of that context and message on the evangelists, is vital to faithful and effective proclamation. Three issues focus the discussion: (1) the meaning of Isa. 7:10-14 in its own context; (2) the meaning of the respective Hebrew, Greek, and English terms 'alma, parthenos, and "virgin"; (3) the appropriation of Isaiah by Matthew, Luke, and early Christian tradition.

Isaiah 7:1-10 sets the scene: early in the reign of Ahaz, king of Judah, the kings of Aram (Syria) and Israel marched on Judah and threatened Jerusalem so that "the heart of Ahaz and the heart of his people shook as the trees of the forest shake before the wind" (Isa. 7:2). God sends Isaiah to chastise Ahaz for his fear and invite him to ask the Lord for a sign of reassurance. When Ahaz demurs, Isaiah blasts back: "Hear then, O house of David! Is it too little for you to weary mortals, that you weary my God also? Therefore the Lord himself will give you a sign. Look, the young woman is with child and shall bear a son, and shall name him Immanuel" (7:13-14). The Old Testament context is clear. Someone known to Ahaz is or will soon be pregnant. The child will be called "Immanuel" to remind all of God's continuing presence. Before the child is two years old or so, the threat to Jerusalem will have entirely dissolved. Raymond Brown summarized as follows, "[The Masoretic Text] of Isa 7:14 does not refer to a virginal conception in the distant future. The sign offered by the prophet

> Fifteen years old—
> The flowers printed on her dress
> Cease moving in the middle of her prayer
> When God, Who sends the messenger,
> Meets His messenger in her Heart.
> Her answer, between breath and breath,
> Wrings from her innocence our
>   Sacrament!
> In her white body God becomes our
>   Bread.
> —Thomas Merton, "The Annunciation"[1]

was the imminent birth of a child, probably Davidic, but naturally conceived, who would illustrate God's providential care for his people. The child would help to preserve the House of David and would thus signify that God was still 'with us.'"[2]

The key term in discussions of 7:14, translated in the NRSV as "young woman," is the Hebrew term 'alma, translated in LXX as *parthenos*, a Greek term itself best rendered in English as "virgin." But 'alma does not mean "virgin." That is the meaning of the Hebrew term *betûlâ*. This does not mean that the Greek translator of Isaiah misunderstood the prophet's intent. Instead the translator sharpened that intent, casting the event in the future tense ("will conceive") believing, as Brown says, "it would be more manifestly reflective of divine providence if a well-known woman who was still a virgin would become pregnant as Isaiah had prophesied."[3]

The tradition, explicitly in Matthew's citation of the Greek text of Isa. 7:14 (Matt. 1:23) and implicitly in the Annunciation, saw an unmistakable connection between Isaiah's prophecy and Jesus' birth, and was indisputably correct to do so. Unless one wishes to argue that Luke did not intend the reader to understand Mary to be a virgin, something 1:34 specifically claims.

LUKE 1:26-38 (ELW, BCP, LFM)

Luke has prepared the reader for the announcement of the birth of Jesus through the earlier, and much longer, annunciation of the birth of John to Zechariah (Luke 1:5-25). The patterns are almost identical:

• The angel Gabriel appears (he greets Mary but not Zechariah) and admonishes, "Do not be afraid" (1:13, 30).

• An explanation—"your prayer has been heard" (1:13); "you have found favor with God" (1:30)—precedes the promise of the birth of a son who will do wondrous things (1:13-17, 31-33).

• Zechariah and Mary respond with some incredulity ("How will I know?" 1:18; "How can this be?" 1:34).

• Gabriel responds by announcing Zechariah's loss of speech (1:19-20), and by telling Mary of Elizabeth's pregnancy and God's power (1:36-37).

• Zechariah accepts the announcement implicitly (1:21-23), Mary with words of affirmation, "Here am I, the servant of the Lord; let it be with me according to your word" (1:38).

The pattern is not unlike Old Testament scenes in which God's messengers announce to an infertile couple that they will "bear a son" (Sarah and Abraham,

Genesis 17; Hannah and Elkanah, 1 Samuel 1; and others)—with of course the inestimable difference: Mary is not infertile, she is a virgin.

As we have seen, focus on Isa. 7:14 as the important Old Testament parallel may miss the point. The pattern of Luke 1:5-25 and 26-38 suggests that Luke wants to depict the announcement to Mary as both continuous with the tradition and radically discontinuous at the same time. Mary stands in a long line of those to whom God or God's messenger, angelic, priestly, or prophetic, has announced an impending and miraculous birth. But Mary also stands alone, for none of the other announcements presume the absence of an earthly father.

Mary's responses throughout the scene are profoundly human. Perplexity at the appearance of an angel seems entirely appropriate, even more so when the angel begins the conversation with a proclamation of divine presence and an assumption of human fear. Give the girl a chance, Gabriel! Her question is not an expression of doubt, but an effort to understand the extraordinary words of the angel. Nor is her acceptance of the divine call—"Behold, the handmaid of the Lord," and so forth—blind obedience. As Elizabeth Johnson has shown us, we must be careful not to so valorize Mary that we rob her of her human courage.[4] Mary was a young woman, confronted within history with an unprecedented proclamation, who accepted her unique calling with faith and trust.

Finally, Luke 1:37, "For nothing will be impossible with God." The Greek, *ouk adunatēsei para tou theou pan rēma*, translates literally, "not impossible for God every word" and is a close rendering of Gen. 18:14, the promise to Sarah and Abraham at the oaks of Mamre, *mē adunatei tō theō rēma* (in the Greek LXX Luke would have known; NRSV: "Is anything too wonderful for the LORD?"). It is here, and not to Isaiah 7, that Luke wants us to look for antecedents.

> Pour your grace into our hearts, O Lord, that we who have known the incarnation of your Son Jesus Christ, announced by an angel to the Virgin Mary, may by his cross and passion be brought to the glory of his resurrection; who lives and reigns with you, in the unity of the Holy Spirit, one God, now and for ever. Amen.
> —Collect for the Feast of the Annunciation, *The Book of Common Prayer*

PREACHING THE FEAST OF THE ANNUNCIATION

My promise of a "homiletical Marian theology" will emerge in this and the other feast days of Mary—the Visitation (May 31), and the Assumption of Mary (LFM)/Mary, Mother of Our Lord (ELW/BCP) (August 15)—on which I write. To anticipate before focusing on the first part, my debt to other scholars will be obvious, especially to the work of Elizabeth Johnson and Roberto Goizueta, and to the scholarship, pastoral ministry, and personal friendship of Msgr. Arturo Bañuelas.[5] As an Episcopalian with a deep love of Mary, I am honored to share reflections on her meaning and message for the life of the church. Those reflections have a threefold focus, all guided by a vision of Mary as a historical figure: Mary within tradition, Mary in community, and Mary in the life of the faithful.

Searches for the "historical Miriam of Nazareth" have not been especially fruitful, a result of the slight biblical material and the profuse apocryphal writings that followed. Yet in many ways we know more than we realize, and considerably more than we often proclaim. Too often, though, we let what we *feel* about Mary delimit what we say about her, and as Johnson and others have pointed out, the language of *theotokos* or *christotokos* so overwhelms consideration of Miriam of Nazareth we lost sight of her historicity, and the meaning of her historical experience for our understanding of her. While not without controversy, Johnson's proposal remains a challenge to all interpreters. We need to ask what happens when we look at "Mary, the historical, graced, human woman, [remembering] her as our companion in the communion of saints. Entirely particular, lived out within the constraints of a patriarchal society, her life with its concrete details in no way function[ing] as culturally normative for women's lives today, lives racing along in a world she never dreamed of. But the memory of her partnership with God through the power of the Spirit can create liberating energies for justice, especially given her low estate as poor and as female."[7]

> Ere by the spheres time was created, thou
> Wast in His mind, who is thy Son and Brother;
> Whom thou conceivst, conceived; yea thou art now
> Thy Maker's maker, and thy Father's mother;
> Thou hast light in dark, and shutst in little room,
> Immensity cloistered in thy dear womb.
> —John Donne, "Annunciation"[6]

What happens? First, we recover Mary as a first-century woman with the power to choose, and so better understand the choice she made. Gabriel was an admittedly formidable presence, but nothing in Mary's response suggests Luke wanted us to see her as intimidated into submission. Her acceptance of God's will for her life was just that, acceptance, not capitulation. It was her choice, and no one else's. Second, we recover Mary as God's partner, God's chosen partner. Of course it was not a partnership of equals. It never is with God. But Mary's choice was preceded by God's choice. Third, we recover an appreciation of the tradition within which the historical Mary is grounded, the traditions of Second Temple Judaism, and the tradition of God's intervention in the birth of God's chosen ones. Mary is both fully a part of those traditions and, in the virginal conception of Jesus, distinct from it. But we can only grasp the distinction if we appreciate the continuities.

On the Feast of the Annunciation we emphasize Mary within tradition. This naturally presents occasion to remind the audience that our love and adoration for Mary must not cause us to lose sight of her as, like us, a person within history. We connect her to the Old Testament traditions of God's intervention to bring about birth where none had been possible, traditions Luke clearly had in view. And we connect Mary to her historical context as a peasant Jewish woman, under Roman authority, in a period of rebellion and dislocation. This important background then serves to accentuate the singularity of her "chosenness" and her choice, the beginning of the radical "scandal" of the incarnation.

That scandal is often identified with its "particularity," a place, a time, a people. All of that is embodied, and truly symbolized, in Mary. One homiletical starting point could be just this, the scandal of particularity, then and now, God choosing to love us. Another might be the continuity and discontinuity of Mary, and the ways we are called to remain faithful to tradition while responding in freedom to a new day and a new time—often a scandal in and of itself.

FOR FURTHER COMMENT

Additional comments on these Scripture texts, in part or in full, may be found in the seasonal volumes of *New Proclamation* as follows:

- Isaiah 7:10-14—Year A, Advent 4
- Psalm 40—Year A, Epiphany 2
- Psalm 45—Year A, Proper 9; Year B, Proper 17
- Hebrews 10:4-10—Year C, Advent 4
- Luke 1:26-38—Year B, Advent 4

Notes

1. Thomas Merton, "The Annunciation," in *The Collected Poems of Thomas Merton* (New York: New Directions, 1977 [1957]), 284.

2. Raymond Brown, *The Birth of the Messiah* (Garden City, N.Y.: Image Books, 1979), 148.

3. Ibid., 149.

4. Elizabeth A. Johnson, *Truly Our Sister: A Theology of Mary in the Communion of Saints* (New York: Continuum, 2003).

5. Roberto S. Goizueta, *Caminemos con Jesús: Toward a Hispanic/Latino Theology of Accompaniment* (Maryknoll, N.Y.: Orbis, 1995); Arturo J. Bañuelas, ed., *Mestizo Christianity: Theology from the Latino Perspective* (Maryknoll, N.Y.: Orbis, 1995).

6. John Donne, "Annunciation," in *John Donne: Selections from Divine Poems, Sermons, Devotions and Prayers*, Classics of Western Spirituality, ed. John Booty (New York: Paulist, 1990), 75.

7. Elizabeth A. Johnson, *Truly Our Sister: A Theology of Mary in the Communion of Saints* (New York: Continuum, 2003).

MARK, EVANGELIST

APRIL 25

CRAIG A. SATTERLEE

LUTHERAN (ELW)	EPISCOPAL (BCP)	ROMAN CATHOLIC (LFM)
Isa. 52:7–10	Isa. 52:7–10	1 Pet. 5:5b–14
Psalm 57	Psalm 2 or 2:7–10	Ps. 89:2–3, 6–7, 16–17
2 Tim. 4:6–11, 18	Eph. 4:7–8, 11–16	
Mark 1:1–15	Mark 1:1–15	Mark 16:15–20

KEY THEMES

- The church's public ministry is established and empowered by Christ.
- Offices in the church exist for the growth and spiritual maturity of the believing community.
- Faith in and loyalty to Christ overcomes disagreements.
- As the recollections of Peter, Mark's Gospel is God's good news for us in Christ.

ST. MARK

In celebrating the feast day of St. Mark, the church historically assumes that the individual referred to in Acts as John Mark (12:12, 25; 15:37), John (13:5, 13), and Mark (15:39), the individual identified as Mark by Paul (Col. 4:10; 2 Tim. 4:11; Philemon 24), and the individual that Peter refers to as Mark (1 Peter 5:13) are the same person. This claim is not as incredulous as it may at first seem. Mark of the Pauline Epistles was the cousin of Barnabas; in Acts, Mark appears to have a special bond or relationship with Barnabas. Moreover, the Mark that Peter calls his son appears to be the son of Mary, Peter's friend in Jerusalem, mentioned in Acts (12:12). The Roman name Marcus was commonly added to the Jewish name John, and the readers of Acts and the Epistles came to know this individual as Mark.

Mark's mother, Mary, owned the house where the infant church gathered (Acts 12:12). Peter returned to Mary's house after being released from prison; many of the members of the church were praying there when Peter arrived. Barnabas and Paul took Mark with them when they returned to Antioch from

Jerusalem, and John Mark accompanied his cousin and Paul as some sort of assistant on the first missionary journey. Unlike Barnabas and Paul, John Mark was
neither selected by the Holy Spirit, nor delegated by the church of Antioch; yet,
Acts 13:5 suggests that John Mark assisted the apostles even in preaching the
word. When Paul and Barnabas resolved to push on from Perga into central Asia

Minor, Mark left the mission and returned to Jerusalem
(Acts 13:13). Acts 15:38 suggests that the work was too
much for Mark. Paul refused to take Mark on the second missionary journey, because Mark left the earlier
mission. The disagreement over John Mark became so
sharp that Paul and Barnabas parted company; Barnabas
took Mark with him to Cyprus. At this point, we lose
track of Mark in Acts, and do not meet Mark again until
he is mentioned as the fellow worker of Paul, and in the
company of Peter, at Rome (Col. 4:10; Philemon 24;
2 Tim. 4:11; 1 Peter 5:13). First Peter was addressed to
various churches of Asia Minor, and Peter sends Mark's
greeting to them. Though Mark refused to accompany
Paul and Barnabas to Asia Minor, Peter confirms that he
went afterwards, and was widely known there.

The Prayer of the Day thanks God for enriching the
church with Mark's proclamation of the gospel. Papias
(second century) asserts, on the authority of an "elder,"
that Mark was Peter's interpreter and wrote Peter's
teaching down accurately, though not in order. Those

Such a ray of godliness shone forth on the
minds of Peter's hearers, that they were not
satisfied with a single hearing or with the
unwritten teaching of the divine proclamation. So, with all manner of entreaties, they
pleaded with Mark, to whom the Gospel is
ascribed (he being the companion of Peter)
to leave in writing a record of the teaching
that had been delivered to them verbally.
And they did not let the man alone until
they had prevailed upon him. And so to
them, we owe the Scripture called the "Gospel of Mark." On learning what had been
done, through the revelation of the Spirit,
it is said that the apostle was delighted with
the enthusiasm of the men and approved
the composition for reading in the churches.
—Clement of Alexandria[1]

teachings are said to be collected and reorganized in the Gospel that bears Mark's
name. A later but widespread tradition claims that Mark founded the church of
Alexandria and was martyred there in 64 C.E. In 829 Mark's supposed remains
were taken from Alexandria to Venice and the famous cathedral that bears his
name. St. Mark is symbolically represented by a lion.

Since the beginning of the seventh century, the West has observed April 25
as a rogation day that included a procession known as the Major Litany, which
replaced an old pagan procession, held on the same day, that was intended to
prevent wheat mildew. In the ninth century, the commemoration of St. Mark
was assigned to this day. For this reason, Mark's feast day is an occasion of prayer
for fertile fields and good crops.

THE GOSPEL

MARK 1:1–15 (ELW, BCP)
MARK 16:15–20 (LFM)

Taken together, the texts appointed by the lectionaries give us both the beginning and end of Mark's Gospel. Both passages are concerned with the launching of public ministry, that of Jesus in the prologue and the apostles in the conclusion. In both instances, public ministry is called for and empowered by God.

In just fifteen verses, Mark presents the ministry of John the Baptizer as fulfillment of prophecy, Jesus' baptism and anointing with the Holy Spirit, Jesus' temptation in the wilderness, and the beginning of Jesus' public ministry. As the pace of this narrative suggests, Mark is in a hurry to proclaim "the gospel of Jesus Christ, the Son of God" (v. 1).

Mark emphasizes that Jesus' public ministry is firmly grounded in the history of Israel. God's prophet, John the Baptizer, prepares for Jesus' ministry. John does not call the people to repentance. Rather, the Baptizer announces a baptism that leads to national repentance and results in forgiveness. God's gift of grace, given in the waters of the Jordan, is God's offer of righteousness to the nation of Israel in anticipation of the final judgment. John's announcement indicates that the end is near, and makes plain that the "one who is more powerful than I" (v. 7), whose arrival is imminent, can be none other than the Messiah. For Mark, the Messiah arrives at the Jordan. Jesus' baptism is the threshold from private life to public ministry. Jesus comes to the Jordan to acknowledge God's judgment on the sin of his people and to commit himself to God's sovereign rule by participating in this ritual of national renewal. At baptism, God calls Jesus to be God's Messiah and empowers Jesus for that role. God then drives Jesus into the hostile wilderness, where Jesus learns he can depend on God's sustaining power. Finally, Jesus begins his public ministry by preaching that the time Israel has waited for, the time promised by the prophets, has come. The reign of God is at hand. John's prophecy is fulfilled in Jesus' public ministry.

> From your childhood the light of truth
>   enlightened you, O Mark,
>   and you loved the labor of Christ the Savior.
> Therefore, you followed Peter with zeal
>   and served Paul well as a fellow laborer,
>   and you enlighten the world with your holy
>   Gospel.
> — *Troparion* (Tone 4)[2]

Mark presents the good news of Jesus Christ as urgent. This good news calls for decision; it demands that we entrust and commit our future to God's activity in the life, death, and resurrection of Jesus. The time is coming as quickly as Mark's Gospel gets going.

Mark 16:15–20 is an added account of the commissioning of the apostles. Jesus commands the disciples to go into the world and proclaim the good news to the

Jesus then ascends to God's right hand. While Jesus was at the Jordan for baptism, the heavens were torn open and God empowered Jesus; now Jesus empowers the disciples, working with them and confirming their preaching with accompanying signs. Called and empowered by Jesus, the disciples go out and proclaim the good news.

SECOND READING

2 TIMOTHY 4:6-11, 18 (ELW)
EPHESIANS 4:7-8, 11-16 (BCP)
1 PETER 5:5B-14 (LFM)

"Get Mark and bring him with you, for he is useful in my ministry" (v. 11). At first glance, it appears that this mention of Mark is the reason *Evangelical Lutheran Worship* appointed these autobiographical remarks and short direct commands, which bring 2 Timothy to a close, as the second reading for this day. Yet putting the two commands found in this passage together (not to mention those in the verses that the lectionary skips) reveals Paul's need and desire for the relationships of Christian faith and loyalty that shape and sustain the individual Christian. Paul tells Timothy, "Do your best to come to me soon. . . . Get Mark and bring him with you" (vv. 9, 11). Paul summons the companionship, strength, and refreshment of faithful and loyal Christians.

> What makes the proclamation of the gospel urgent in your context?

Paul's need arises from the situation in which he finds himself. Paul's death is unquestionably close at hand. Paul describes himself as "already" being poured out as a libation, and declares that the time of his "departure" has come. Paul sums up his ministry by saying that he has fought the good fight, kept the faith, and finished the race. He anticipates the crown of righteousness, which the Lord will give him (vv. 6-8). But in the present moment, Paul has sent off, or been abandoned by, all of his coworkers except Luke. Paul wants Timothy and Mark to come to him and to be with him in his final days.

It is not surprising that Paul desires the companionship of Timothy, whom he regarded as a son. We cannot say the same thing about Paul's relationship with Mark, however. Remember that Paul refused to take Mark with him on his second missionary journey, and that Paul's disagreement with Barnabas about Mark was so strong that it caused a break in their relationship. This simple mention of Mark's name at this pivotal moment in Paul's life speaks of the hope and call for reconciliation that is the gift, sign, and calling of Christian faith and loyalty. We can all name relationships in which disagreements cause strain and distance. A sermon on Mark's relationship with Paul might provide an occasion to help people to reconsider those relationships from the perspective of their faith. The preacher might remind people that, like Paul we will all face circumstances, which cast long-standing disagreements into the background as they call for the strength and support of companions in the faith. In Christ we can set our disagreements aside and request the companionship and help that we need.

The Roman Catholic lectionary likewise seems to appoint an epistle reading that mentions Mark. First Peter highlights Mark's close relationship with Peter and association with the church in Rome. "Your sister church in Babylon . . . sends you greetings; and so does my son Mark" (1 Peter 5:13). Babylon is a cryptic way of referring to Rome. Moreover, commentators suggest that the Greek construction of verses 12–14 raise the possibility that these verses came from Peter's own hand. These verses provide the basis for the tradition that Mark's Gospel is the teaching of Peter as recorded by Mark.

If ELW and LFM appointed epistle readings for their mention of Mark, BCP may have turned to Ephesians because of Paul's inclusion of the word *apostles*. Apostleship is one of several gifts mentioned by Paul, which the ascended Christ bestows on individual Christians for the well-being of the church. Christ's purpose in conferring these gifts is to help and guide the church so that all members exercise their individual gifts and carry out their ministries for the common good. We are not to regard apostleship (or any other office) as an elite status, but as a gift that Christ gives for the healthy growth and spiritual maturity of the believing community. For Paul, we come to appreciate fully what is involved in Christian faith and life in community, that is, in fellowship with one another. Christ established the office of apostle, which we lift up this day, to serve and support this fellowship.

First Reading ·
ISAIAH 52:7-10 (ELW, BCP)

In this context, Isaiah portrays an evangelist as God's messenger of good news. More than witnesses and reporters, evangelists speak for God, announcing good news to God's people. God's good news is the proclamation of peace and salvation that result from God's action and reign. Thus Mark's Gospel is nothing other than God addressing us. Taken together with the reading from 1 Peter, the preacher might construct a sermon celebrating Mark's relationship with Peter, which resulted in God's good news for us in Christ, which is the Gospel that bears Mark's name.

Additional comments on these Scripture texts, in part or in full, may be found in the seasonal volumes of *New Proclamation* as follows:

- Isaiah 52:7–10—ABC, Christmas Evening (Nativity 3)
- Psalm 2—Year A, Last Epiphany/Transfiguration
- Psalm 89—Year A, Proper 8; Year B, Advent 4
- 1 Peter 5:5b–14—Year A, Easter 7
- 2 Timothy 4:6–11, 18—Year C, Proper 25
- Ephesians 4:7–8, 11–16—Year B, Proper 13
- Mark 1:1–15—Year B, Advent 2; Year B, Baptism; Year B, Lent 1; ABC, Easter Sunday

Notes

1. Clement of Alexandria, "Letter to Theodore," Cited in Eusebius, History of the Church, 6.14 http.www.catholic-resources.org/Bible/Eusebius_Gospels.htm

2. http://orthodoxwiki.org/Apostle_Mark#Hymns (accessed June 28, 2007).

PHILIP AND JAMES, APOSTLES

May 1 (ELW/BCP) / May 3 (LFM)

Bill Doggett

Lutheran (ELW)	Episcopal (BCP)	Roman Catholic (LFM)
Isa. 30:18–21	Isa. 30:18–21	1 Cor. 15:1–8
Ps. 44:1–3, 20–26	Ps. 119:33–40	Ps. 19:2–3, 4–5
2 Cor. 4:1–6	2 Cor. 4:1–6	
John 14:8–14	John 14:6–14	John 14:6–14

KEY THEMES

• Trust in earthly powers blinds us to God's way.
• Sending forth.
• Seeing God in Jesus and Jesus in others.

The name James, which is the English version of Jacob, is a common one in the New Testament, and there are at least three and possibly as many as eight men so named: James the Greater (or Elder), son of Zebedee, whose feast day is July 25; James the Less, son of Alphaeus, the subject of this commemoration; James the Just, called "brother of the Lord" and leader of the Jerusalem congregation (Acts 12:17, 15:13; 21:18; 1 Cor. 15:7; Gal. 1:19; 2:9, 12); James the Writer, author of the epistle of James (Jas. 1:1); James the son of Cleopas (Mark 15:40ff.); James the Nazarene (Matt. 13:55; Mark 6:3); James the kinsman of Judas the apostle (Luke 6:16; Acts 1:13); and James the brother of Jude the Writer (Jude 1:1). Historically, James the Less has sometimes been identified with James the son of Cleopas, but this makes the linguistically doubtful assumption that Cleopas and Alphaeus are both attempts to transliterate the same Hebrew name. James the Less has also been identified with James the Just, but one difficulty with that identification is in John's Gospel, which says that the brothers of Jesus did not believe in him (John 7:5), so they could not have been apostles.

It is more common, anyway, to identify James the Just with James the Writer, and to either identify the other men named James with James the Just as well or to ignore them, at least for the sake of festivals. The James remembered on this day, then, if he is not to be identified with any other James, is known only from the various lists of the apostles (Matt. 10:3; Mark 3:18; Luke 6:15; Acts 1:13). Tradition holds that James was martyred in Ostrakine in lower Egypt by crucifixion. His body was said to have been later dismembered, which is why his symbol is the saw.

Philip, who shares this day, is also, in the Synoptics, only known from the lists of apostles, but John's Gospel names Philip four times in the narrative: he was among the first to be called to follow Jesus (John 1:43) and immediately brought Nathaniel to Jesus. It is to Philip that Jesus turned before the feeding of the five thousand and asked where bread might be bought (John 6:5); Luke's Gospel places the feeding near Philip's hometown of Bethsaida, so Philip would have been a likely person to ask. When some Greeks wished to speak with Jesus, they first came to Philip (John 12:20), possibly because Philip had a Greek name. Philip brought them to Andrew, and Andrew brought them to Jesus. It is Philip who at the Last Supper says to Jesus, "show us the Father, and we shall be satisfied" (John 14:8), prompting Jesus' discourse on his identity with the Father.

Tradition holds that Philip preached in Greece, Syria, and Phrygia. Clement of Alexandria reports that Philip was married, had children, and that one of his daughters married.[1] The third-century *Acts of Philip* recounts that Philip, Bartholomew, and Mariamme preached and baptized in Hierapolis in Phrygia, and that the proconsul, enraged that his wife had become a Christian convert, had the three tortured, and then crucified Philip and Bartholomew upside down. Philip continued to preach from the cross, and due to the power of his preaching, the crowd freed Bartholomew, but Philip refused to be freed, and died on the cross.[2] There seems to be some confusion, however, as to whether this story refers to Philip the apostle or Philip the deacon named in the book of Acts. He is said to have been buried in a shrine in Hierapolis, in present-day Turkey, but his relics were moved to Constantinople and then to the Church of the Twelve Apostles in Rome. Loaves of bread, either by themselves or in a basket, are the traditional symbol for Saint Philip.

> O Saint Philip, chosen disciple of the Lord, who brought Nathaniel to Christ, who most zealously preached thy Lord, Jesus Christ, and out of love to Him willingly gave thyself to be nailed to the cross, and put to death, obtain, I beseech thee, for me, and for all men, grace with zeal to bring others to the practice of good works, to have a great desire after God and His truths, and, in hope of the eternal blissful contemplation of God, to bear patiently the adversities and miseries of this life. Amen.
> —Prayer to St. Philip[3]

THE FEAST

In the Roman calendar, the feast of Saints Philip and James was moved from May 1 to May 13 in 1955 to make room for the feast of Joseph the Carpenter. It was then moved to May 3 during the revision of the Roman calendar in 1970.

The Episcopal and Lutheran calendars maintain the traditional date of May 1. The two saints have shared a feast since it began to be celebrated—as there is nothing to link the two saints in Scripture or in their legends, most probably the date commemorates the coincidental dates of their martyrdoms as preserved in their communities.

Historically, the feast of two apostles about whom so little is known was never sufficient to supplant pagan May Day rituals. Some medieval images of Philip and James even show them carrying branches of May Day flowers themselves. It might be fitting for a congregation to mark the day by sharing food with the needy in some way, in commemoration of the feeding of the five thousand.

THE READINGS

The reading from Isaiah was clearly chosen to foreshadow the Gospel lesson. The end of the Isaiah passage, "This is the way; walk in it" (Isa. 30:21), cannot help but resonate on this day with the beginning of the passage from John's Gospel: "I am the way, and the truth, and the life." The Isaiah passage, however, has a strong message independent of any messianic foretelling. Isaiah 30 instructs the people of Israel not to depend on Egypt for help against an unnamed enemy. On the one hand, Egypt considers Israel to be worthless, and on the other hand, Egypt's help will be worthless to Israel (Isa. 30:1-14). Seeking help from an earthly power means, Isaiah says, abandoning the help of God. The passage for today concludes the prophecy of the woe that will ensue with words of hope for those who return to God. And the blessing that God offers is complimentary: "The LORD waits to be gracious to you.... blessed are all those who wait for him" (v. 18). When the people of God stop turning toward Egypt, they will be able to hear the voice that is trying to tell them which way they should go.

> O Saint James, who lived so temperately and strictly, who, like thy master, prayed so earnestly and constantly for thy tormentors, I beseech thee that thou wouldst procure us from Jesus' grace, after thy example, to live sober and penitential lives, and to worship God in spirit and in truth. Obtain for us, therefore, the spirit with which thou didst write thine epistle, that we may follow thy doctrine, be diligent in good works, and, like thee, love and pray for our enemies. Amen.—Prayer to St. James[4]

The passages from 1 and 2 Corinthians are, not surprisingly, about evangelism. Since there is so little in their biographies to lead us, one of the themes for Philip and James is easily found in what it means to be an apostle. The apostolic mission is expressed in 2 Cor. 4:5-6: "For we do not proclaim ourselves; we proclaim Jesus Christ as Lord and ourselves as slaves for Jesus' sake. For it is the God who said, 'Let the light shine out of darkness,' who has shone in our hearts to give the light of the knowledge of the glory of God in the face of Jesus Christ." The good news that Jesus sends the apostles forth to proclaim is summarized in 1 Cor. 15:3-4, "that Christ died for our sins in accordance with the scriptures, and that he was buried, and that he was raised on the third day in accordance with the scriptures." Note that both of these passages tie the evangelical imperative to the God of the Hebrew Scriptures. The passage quoted from 1 Corinthians, which is a familiar liturgical formula (and probably was in Paul's day as well), emphasizes that connection by repetition: Christ's death was predicted in Scripture and Christ's resurrection was predicted in Scripture. This insistence that death and resurrection are both essential to a biblical messiahship spoke in Paul's day to those who denied Jesus as Christ because of his death. In our day, it may speak just as strongly of the promise that for God, death and new life are linked. We know the certainty of death, we may be equally confident that new life follows.

The passage from the Gospel of John that is shared by all three lectionaries is one of the stories about Philip mentioned above. Philip asks Jesus to show the disciples the Father, and Jesus responds with a discourse about his identity with the Father. One interesting facet of this discourse is brought up in John 14:11, where Jesus says, "Believe me that I am in the Father and the Father is in me; but if you do not, then believe in me because of the works themselves." This is a theme that is common to all the Gospels—that Jesus' miracles do not primarily matter in and of themselves, but they are meant to validate Jesus' teaching. The passage goes on to proclaim that the disciples will be able to work even greater wonders, with the implication that their teaching of the same message will need the same validation, "so that the Father may be glorified in the Son." In an age when those who still believe in miracles generally pray for them for their own sake, it might be well to consider what kinds of works would actually validate our words in our time. Feeding the poor, caring for the sick, sheltering the needy, and freeing the captives might be signs enough to validate our proclamation of the reign of God. Indeed, they might even bring it closer. Another preaching point might be the relationship between seeing God in Jesus and seeing Jesus in his followers.

FOR FURTHER COMMENT

Additional comments on these Scripture texts, in part or in full, may be found in the seasonal volumes of *New Proclamation* as follows:

- Psalm 19:2-5—Year A, Proper 22; Year B, Lent 3, Proper 19; Year C, Epiphany 3
- Psalm 119:33-40—Epiphany 7, Proper 18
- 1 Corinthians 15:1-8—Year B, Easter; Year C, Epiphany 5
- 2 Corinthians 4:1-6—Years B & C, Transfiguration
- John 14:6-14—Year B, Easter 5; Year C, Pentecost

Notes

1. Clement of Alexandria, *Miscellanies*, 3.6.52, available online at http://www.earlychristianwritings.com/text/clement-stromata-book3-english.html (accessed July 9, 2007).

2. *The Acts of Philip,* in *The Apocryphal New Testament*, trans. M. R. James (Oxford: Clarendon Press, 1924).

3. Goffine's Devout Instructions, http://www.catholic-forum.com/saints/gdi219.htm (accessed July 5, 2007).

4. Ibid.

VIGIL OF PENTECOST

MAY 9 (EARLIEST)–JUNE 12 (LATEST)

GAIL RAMSHAW

LUTHERAN (ELW)
Exod. 19:1-9 or
   Acts 2:1-11

Ps. 33:12-22 or
   Psalm 130

Rom. 8:14-17,
   22-27

John 7:37-39

EPISCOPAL (BCP)
Gen. 11:1-9; or
   Exod. 19:1-9a,
   16-20a; 20:18-20;
   or Ezek. 37:1-14;
   or Joel 2:28-32
Ps. 33:12-22; or
   Canticle 2 or 13;
   or Psalm 130; or
   Canticle 9; or
   Ps. 104:25-32
Acts 2:1-11 or
   Rom. 8:14-17,
   22-27
John 7:37-39a

ROMAN CATHOLIC (LFM)
Gen. 11:1-9 or
   Exod. 19:3-8a,
   16-20a; 20:18-20
   or Ezek. 37:1-14
   or Joel 3:1-5
Ps. 104:1-2, 24, 35,
   27-28, 29b-30

John 7:37-39

KEY THEMES

• The Vigil of Pentecost may serve a parish well as a baptismal festival event.
• This vigil prepares us for the next morning's Pentecost celebration.
• The water imagery in John is appropriate for the baptisms that may occur at the vigil.

THE DAY

Several different strands weave together in the tradition of Christians keeping vigil. One strand comes to us from the ancient Mediterranean world, in which each day was understood as beginning at sundown. When the sun went down, the day was over, and the next day began. Thus any celebration that was set on a certain day began, by contemporary standards, on the night before. Our culture retains this historic method of keeping time, for example on Christmas

Eve and New Year's Eve. On both these occasions, for many people the greater part of their celebration occurs on the evening before the actual day that is being observed. This idea of the day beginning at sundown has allowed contemporary Roman Catholics to schedule "Sunday" services on Saturday evening after sundown.

The current revival of the Easter Vigil demonstrates a similar logic. A full paschal Vigil is not preparatory to Easter: by many communities it is understood as the primary celebration of Easter, and it begins and usually concludes on Saturday evening. Most people who participate in an Easter Vigil do not return to church the next morning for another Easter celebration.

One reason that Pentecost maintained its vigil is that Pentecost was designated as one of the primary occasions for baptism. If for some reason a catechumen who was scheduled to be baptized at the Easter Vigil had to cancel, that baptism was transferred to a vigil at Pentecost. Many liturgical reformers who are urging parishes to conduct baptismal festivals indicate Pentecost as one of the most appropriate days for the celebration of multiple baptisms. It may be that the Vigil of Pentecost serves a parish well as a baptismal festival event.

> The Holy Spirit is therefore a river, the supreme river, which flowed from Jesus down to the earth. Mighty is this river, which flows forever and never grows less: and not alone the river, but also the rushing of the torrent with its overflowing splendor. For if a river, overflowing the tops of its banks, spreads out, how much more will not the Spirit, overtopping every created thing, make joyful with a more abundant richness of grace the creatures of heaven, when it pours out over the lowlier fields of our soul!
> —St. Ambrose[1]

A second strand in the history of Christian vigils arose in the primitive church when Christians held the belief that the second coming of Christ was imminent and that the faithful were to watch for his coming, which might come "like a thief in the night." Praying throughout the night became symbolic of the lifelong "waiting on the Lord" and signified the need to be always ready for the arrival of the Savior. Such a prayer service is clearly preparatory in style and tone to the primary event on Sunday morning.

Because Pentecost is understood as at least the third if not the second most significant celebration in the liturgical year, current lectionaries have appointed readings for a Vigil of Pentecost. In our time and culture, Roman Catholics speak of the Vigil of Pentecost as the first Eucharist of Pentecost. Among the small number of Protestant and Anglican parishes that keep a Vigil of Pentecost, it is largely a preparatory Eucharist for the festival Eucharist on Sunday morning, at which it is common to include various rites of inclusion, such as baptisms, confirmations, affirmations of baptism, and the welcome of new members. The vigil prepares the worshipers for the Pentecost celebration of the next morning, rather than paralleling, or even supplanting, the Sunday liturgy.

Pentecost is observed by Christians as the date, fifty days after Easter, that the Spirit of Christ came into the gathered community. One reason that the church counts fifty days arises from its Jewish roots that also held a festival fifty days after Passover. Pentecost is the Jewish commemoration of the giving of the law on Sinai. God descends onto the mountain, and the faithful witness that presence in fire and a cloud. Likewise, in Luke's narrative of Pentecost the Spirit of God descends, but this time onto the forehead of each believer. Fire is on each faithful Christian, and the wind of the divine Spirit blows through the room, enlivening all who are present. Luke means to say that the presence of God, once far removed on the top of a mountain and mediated by Moses, is now, thanks to the resurrection of Jesus Christ, available to all who believe.

Luke's way of telling the story of Jesus and of the church provides the timeline used by most Christians. The liturgical year follows the chronology of Luke, rather than that of John, perhaps because Luke is such a fine storyteller. We smile to read the evangelist's defense of his Luke-Acts writing project, when in Luke 1:3 he describes his account as "orderly." Indeed, it is not only orderly, but also ordered: this happened this day, this happened six months later; this occurred forty days later, and that fifty days later. Luke's memorable chronological approach governs the liturgical calendar, and thus we come to the feast of Pentecost, with an optional vigil, fifty days after Easter.

Yet it is striking that the Gospel readings for the Vigil of Pentecost and for all three years of the Day of Pentecost come from the Gospel of John, which does not adhere to any fifty-day chronology. We recognize here one of the riches of the lectionary, in that thanks to the three readings, we are provided with several different layers to the meaning of each liturgy. We meet on the fiftieth day, or on the evening before, and listen to John whose witness to the resurrection knows nothing of fifty days. For John, Christ appears always "after eight days," that is, on every Sunday morning, and when Christ appears, he brings to us his Spirit. Thus, for our three-year lectionaries, we meet on the fiftieth day to celebrate the gift of the Spirit, and on that day we hear that every Sunday is both the first day and the fiftieth.

THE GOSPEL
JOHN 7:37-39 (ELW, BCP, LFM)

The liturgical setting for the short Gospel reading from John 7 is the Feast of Tabernacles, Succoth, the festival of the wheat harvest. This agricultural festival, a kind of Thanksgiving Day, acquired as a historical religious layer the commemoration of the Jewish wilderness wanderings. Part of this pilgrimage festival was a ritual in which water was poured down the Temple steps. The rushing water was to recall the miracle of the water gushing from the rock in the wilderness and to anticipate the freely flowing water of eschatological Jerusalem. John's use of the water imagery makes this passage particularly appropriate for the baptisms that may take place at the vigil or the next day on Pentecost. Yet even without parish baptisms, the celebration of Pentecost always recalls baptism, since it is through the waters of baptism that the Spirit comes to the believer. This focus on baptism also brings the fifty days of Easter full circle, since the Vigil of Easter celebrates Christ's resurrection with continual reference to our own death and resurrection in baptism.

Although the passage from John 7 is brief, it has generated a massive amount of critical study because the Greek can be translated in several different ways. In Raymond Brown's magisterial study of the Gospel of John, these three verses occupy over ten pages of small-print commentary, and readers are encouraged to consult Brown for fascinating detail about what this passage might mean, which church fathers adopted which interpretation, and which Old Testament links support each possible reading.[2]

Jesus calls to himself everyone who is thirsty. According to the evangelist, Christ is now the rock from which pours out living water. The scholarly debate focuses largely on verse 38: Is the source Christ himself, or is it the believers, or does the Greek intend ambiguity? The ambiguity actually serves well on Pentecost. For from Christ, the living water, comes the life of the believers, who once they receive the gift of the Spirit of Christ, themselves become water for all who thirst.

THE READINGS

A considerable number of biblical texts are suggested for the Vigil of Pentecost. Here we shall attend to only several. In contrast to the usual pattern that the first reading in some way complements the Gospel, these readings relate far more closely to the Acts 2 narrative of the day of Pentecost than they do to John 7.

Exodus 19:1-9 stands as a mirror of the narrative in Acts 2. God descends onto the top of a mountain in a cloud, just as on Pentecost the Spirit descends in wind. Moses declares that the people can choose whether to accept the covenant relationship, just as Peter calls the crowd to accept Jesus as Messiah. The Exodus passage includes one of the Old Testament's evocations of the image of the mother eagle, who flies beneath the fledglings so that she can catch them with her wings if they fall. God calls the people into a relationship in which they are a treasured nation, a priestly kingdom, and a holy nation. The people will be especially cared for by the Almighty; they will all be able to access God, and they will be ordained to intercede for others, just as if each person is a priest; and they will be set apart from other nations, separated out, as whole unto God. The early Christian community sees itself as the inheritor of these labels.

If Exodus 19 is a mirror of the narrative in Acts 2, *Genesis 11:1-9* is the foil. Although Genesis 10 presents a genealogy in which peoples of different languages are listed, Genesis 11 records the well-known etiological myth that explains the origins of humankind's many languages. The myth concludes the prehistory of Genesis 1–11. If Genesis 3 told of the sin of the first couple and the alienation of humans from God, Genesis 11 tells of the sin of a powerful civilization and the alienation of peoples from one another. The stage is then set for Abraham to enter the story. Babel means "gate of God," but has been elided with the Hebrew *bll*, meaning "to confuse." In this myth, the world's differing languages come from God as a punishment for human arrogance. The Acts narrative, then, provides the opposite story, when the peoples who speak many languages come together in recognition of Jesus as Messiah. The coming of the Spirit is then seen as the repair of the rift between peoples. The many languages are not a curse, but become the vehicle for blessing throughout the world.

A good-sized book could be written about *Romans 8:14-17, 22-27*. Here we will list the emphases that are particularly appropriate to Pentecost. Christian baptism, by putting to death our old selves and joining us to Christ's resurrection, grants to us the gift of the Spirit. That Spirit of Christ bonds us to God as children to parents, and we can stand in relation to God as did Jesus, who was remembered as having called God *Abba*. Humans are not naturally heirs of divinity: only in Christ can believers gain the promised inheritance. Yet although we already enjoy the Spirit of Christ, we and all creation are still merely in labor. We are not yet fully borne into God, and at the end time, not only believers, but all creation will be saved. Paul here refers to the biblical ideas that in the fall, even nature has fallen, and that at the eschaton also nature will be saved.

> I had a kind of vision of all of us coming together, bearing our different wounds, offering differing gifts. The preachers, prophets, healers, and discerners of spirit. Those who can describe the faith and those who can only live it. Those who speak in tongues, and those who interpret. Those who write, and those who sing. Those who have knowledge, and those who are wise only in the sight of God. Each of us poor and in need of love, yet rich in spirit. Each of us speaking in the language we know, and being understood. Pentecost, indeed.
> —Kathleen Norris[3]

Considerable scholarship has addressed the meaning of *Abba*. Although in mid-century many interpreters asserted that *Abba*—a child's designation for the father, similar to "Papa"—was unique to Christ, both of these claims are now questioned. Paul, not himself a member of Jesus' community, does cite the term in Aramaic, and thus it is clear that *Abba* had honor in the primitive church. Yet in the Synoptics, Jesus is quoted as having prayed with this word only in Gethsemane, while his followers were asleep. What becomes commonplace in the New Testament is calling God "Father," which although surprising for first-century Jews, would have been normal for Greco-Romans, for whom Jupiter was Father of fathers. The Romans passage uses this term, however, for what we understand as trinitarian proclamation: God grants to believers the Spirit of the resurrected Christ, and with that Spirit, we are brought to God.

The verse about all nature groaning has become increasingly cited as Christians think more profoundly about ecological concerns. Here is a biblical warrant for the idea that God loves not only humans, but all the created order, all the animals, all the plants, indeed, all the planets, and that God's original intention for everything will finally come to fulfillment. Throughout most of Christian history, a thoroughgoing anthropomorphism has suggested that God cared only for humankind. This verse calls us to share God's care for the entire created universe.

The Vigil of Pentecost, then, appoints exceedingly complex readings, such as John 7 and Romans 8, for a liturgy that few parishes schedule. Yet for any celebration of Pentecost, these readings are excellent Bible study, since each one in its way sheds some light on the mystery of the coming of the Spirit to the faithful.

FOR FURTHER COMMENTARY

Additional comments on these Scripture texts, in part or in full, may be found in the seasonal volumes of New Proclamation as follows:

- Genesis 11:1-9—Year C, Pentecost Sunday
- Exodus 19:1-9a, 16-20a; 20:18-20—Year A, Proper 6, Proper 22
- Ezekiel 37:1-14—Year A, Lent 5; Year B, Pentecost Sunday
- Joel 2:28-32—Year C, Proper 25
- Psalm 33—Year C, Proper 14
- Psalm 104—Years ABC, Pentecost Sunday
- Psalm 130—Year A, Lent 5; Year B, Proper 5, Proper 8, Proper 14
- Acts 2:1-11—Years ABC, Pentecost Sunday
- Romans 8:14-17, 22-27—Year A, Proper 11; Year B, Trinity Sunday; Years B & C, Pentecost Sunday
- John 7:37-39—Year A, Pentecost Sunday

Notes

1. Ambrose, *The Sunday Sermons of the Great Fathers*, vol. 3, ed. M.F. Toal (Chicago: Henry Regnery, 1959), 12–13.

2. Raymond E. Brown, *The Gospel According to John I–XII* (New York: Doubleday, 1966), 320–24, 326–31.

3. Kathleen Norris, *Amazing Grace: A Vocabulary of Faith* (New York: Riverhead, 1998), 349.

MATTHIAS, APOSTLE

MAY 14 (ELW/LFM) / FEBRUARY 24 (BCP)

CRAIG A. SATTERLEE

LUTHERAN (ELW)	EPISCOPAL (BCP)	ROMAN CATHOLIC (LFM)
Isa. 66:1–2	Acts 1:15–26	Acts 1:15–17, 20–26
Psalm 56	Psalm 15	Psalm 114
Acts 1:15–26	Phil. 3:13b–21	
Luke 6:12–16	John 15:1, 6–16	John 15:9–17

KEY THEMES

- God works in and through the Christian community to keep God's promise and fulfill God's will.
- Jesus provides and empowers witnesses through the church, so that neither God's people nor the world will forget the gospel.
- The most important quality of Christian witnesses is their experience of Christ.

ST. MATTHIAS

If ever there is an occasion to remember that saints' days are about God in Christ, and not the saint, this is it. Here is everything we know about Matthias: Matthias was with Jesus from baptism to ascension. After Pentecost, when the apostles prayed and cast lots, flipped a coin, rolled the dice, or cut cards to select someone to replace Judas Iscariot, Matthias won. Matthias was then named one of the apostles. Immediately following his election, Matthias disappeared from both Scripture and church history. While some traditions hold that Matthias was one of the seventy disciples sent out by Jesus (Luke 10:1), and stories circulate that he preached in Judea and Ethiopia and was martyred, these things cannot be verified.

Matthias will be linked forever with the person not elected an apostle. Joseph called Barsabbas (also known as Justus) also had been with Jesus from baptism to ascension. For all we know, Joseph went on being a Christian and, like Matthias, disappeared from Scripture and church history. The only difference between these two is that Matthias won the coin toss and was elected an apostle; Joseph lost and was not. Matthias was granted a saint's day. Joseph called Barsabbas (also known as Justus) is still waiting for one.

Matthias's feast day was one of the last apostles' days to be added to the calendar; it was not celebrated before the eleventh century. The LFM celebrates St. Matthias on May 14 to place it in the Easter season and emphasize that Matthias was a witness to Christ's resurrection. The rationale for commemorating Matthias on February 24 is unknown.

This saint's day is not about Matthias at all. This saint's day is about Jesus, who as an expression of great love for the church and the world, sets individuals apart, appoints them as apostles, and sends them to witness publicly to the good news, so that neither God's people nor the world will ever forget about God's incredible love. And, when these witnesses are no more, Jesus through the church calls and sends other witnesses to replace them.

The most important credential that these witnesses carry as they go is that the church sees in them what the New Testament church saw in Joseph and Matthias. They have witnessed Jesus in baptism. They have seen Jesus heal and heard Jesus teach. They have experienced the power of Jesus' forgiveness, and seen Jesus reveal God's love in suffering and death. They can point to Christ's resurrection, and trust that Jesus will always bring new life. In other words, they have experienced the power of God at work in Jesus Christ. And, in response to our church's process of casting lots, and sometimes even in spite of it, these witnesses, like both Matthias and Joseph, follow Jesus from death to new life so that the world never forgets God's incredible love.

O Glorious Saint Matthias, in God's design it fell upon you to take the place of the unfortunate Judas who betrayed his Master. You were selected by the twofold sign of the uprightness of your life and the call of the Holy Spirit.

Obtain for us the grace to practice the same uprightness of life and to be called by that same Spirit to wholehearted service of the Church. Then after a life of zeal and good works let us be ushered into your company in heaven to sing forever the praises of Father, Son, and Holy Spirit. Amen.[1]

First / Second Reading

ACTS 1:15-26 (ELW, BCP, LFM)

The passage from Acts, the principal reading for this day, takes up a problem left unresolved in Luke's Gospel. One of the apostles chosen by Jesus, appointed by God, and given authority to preach and to heal, and even to rule over the twelve tribes of Israel (Luke 6:12-16; 9:1; 22:29-30; see comments below) betrayed Jesus and led Jesus' enemies to arrest him. This is very serious. Yet Acts 1:15-26 is concerned with a matter more serious than either the scandal caused by

Judas or the need to replace a failed, fallen apostle. The circle of apostolic leadership has been shattered. Eleven apostles simply will not do.

The number twelve is significant in Luke for its connection to the twelve tribes of Israel. Luke refers to the apostles as "the Twelve" six times. Luke emphasizes the number twelve to indicate that Jesus is restoring the people of Israel. Perhaps this is why the leftovers from the feeding of the five thousand are gathered up into twelve baskets (9:17). In the Acts text, the crowd of believers numbered 120 persons, or ten times twelve (v. 15). We see, if you will, the "twelve tribes" of the restored Israel gathered around the twelve apostles, the new leadership appointed by Jesus. This image of a restored Israel is flawed by the one missing apostle. Jesus' promise and God's plan are at stake. Judas is gone and another must be *numbered* among the apostles (v. 17). The Twelve had to be unequivocally reestablished at the heart of the people so that the promised Spirit might be bestowed, the faithful Israel established, and God's promise fulfilled.

So Peter cites and joins two psalms (LXX 68:26 and 108:8) to interpret definitively Scripture as prophecy verifying that both Judas's defection and the appointment of another to replace him are in keeping with God's will and purpose (v. 20). Scripture was fulfilled in Judas; now the community must fulfill Scripture by appointing someone to replace him. The community proposes two candidates. The personal qualities of these candidates do not appear to be important; what matters is their experience of Jesus. The two identified candidates both accompanied the apostles and were part of Jesus' ministry from baptism to ascension, in Luke's Gospel from beginning to end, and so witnessed the resurrection.

> And they all prayed together, saying: "You, Lord, know the hearts of men; make your choice known to us. You, not we." Appropriately they said that he knew the hearts of men, because the choice was to be made by him, not by others. They spoke with such confidence, because someone had to be appointed. They did not say "choose" but "make known to us" the chosen one; "the one you choose," they said, fully aware that everything was being preordained by God.—St. John Chrysostom[2]

In keeping with the pattern established by Jesus (Luke 6:12-16), the choice is made following a time of prayer. Since both candidates are equally qualified, discerning God's will can be entrusted to the casting of lots. The first reading from Isaiah (66:1-2), appointed by *Evangelical Lutheran Worship*, perhaps is intended to indicate how God made the choice: "But this is the one to whom I will look, to the humble and contrite in spirit, who trembles at my word" (66:2). Yet, both candidates appear to fit this description. "The lot fell on Matthias; and he was *added* to the eleven apostles" (1:26). Matthias restores the total of twelve apostles. Symbolically, the twelve tribes of the restored people of God are reestablished, and the promise of Christ fulfilled. This story is not about Matthias at all. It is about God keeping God's promise and fulfilling the divine will in and through the Christian community.

THE GOSPEL
LUKE 6:12-16 (ELW)
JOHN 15:1, 6-16 (BCP)
JOHN 15:9-17 (LFM)

The Gospel readings make the point that the apostles were appointed by Jesus, and their ministry is empowered by God. These leaders did not emerge by accident or vote, but according to God's plan. Luke 6:12-16 relates how Jesus established the role of apostle and handpicked twelve individuals to fill it. Jesus chose these twelve from a larger group of disciples after spending the night praying to God. Jesus selects these twelve in the context of humility and dependence upon God's guidance; therefore, we are to understand Jesus' choices as divinely inspired. Jesus chose ordinary people from a variety of life experiences, including a fisherman, tax collector, political revolutionary, skeptic who would demand proof of Christ's resurrection, and the traitor who betrayed Jesus. Yes, Judas Iscariot is included as part of a divinely guided process. These were the first followers that Jesus sent out in mission. Jesus trained them and gave them special authority for their ministry (9:1; 22:29-30). Moreover, the apostles chosen by Jesus comprise the pool from which almost every major leader of the early church is drawn.

> What process does your congregation use to select its leaders? How important are leaders' experience of and relationship with Jesus in the process?

In the reading(s) from John's Farewell Discourse, Jesus tells the disciples (after Judas left to betray him), "You did not choose me but I chose you. And I appointed you to go and bear fruit, fruit that will last, so that the Father will give you whatever you ask him in my name" (John 15:16). Jesus describes his relationship to the disciples using the symbol of a vine and its branches. In verse 1, Jesus is the vine in relation to God, who is the vine grower; in verse 5, Jesus is the vine in relation to the community of his disciples. Taken together, these verses present Jesus as the vine that connects the gardener and the branches and results in the production of fruit. The community of disciples is not only appointed by God; this community is empowered by God to bear fruit through its connection to Jesus Christ. Jesus is the middle ground between God and the community of faith. Jesus remains with the community so that the disciples can do the same works of love that Jesus does, and continue the glorification of God. In other words, God empowers the community to continue Jesus' own ministry.

Jesus is so intimately involved in this community that he calls the disciples his friends, those whom he loves, because Jesus has included them in his intimate relationship with God (v. 15). Jesus appoints these friends to share in his life and work. Unlike Luke, John makes no mention of the number and composition of the group that Jesus appoints. John's concern is that the disciples' relationship to

Jesus (and ours) results from Jesus' initiative. Friendship with and appointment by Christ is the gift of God's grace and does not result from our effort or merit. For John, the most important quality of Christian witnesses is their relationship with Christ. Friendship *with* Jesus leads to commissioning *by* Jesus. The vocation of Jesus' friends is to bear fruit, to do works of love, and participate in and continue Jesus' glorification of God.

FOR FURTHER COMMENT

Additional comments on these Scripture texts, in part or in full, may be found in the seasonal volumes of *New Proclamation* as follows:

- Psalm 15—Year A, Epiphany 4; Year B, Proper 17; Year C, Proper 11
- Psalm 114—Year A, Proper 19; Years ABC, Easter Vigil, Easter Evening
- Acts 1:15-26—Year B, Easter 7
- Philippians 3:13b-21—Year C, Lent 2, Lent 5
- John 15:1, 6-16 (17)—Year B, Easter 5, Easter 6

Notes

1. Catholic Community Forum, Patron Saints Index; http://www.catholic-forum.com/saints/pray0156.htm (accessed May 23, 2007).

2. St. John Chrysostom, Homily on the Acts of the Apostles, at Catholic Community Forum, Patron Saints Index; http://www.catholic-forum.com/saints/saintm17.htm (accessed May 23, 2007).

THE SOLEMNITY OF THE MOST HOLY BODY AND BLOOD OF CHRIST / CORPUS CHRISTI (LFM)

SUNDAY AFTER TRINITY SUNDAY:
MAY 24 (EARLIEST)–JUNE 27 (LATEST)

GERARD S. SLOYAN

YEAR A	YEAR B	YEAR C
Deut. 8:2–3, 14b–16a	Exod. 24:3–8	Gen. 14:18–20
Ps. 147:12–13, 14–15, 19–20	Ps. 116:12–13, 15–16, 17–18	Ps. 110:1, 2, 3, 4
1 Cor. 10:16–17	Heb. 9:11–15	1 Cor. 11:23–26
John 6:51–58	Mark 14:12–16, 22–26	Luke 9:11b–17

KEY THEMES

• Adoration by a protracted gaze.
• Christ's body eaten and his blood drunk.
• The many who no longer believed.

The origins of this feast go back to the lifetime of an Augustinian nun, Juliana of Liège, who claimed a vision in support of the institution of a feast of the publicly displayed eucharistic body of Christ. The fathers of the early church had been so successful in preaching awe in the presence of the sacramental Christ that from the year 300 onward his body and blood were less and less frequently eaten and drunk. A visual piety gradually replaced the piety of a ritual meal. Two elevations of the sacred host and chalice for a protracted gaze gradually made their way into the rite. The first of these occurred at the midpoint of the canon or prayer of the people that effected the change of the elements; the second, called the minor elevation, took place at its end as the people affirmed their eucharistic faith with a sung "Amen." By the year 1000 the static adoration of the body of Christ both at the Mass and as reserved between Masses for the Sacrament of the Dying (*Viaticum*, "On the way with you") had all but replaced a dynamic act, the rite in which congregations by this time were participating only as silent spectators. By the year 1215, communicating in the sacred species (as what appeared to the eye were called) had become such a rarity that the Fourth Council of the Lateran, a Roman basilica, mandated "reverent reception of the Paschal Sacrament of the Eucharist" at least once a year. Those who failed to receive the Body of Christ in the Easter season were forbidden entry to the church and, if they persisted in their abstention, not allowed Christian burial. This legislation was passed by the whole body of bishops of Europe and parts of Asia as binding their populations—Jews, Muslims, and heretics excepted. Written acknowledgment that one had conformed called a *libellus* was issued, confirming that sacramental reception had been preceded by the confession of grave sins. While these measures at law had a certain effect, their chief result in the popular mind was a heightened awareness of the Christ made present sacramentally by the Mass, to be adored visually rather than consumed as food and drink. The dynamic was thus almost thoroughly eclipsed by the static. Seven hundred years would pass before Pope Pius X, a man of simple piety, was canonized a saint for his promotion of early and frequent reception of the Eucharist and his plea for "full active participation" in the rite, in a document on song in the melodies of Gregorian chant.

YEAR A

John 6:51-58. The biblical choices of *Lectionary for Mass* in this, the Matthew year, present few problems. The "bread of life discourse" delivered by Jesus in the synagogue at Capernaum as reported in the Gospel according to John (6:59) seems throughout to be a demand for faith in Jesus' person under the symbolism of bread that nourishes and wine that stimulates. It is part of the evangelist's literary technique of following a "sign," elsewhere a "work," of Jesus with an exposition that explains. The metaphor of bread as a latter-day manna sustaining a life of faith in Jesus, God's Christ, seems to come to an end with the explanation in response to a challenge. Jesus himself is presented as the expositor of what it means for his flesh to be eaten and his blood to be drunk. Doing so achieves the receiving of life, a life that will last forever (v. 51). Up to this point the phrase about eating him as bread is obviously a continued metaphor. An element of realism, however, enters in at verses 52-58. The adjective *true*, describing first Jesus' flesh, then his blood, raises the question: "Real, genuine, yes, but in what sense?" There must be an eating and drinking possible in some sense other than the literal, namely anthrophagy. What is the sense that John intends?

One clue may be that he deserts the ordinary Greek word for eating that has been used throughout the discourse for another word in these seven verses that means to chew or eat audibly. Is this a sign that the physical act of eating and drinking is meant here? This evangelist has arrived at the initiatory rite of baptism

103

BODY AND
BLOOD OF
CHRIST

MAY 24–
JUNE 27

in the Nicodemus story in just such an oblique way. There is the further fact that John has no account of Jesus' words over bread and wine at the Last Supper like those of the Synoptic Gospels and Paul's one epistle. Can this be John's eucharistic discourse? Many think so. Jean Cauvin did not. He was convinced that since the body of Christ existed in heavenly glory there is no way it could be on all the altars of the world. We have come to the meaning of sacrament. Can one meaning be unique here among the others of this multivalent term?

The Deuteronomic narrative as proclaimed in this liturgy (*Deuteronomy 8:2-3, 14b-16a*) has no puzzling elements. The manna is evidently viewed as a type of future nourishment, accompanied by the warning that bread alone does not suffice. The word of God is the essential complement to the bread. In two places, verses 3 and 6, manna is described as a total *novum*, "a food unknown to you and your fathers." Christian faith sees here a foreshadowing of bread become Christ's eucharistic body, a new reality if ever there was one. God sends his commands to earth in the psalm of response, proclaiming his word to Jacob that sees God's decrees and laws as Israel's food. This people has been given the gift of peace up to its very borders, with finest wheat as its token. So, too, does the Prince of Peace come to earth as finest wheat to be harvested, milled, and served to be consumed.

> Lord Jesus Christ, You gave us the Eucharist as the memorial of Your suffering and death. May our worship of this sacrament of Your Body and Blood help us to experience the salvation You won for us and the peace of the kingdom where you live with the Father and the Holy Spirit, one God, for ever and ever. Amen.
> —Collect for the Feast of Corpus Christi[1]

1 Corinthians 10:16-17. Paul reminds the church at Corinth that the consuming of food and drink in the eating places attached to pagan shrines is empty of symbolic meaning, there being no pagan gods behind the idols (1 Cor. 8:4). The pita bread and the cup of wine, on the other hand, are fraught with meaning for the baptized. Consuming them is no less than a "participation in the blood of Christ," the draught from the common cup, while "the bread that we break, is it not a participation in the body of Christ?" (10:10-11). The apostle could not be clearer in expounding the sacramental realism of the act. Its sacramental significance both preceded and followed his description of the eating and drinking.

YEAR B

Turning to *Hebrews 9:11-15* we find a perfect expression of the one theme of this book, namely that Christ acted as both high priest and victim in offering his blood in unblemished sacrifice. An important question is, How did the apostolic church arrive so soon and so certainly at the conviction that Jesus crucified and risen did, under God and for all, what God had earlier appointed to be done for Israel in Jerusalem's temple? Luke, in his book two, later called the

105

BODY AND
BLOOD OF
CHRIST

MAY 24–
JUNE 27

Acts of the Apostles, places on Peter's lips a succession of public discourses as if delivered a scant seven weeks after Jesus' death and resurrection. Accepting in faith this deed of God, coupled with repentance and baptism, would mean remission of sins (Acts 2:38; 3:19; cf. 8:38).

These homilies in aid of faith and repentance were clearly crafted and delivered often, well after the events of the Passover season in Jerusalem they describe. Still, Paul's earliest extant correspondence, combined with his assurance that after an interval he had made sure that his gospel coincided with that of the Jerusalem apostles, is the way we know that Jesus' death on the cross was being deemed not only *an* but *the* acceptable blood sacrifice while the Temple still stood. It was left to this treatise called To the Hebrews to spell out the self-offering of Jesus on the cross as continuing in a liturgy in the sanctuary beyond the veil of the heavens. Paul's first Corinthian letter had spoken of eating the meat that had been offered in the Temple as participating in the sacrifices (1 Cor. 10:18). When the author of Hebrews later than in the present passage speaks of Jesus' "one sacrifice" (10:12) and of the "consecration of the people through Jesus' own blood" (13:12), he does so in a context of the continued offering of a "sacrifice of praise," an act that is the fruit of praise upon the lips. It is not certain what he means to include with doing good and sharing what you have when he speaks of "sacrifices of that kind" (v. 16).

More sure of what is meant by sacrifice in this context is the description of the eucharistic meal toward the end of the first century and following by the use of the word *thusía*. Calling the rite a sacrifice is a logical development from Jesus' words over wine at the supper table, "This is my blood of the covenant poured out for the many" (Mark 14:24; Matt. 26:28) and the eating and drinking of bread and cup as a proclamation "of the death of the Lord until he come" (1 Cor. 11:26). The worshipers at the Corpus Christi Eucharist are alerted first to the mystery of Jesus' blood poured out in sacrifice by the narrative of Moses' proclamation of the book of the covenant (Exod. 20–23) in *Exodus 24:3-8*. The Lawgiver wrote down all the words of the Lord on a scroll, then read them out, and having received the people's assent to its terms sealed this covenant by sprinkling the people with the blood of young bulls. "The new covenant in my blood" in Mark and Matthew, likewise in Luke 22:20, and 1 Cor. 11:25 can only mean a renewal of this covenant sealed in blood.

> The desire of Jesus Christ and of the Church that all the faithful should daily approach the sacred banquet is directed chiefly to this end, that the faithful, being united to God by means of the Sacrament, may thence derive strength to resist their sensual passions, to cleanse themselves from the stains of daily faults, and to avoid these graver sins to which human frailty is liable; so that its primary purpose is not that the honor and reverence due to our Lord may be safe-guarded, or that it may serve as a reward or recompense of virtue bestowed on the recipients. Hence the Holy Council calls the Eucharist "the antidote whereby we may be freed from daily faults and be preserved from mortal sin.
> —Pope Pius X, *Sacra Tridentina*[2]

The Gospel portion in today's Mass, *Mark 14:12–16, 22–26*, speaks of the eve of the first of eight Yeastless Days (*Azyma/Matsoth*) in describing the booking of a guest room in Jerusalem for Jesus and his fellow Passover pilgrims. Would the company of men have prepared the meal? It was entirely unlikely. Succinctly, in the description of the meal, only Jesus' blessing of bread and wine is reported, which he declares to be his body and blood. His vow of abstention from wine "again" until he would drink it new in the kingdom of God is the evangelist's anticipation of Jesus' reign in glory at the end of the age, a vow that Matthew repeats. The hymn that all sang would probably have been the Great *Hallel*, Psalm 136. This song in praise of God for releasing the people from Egyptian captivity, among other blessings, was fittingly sung on the feast of *Pesah*, the passing over of a destructive angel on the houses in Egypt while those of the Egyptians were struck down.

YEAR C

On this feast in the Lukan year the Gospel passage chosen is *Luke 9:11b–17*, the multiplication of pocket breads and fish from an initial five and two to become enough to feed five thousand men. Luke copies out the first of Mark's two accounts of the miracle (6:35–44), editing it only slightly. Certainly to be observed in the accounts in the two Gospels, and in Matthew as well, is Jesus' looking up to heaven, blessing, breaking, and giving the disciples the broken bread and fish to distribute; this is almost identical in the wording spoken over the bread at the supper in Luke 22:19. These would be the words and acts of the oldest male at any Jewish meal but, in light of the direction Jesus gave to his disciples, "Take this and divide it among yourselves" (Luke 22:17) and "Do this as my memorial" (1 Cor. 11:24, 25), we can assume that the Synoptic writers were obeying that meal command in their respective communities and had Jesus' words at the rite very much in mind as they retold the multiplication story. They would now, years later, have viewed it in retrospect as anticipatory.

> How many of you say: I should like to see His face, His garments, His shoes. You do see Him, you touch Him, you eat Him. He gives Himself to you, not only that you may see Him, but also to be your food and nourishment.
> —St. John Chrysostom[3]

The Genesis author means his brief account of Melchizedek's bringing out bread and wine and invoking the blessing of his Canaanite deity God Most High (*El Elyon*) on these gifts and on Abram (*Gen. 14:18-20*) to be an acknowledgment of the true God of the Hebrews. They later adopted the title, the Most High, for their Lord. Not only are bread and wine the symbols of gift giving in the Genesis passage but also of victory (v. 22). The shadowy king of Salem who offers them will reappear in Psalm 110:4 as the type of a Davidic king who is precisely a non-Aaronide, one whose priesthood moreover will be forever. This attribution of priesthood to a member of the royal line is applied to Jesus in Heb. 5:6, 10; 7:11–17. The latter verse makes the specific point that Jesus is God-appointed as "another priest arising according to the order of Melchizedek, rather than one according to the order of Aaron" (v. 11; see v. 17). This provides the homilist with the opportunity to speak of the eucharistic action as an exercise of the priesthood of Christ, which is true of all the sacraments. Today's feast is a second celebration of the Holy Thursday Mass of the Lord's Supper, not of the body of the Lord in reservation or on display. *Psalm 110:1, 2, 3, 4* for its part is an obviously sung responsory to the Genesis reading.

In 1980 I participated in a Corpus Christi procession through the streets of a largely Protestant town not far across the River Neckar from Heidelberg. The concrete aprons in front of all the police and fire stations had ingenious carpets made of flower petals showing hosts surmounting chalices, the IHS of *Iēsoús,* and monstrances with their gleaming rays done in goldenrod with a host at the center. In an inescapable paradox, the Protestant townsfolk were at every window along the way as silent, respectful spectators while the Catholic parishioners were full, active participants in a paraliturgical rite. They had had seven hundred years of practice for it, but at the time only ten years for full, active participation in the liturgy of the Mass.

For Further Comment

Additional comments on these Scripture texts, in part or in full, may be found in the seasonal volumes of *New Proclamation* as follows:

- Deuteronomy 8:2-3, 14b-16a—Year A, Thanksgiving
- Psalm 116:12-13, 15-16, 17-18—Year A, Easter 3, Proper 6; Years ABC, Holy Thursday
- Psalm 147:12-13, 14-15, 19-20—Years ABC, Christmas 2
- 1 Corinthians 11:23-26—Years ABC, Holy Thursday
- Hebrews 9:11-15—Year B, Proper 26; Years ABC, Monday of Holy Week
- Mark 14:12-16, 22-26—Year A, Proper 13, Proper 14
- John 6:51-58—Year B, Proper 15, Proper 16

Notes

1. http://www.thesundayliturgy.com/lent/gpage20.html (accessed June 29, 2007).

2. Pope St. Pius X, *Sacra Tridentina: On Frequent and Daily Reception of Holy Communion;* http://www.ewtn.com/library/CURIA/CDWFREQ.HTM (accessed May 24, 2007).

3. http://www.therealpresence.org/eucharist/tes/a7.html (accessed June 29, 2007).

107

BODY AND
BLOOD OF
CHRIST

MAY 24–
JUNE 27

THE SOLEMNITY OF THE MOST SACRED HEART OF JESUS (LFM)

FRIDAY AFTER THE SECOND SUNDAY AFTER PENTECOST: MAY 29 (EARLIEST)–JULY 2 (LATEST)

GERARD S. SLOYAN

Year A	Year B	Year C
Deut. 7:6–11	Hos. 11:1, 3–4, 8c–9	Ezek. 34:11–16
Ps. 103:1–2, 3–4, 6–7, 8+10	Isa. 12:2–3, 4, 5–6	Ps. 23:1–3a, 3b–4, 5, 6
1 John 4:7–16	Eph. 3:8–12, 14–19	Rom. 5:5b–11
Matt. 11:25–30	John 19:31–37	Luke 15:3–7

KEY THEMES

- From the dawn of the second millennium there developed in the West an intense appreciation of the human Jesus in whom the Spirit of love dwelt, leading to a warmhearted piety of response.
- Mutual love sustained among believers is the guarantee that God's love is brought to perfection in us.
- Devotion to the Sacred Heart of Jesus has always been a matter of sorrow at his sufferings and death but joy at his resurrection.

This observance is not very old in the Catholic Church of the West but devotion to the love that Jesus Christ bears the Church and every individual in it, not to speak of everyone in the world, goes back to the apostolic age. The heart has for millennia in the Western Hemisphere been considered the symbol of love and affection whereas in the Semitic world of the Bible the heart represented thought or mind: knowledge, wisdom. The symbolism, therefore, cannot be the important matter. The reality symbolized is of great importance: God's love for the human family and every member in it. With the incarnation, the enfleshment of God's Son whom John in his Gospel calls the Word, the love of God for the human family began to be appreciated in a new way. But, of course, human love had been the analogue for divine love all along.

In the patristic period the lance-thrust in Jesus' side of Mark 15:39 (see, too, John 19:34; 20:27, "put your hand into my side") became the wound of special devotion. It was clear that the statement "blood and water flowed out" described a physiological impossibility, there being no appreciable water in the human chest cavity. Various interpretations of the Johannine symbolism were proposed. Some saw in the twofold flow baptism and eucharist, others John's specification of the word of Jesus: "Whoever believes in me, as Scripture says, 'Streams of living water shall flow from within him.' He was speaking of the Spirit, which believers in him would later receive" (John 7:38-39; REB). Ephesians made a husband's loving concern for his wife the archetype of Christ's love for the church. The church meant, then as now, all the people who make it up (5:25-27).

From the dawn of the second millennium there developed in the West an intense appreciation of the human Jesus in whom the Spirit of love dwelt. This led to a warmhearted piety of response to the love Jesus bore toward all whom by his love he had redeemed. In the spirit of the age Jesus' beating, throbbing heart was taken as the sign of that love. All sorts of visionary experiences began to be reported by mystics in the eleventh and twelfth centuries, bleeding linen corporals and the like. As the Middle Ages flowered into the Renaissance, numerous devotions were developed that centered on that sacred heart of Jesus. Religious congregations of men and women were founded under that title, art both good and bad was created that showed Jesus pointing to his open chest where a heart was surmounted by a flame of love. In 1765 Pope Clement VII authorized a Mass and Office of the Sacred Heart. By the nineteenth century the depiction was everywhere, often in family homes with a light of vigil burning before it. Pius IX in 1856 extended the feast to the Western Church. In 1875 he consecrated the entire world to the Sacred Heart of Jesus. To this day one can see on television bombed-out, flooded-out, totally ravaged dwellings with one wall standing on which hangs the pictured Jesus displaying his inflamed heart.

> So when we say "heart of Jesus" we evoke the innermost core of Jesus Christ, and we say that it is filled with the mystery of God. We say in a way that frightens us to death while yet making us utterly happy, in a way that contradicts all our experiences of emptiness, futility and death, that there reigns in this heart the infinite love of God's self-giving.—Karl Rahner[1]

YEAR A

As with all Sundays and major feasts, the Bible readings are three with a psalm chosen to echo the first of these. In the Matthew year the initial lection is *Deuteronomy 7:6-11*, which proclaims a people consecrated to the Lord, Israel's God. It is not a numerous people, far from it. But despite its small size the Lord has chosen it, made it peculiarly his own. God has loved this people, sworn fidelity to it with an oath the covenantal terms of which God has not departed from. Indeed, as a result of that love the Lord has ransomed this people from the hand of the Pharaoh of Egypt. But if Israel fails to reciprocate the Lord's covenanted love, if it ceases to keep all the commandments, statutes, and decrees, it may expect punishment. The God who is patient and merciful down to the thousandth generation will have to repay this people with a chastisement that is just. A cantor or schola that provides the antiphon in clear tones will be rewarded by hearing the congregation come back strongly with "The earth is full of your riches, O LORD. In your wisdom you made them all." The LORD "surrounds you with love and compassion, / Fills your days with good things." Psalm 103:4-5 is a fitting echo of, "The LORD set his heart on you . . . loved you and because of his fidelity to the oath he had sworn . . . brought you out from the place of slavery . . ." (Deut. 7:7-8).

Matthew 11:25-30. This affection of Israel's God for an elect people often expressed in the First Testament prepares hearers of the Second Testament for what has been called "a Johannine thunderbolt in the synoptic sky." That would be Matt. 11:25-27 (parallel, Luke 10:21-22), to which verses 28-29, uniquely Matthean, have been appended. The much-cherished yoke that does not chafe and the burden that lies lightly on the laboring classes comes from this passage that offers rest for the weary at Jesus' invitation. Job had said of the grave that "there the weary be at rest" (3:17), but Jesus promises a cessation of back-breaking toil in this life, not in death (Matt. 11:27). His prayer is

Most Sacred Heart of Jesus, have mercy on me.
O God, forgive me for all the sins of my life;
The sins of my youth and the sins of my age,
The sins of my body and the sins of my soul,
The sins I have confessed and the sins I have forgotten,
The sins against others in thought, word, and deed,
My sins of omission.
—Traditional Prayer of Reparation from the Irish[2]

in praise of the Father whose gracious will it has been to hand all things over to him. Jesus speaks of revealing the Father, whom he alone knows, to anyone he chooses to reveal him. The rhythmic verse is poetic hyperbole, for in New Testament thought God has been revealed freely to all. Such is the choice the One whom the Gospels call the Son has made. The childlike have now received what the wise and learned have not, in the sense that those who have become as little children have known what to make of it. *1 John 4:7-16* spells out God's love for us as so great that "he sent his Son as expiation for our sins" (v. 10). Love of this depth requires a return in kind, a love not only for God but for one another (v. 11). Such is the love Jesus bears those who have come to know God through him. Mutual love sustained among believers is the guarantee that God's love is brought to perfection in us (v. 12). All this is symbolized by devotion to the Sacred Heart of Jesus in the Catholic West. Needless to say, the East is committed to this love fully, expressing it through iconography, while Protestants in the Lutheran,

Methodist, and other traditions do the same through hymnody. Pentecostals and "evangelical Christians," latecomers in the use of that adjective, and the self-described "Christians" of recent date, in simple verbal imagery feature the love Jesus bears them and they him.

YEAR B

John 19:31–37 speaks of the practice known in Roman writings as *crurifragium*, leg-breaking, done not as an additional cruelty to victims of crucifixion but as a means of hastening death. With the body taken off the wooden cleat known as a saddle between the buttocks and with the legs no longer rigid the abdominal cavity would sag and bring on death by asphyxiation. But that action by Jesus' executioners is part of the Gospel reading on this feast as preliminary to the flow of blood and water from Jesus' side (v. 34). The eyewitness who testifies to these events (v. 35) has to be the one spoken of in 21:24 as the authenticator of all that is told in the Gospel. It is the evangelist who finds a symbolism of the paschal lamb, not one of whose legs is to be broken (Exod. 12:46). There is the further type of one unnamed who is as if an only son looked on in sorrow by Jerusalemites as he is thrust through (Zech. 12:10). The grief over him as over a firstborn seems to identify this cryptic figure as Israel, the identification that verse 1 has made. This is no cause for surprise since John and the other New Testament writers tend to see in Jesus Israel typified—in this passage, dying as a victim out of love.

The Gospel pericope is the antitype to the type provided by *Hosea 11:1, 3-4, 8c-9*, a man of the North, hence Ephraim repeatedly, in the days of the Assyrian threat and successful siege. The love of the LORD for this infant son Ephraim is total; the divine pity is stirred (v. 8). It is true, God has given vent to his blazing anger against the people's sins by using the invader from Nineveh as his agent, but God vows not to let Ephraim be destroyed a second time (v. 9).

The second lection (*Ephesians 3:8-12, 14-19*) is convoluted and the lector must read it very well so that attentive worshipers may grasp some part of it. Writing as if Paul, the author says that his ministry is to convey "the mystery hidden from ages past in God" (v. 9). God's eternal purpose, accomplished in Christ, is to have him dwell in believers' hearts through faith rooted and grounded in love (v. 17). Thus will they come

As I look, my eyes begin to recognize the anguish and agony of all the people for whom you gave yourself. Your broken heart becomes the heart of all of humanity, the heart of all the world. You carry them all: abandoned children, rejected wives and husbands, broken families, the homeless, refugees, prisoners, the maimed and tortured, and the thousands, yes millions, who are unloved, forgotten and left alone to die. I see their emaciated bodies, their despairing faces, their anguished looks. I see them all there, where your body is pierced and your heart is ripped apart. O compassionate Lord, your heart is broken because of all the love that is not given or received.
—Henri Nouwen[3]

to know in his body, the church, the love of Christ that outruns all knowledge, becoming vessels to receive deity in its fullness (vv. 18-19). The love of Christ comes at the hearers like a cascade. It must be channeled if some portion of it is to be received.

YEAR C

Ezekiel 34:11-16 employs imagery from the grazing and shepherding industry familiar to his audience now in exile, to make a variety of points about their situation. In today's passage the Lord God is the speaker. Like any good shepherd solicitous for his not overly intelligent beasts, he will rescue the scattered flock from cloud-enshrouded places. The "peoples" and the "lands" of the flock's present dispersion are the Chaldeans and the city of Babylon, their own country and land the good pastures of the mountains of Israel. The present writer, returning once from the site of ancient Troas on the winding road along the Aegean Sea on a moonless night, was startled to capture a shepherd in his headlights standing in a field. The hazard to the sheep would not have been the rocky crevices in which they at times became trapped by day but a startled leap onto the road and into the glare. The LORD's promise of rescue of scattered sheep in 34:11-16 makes a single point: the love the God of Israel has for his people, a love on which God intends to act. No better psalm passage could have been chosen as responsory than the beloved *Psalm 23.*[5]

> We must eventually, in the luminous and in the dark hours of life, try to pray: "Heart of Jesus, have mercy on me." We should perhaps try to practice a prayer like the Jesus prayer of the Russian pilgrim. We might venture to use this word like a mantra in Eastern style meditation. But over and above all that, we must experience in life that it is most improbable, most impossible, and so most evident that God, the incomprehensible, truly loves us and that in the heart of Jesus Christ this love has become irrevocable.—Karl Rahner[4]

The rescue of the one sheep who has strayed from the ninety-nine may be the Gospel passage that a weekday congregation expects after the Ezekiel reading. *Luke 15:3-7* will not disappoint. A question is, do they know it in its briefer form, Matt. 18:12-14, or as here in Luke, who adds what is a familiar concern throughout his Gospel, the one–hundred-and-eighty-degree turn of mind of sinners known as repentance with its resultant joy in heaven (15:7)? Devotion to the Sacred Heart of Jesus has always been a matter of two emotions over one belief: sorrow at his sufferings and death but joy at his resurrection. Hence the feast serves as a paradigm of the redemptive act. In the Isaian phrase, "He was crushed for our offenses, pierced for our sins, / Upon him was the chastisement that makes us whole, by his stripes we were healed" (Isa. 53:5).

Romans 5:5b-11. Paul identifies "the love of God poured into our hearts through the holy Spirit" as a matter of "Christ's having died for us at the appointed time" (5:5-6). The "we" or "us" who were in that desperate need continue to be called the ungodly in most contemporary translations. "Ungodly" in modern parlance has come to mean outrageous in behavior or frightful in appearance, "an ungodly sight." Neither description of a person or event is the actual meaning of the Greek word, an adjective used substantively. As a result, some translations have deserted a word that has become archaic in favor of its original meaning, wicked or sinful. The proof of God's love (v. 8) is where we belong in this passage from Romans, a proof demonstrated by the death of God's Son (v. 10) that justified us by his blood (v. 9). That love was the reason for a Feast of the Sacred Heart in the first place.

FOR FURTHER COMMENT

Additional comments on these Scripture texts, in part or in full, may be found in the seasonal volumes of *New Proclamation* as follows:

- Ezekiel 34:11-16—Year A, Reign of Christ
- Hosea 11:1, 3-4, 8c-9—Year C, Proper 13
- Psalm 23—Year A, Lent 4, Proper 23; Year B, Proper 11; Years ABC, Easter 4
- Psalm 103:1-4, 6-8, 10—Year A, Proper 19; Year B, Epiphany 8/Proper 3; Year C, Proper 16
- Isaiah 12:2-6—Year C, Advent 3, Proper 28; Years ABC, Easter Vigil
- Romans 5:5b-11—Year A, Lent 3, Proper 6; Year C, Trinity Sunday
- Ephesians 3:8-12, 14-19—Year B, Proper 12; Years ABC, Epiphany
- 1 John 4:7-16—Year B, Easter 5
- Matthew 11:25-30—Year A, Proper 9
- Luke 15:3-7—Year C, Proper 19
- John 19:31-37—Years ABC, Good Friday

Notes

1. Karl Rahner, *Theological Investigations* (New York: Crossroad, 1992), 23:127.

2. http://www.2heartsnetwork.org/SacredHeart.htm (accessed June 29, 2007).

3. Henri J. M. Nouwen, adapted from *Heart Speaks to Heart: Three Prayers to Jesus* (Notre Dame, Ind.: Ave Maria Press, 1989); http://www.beliefnet.com/story/213/story_21397_1.html (accessed May 29, 2007).

4. Rahner, *Theological Investigations*, 23:129.

5. See William L. Holladay, "How the Twenty-third Psalm Became an American Secular Icon," in *The Psalms through Three Thousand Years: Prayerbook of a Cloud of Witnesses* (Minneapolis: Fortress Press, 1993).

VISIT OF MARY TO ELIZABETH (ELW/BCP) / VISITATION OF THE BLESSED VIRGIN MARY (LFM)

MAY 31

WILLIAM F. BROSEND II

LUTHERAN (ELW)	EPISCOPAL (BCP)	ROMAN CATHOLIC (LFM)
1 Sam. 2:1–10	Zeph. 3:14–18a	Zeph. 3:14–18a or Rom. 12:9–16b
Psalm 113	Psalm 113 or Canticle 9	Isa. 12:2–3, 4bcd, 5–6
Rom. 12:9–16b	Col. 3:12–17	
Luke 1:39–57	Luke 1:39–49	Luke 1:39–56

KEY THEMES

- Mary had received an unprecedented announcement, and it had to be shared.
- Mary went to visit Elizabeth not to see if what the angel said was true, but because she believed what the angel said was true.
- As important as the Magnificat is for Lukan theology and Christian devotion and worship, it does not exhaust the meaning of the passage.

Something usually becomes a cliché because, at some basic level, it is true. Images of family and friends gathered in celebration, or of expectant mothers exchanging updates on their condition, are the stuff of popular media and medieval art. When something good has happened to us we simply cannot keep it to ourselves. Neither could Mary. Cliché or not, Mary sought out the one person she thought had the best chance of appreciating just how good the news really was.

The Visitation of Mary to her kinswoman Elizabeth, Luke 1:39–56, is treasured by most Christians primarily for verses 46–55, the "Magnificat." As important as this canticle is, for Lukan theology and Christian devotion and worship, the Magnificat does not exhaust the meaning of the passage. In fact, if the late

Raymond Brown was correct, it is not even the only canticle in the passage. We will examine the Gospel text closely, after looking at the other texts for the feast day, then continue the development of the "homiletical Marian theology" first discussed under the Feast of the Annunciation.

OLD TESTAMENT READINGS
1 SAMUEL 2:1–10 (ELW)
ZEPHANIAH 3:14–18A (BCP, LFM)

Depending on your communion, you are assigned either a rather generic passage in praise of God's goodness from Zephaniah 3 or the passage upon which Luke (or earlier tradition, depending on how one understands the composition history of the Lukan canticles) based the Magnificat. Zephaniah 3:14 begins, "Sing aloud, O daughter Zion; shout, O Israel!" much like the passage from like 1 Sam. 2:1, "My heart exults in the Lord." Both passages resonate with psalm-like joy and exaltation, but the key is not really the joy, but the assurance that, "The LORD, your God, is in your midst" (Zeph. 3:17). God's presence—incarnation?—is the theme.

The story of Hannah and Elkanah, the parents of Samuel, is one of the important foreshadows on which the narrative shape of the story of the births of John the Baptist and Jesus was based. The story has its own unique features, but the basic outline—infertility, petition, divine promise in response, and birth—is a classic evocation of Paul's wonderful phrase, referring to the earlier pattern of Abraham and Sarah, that God, "calls into existence the things that do not exist" (Rom. 4:17). We will consider the text itself in relation to the Magnificat below, but before moving on to the epistle(s) for the Visitation note should be made of Hannah herself, who recalls Rachel and anticipates Elizabeth. One of two wives of her husband, like Rachel, she is when we meet her in 1 Samuel 1 also, like Rachel, the favorite of her husband, but childless. "She was deeply distressed and prayed to the LORD, and wept bitterly. She made this vow: 'O LORD of hosts, if only you will look on the misery of your servant, and remember me, and not forget your servant, but will give to your servant a male child, then I will set him before you as a nazirite'" (1 Sam. 1:10–11). Her prayer was heard by the priest Eli, who mistook her fervor for intoxication, and by God, who answered her prayer. Hannah kept her vow, and in presenting Samuel to the Lord after he was weaned,

> Father in heaven, by your grace the virgin mother of your incarnate Son was blessed in bearing him, but still more blessed in keeping your word: Grant us who honor the exaltation of her lowliness to follow the example of her devotion to your will; through Jesus Christ our Lord, who lives and reigns with you and the Holy Spirit, one God, for ever and ever. Amen.
> —Collect for the Feast of the Visitation, *The Book of Common Prayer*

rejoiced greatly. "My heart exults in the LORD; my strength is exalted in my God. My mouth derides my enemies, because I rejoice in my victory" (1 Sam. 2:1).

EPISTLE READINGS
ROMANS 12:9–16B (ELW, LFM ALT.)
COLOSSIANS 3:12–17 (BCP)

The passage from Romans (12:9–16b) and Colossians (3:12–17) represent Pauline exhortation at its finest. (I consider Colossians more likely from Paul than not, an argument not important for this feast in the least.) The theological claims have been staked and the faith proclaimed, and the author now turns to instruction in the shape of Christian living. Love (*agapē* in all verses) is central in both passages ("love one another with mutual affection" [Rom. 12:10]; "Above all, clothe yourselves with love" [Col. 3:14]), with strong emphasis on forgiveness ("forgive each other; just as the Lord has forgiven you, so you also must forgive" [Col. 3:13]), joy ("Rejoice in hope," "Rejoice with those who rejoice" [Rom. 12:12, 15]), and classical virtues ("clothe yourselves with compassion, kindness, humility, meekness, and patience" [Col. 3:12]).

Two things are worth noting in these lists. First, there is nothing really extraordinary about them. They are not even especially or distinctively Christian—one does not need faith in Christ to be kind, humble, or compassionate. In a way the emphasis is not on what we are exhorted to do, but how and why, wonderfully summed up in Col. 3:17, "And whatever you do, in word or deed, do everything in the name of the Lord Jesus, giving thanks to God the Father through him." Second, far, far too often such exhortation, and concrete discussion of the hows and whys of the Christian life, are missing from our sermons. We should not be afraid to follow the example of the apostle.

THE GOSPEL
LUKE 1:39–57 (ELW)
LUKE 1:39–49 (BCP)
LUKE 1:39–56 (LFM)

Mary was told by Gabriel that her "kinswoman" Elizabeth (exactly what the relationship was is a matter of speculation, not precision, *sungenis* being an imprecise term) was pregnant (Luke 1:36), so Mary set out "with haste" to see for herself (1:39). The text gives absolutely no reason to think that Mary was looking for confirmation of the angel's words, however. But under the circumstances, she may have been looking for someone who would be in a position to appreciate what was taking place. So Mary went to visit Elizabeth not to see if what the angel said was true, but because she believed what the angel said was true.

We do not know how far she needed to go, because the town in Judea was either unknown to Luke, or not important to him. The important matter was the response of Elizabeth to Mary, prompted by a timely kick from the child in her own womb, and the response of Mary to Elizabeth's words. (The manuscript evidence overwhelming rejects Irenaeus's contention that it was Elizabeth, not Mary, who sings the Magnificat.) These responses provide the first two canticles in Luke.

Brown argued persuasively that the words of Elizabeth, which provide the foundation for our *Ave Maria*, should be treated as a canticle.[1] When one removes the explanatory doublet in 1:44 it is easy to see why:

> And Elizabeth was filled with the Holy Spirit and exclaimed with
> a loud cry,
> > "Blessed are you among women,
> > > and blessed is the fruit of your womb.
> > And why has this happened to me,
> > > that the mother of my Lord comes to me?
> > And blessed is she who believed that there would be a fulfillment
> > > of what was spoken to her by the Lord."

Scholars are evenly divided about credit for the composition of the *Magnificat* and the other canticles in the Gospel of Luke, whether to the third evangelist or a liturgical source. All agree on the importance of Hannah's song at the presentation of Samuel to the Lord at Shiloh (1 Sam. 2:1-10). The correspondences are remarkable in tone, theme, and specific content:

1. "Hannah prayed and said, 'My heart exults in the LORD; my strength is exalted in my God. My mouth derides my enemies, because I rejoice in my victory.'" (1 Sam. 2:1)
   "And Mary said, 'My soul magnifies the Lord, and my spirit rejoices in God my Savior, for he has looked with favor on the lowliness of his servant. Surely, from now on all generations will call me blessed . . . .'" (Luke 1:46-48)
2. Hannah—"There is no Holy One like the LORD, no one besides you; there is no Rock like our God." (1 Sam. 2:2)
   Mary—"[F]or the Mighty One has done great things for me, and holy is his name. His mercy is for those who fear him from generation to generation." (Luke 1:49-50)

3. Hannah—"Talk no more so very proudly, let not arrogance come from your mouth; for the LORD is a God of knowledge, and by him actions are weighed. The bows of the mighty are broken, but the feeble gird on strength." (1 Sam. 2:3-4)

    Mary—"He has shown strength with his arm; he has scattered the proud in the thoughts of their hearts. He has brought down the powerful from their thrones, and lifted up the lowly . . ." (Luke 1:51-52)

4. Hannah—"Those who were full have hired themselves out for bread, but those who were hungry are fat with spoil. . . . The LORD makes poor and makes rich; he brings low, he also exalts. He raises up the poor from the dust; he lifts the needy from the ash heap, to make them sit with princes and inherit a seat of honor." (1 Sam. 2:5, 7, 8a)

    Mary—"[H]e has filled the hungry with good things, and sent the rich away empty."
    (Luke 1:53)

The themes introduced in the Magnificat, whatever their origin, are the themes of the Gospel of Luke. Praise of God, reversal, suspicion of political/military forms of power, and a particular concern for the poor resound throughout the Gospel and the Acts of the Apostles. Mary, Luke, and the early Christian tradition built their witness on a solidly Jewish foundation. The radical continuity of concern cannot be overstated, and in case we miss it elsewhere, we cannot miss it in the Magnificat. Here, as elsewhere in his narrative, Luke was careful to connect the story of the birth of Jesus to the story of Israel's experience and expectations, a strategy the preacher does well to follow by connecting our own retelling of the story to the experience and expectations of our audience.

PREACHING THE VISITATION OF MARY

Building on the work of renowned Marian scholars, I introduced the idea of a "homiletical Marian theology" in my discussion of the Annunciation. Seconding Elizabeth Johnson's emphasis on Mary as a historical figure, I suggested such theology should include consideration of Mary from and within her Jewish background, Mary in community, and Mary in the life of the believer. While the Visitation, most especially in the songs of Elizabeth and Mary, clearly evidence continuity with the tradition, I recommend on this day we focus on Mary in community.

If a tree falls in the forest and no one hears it, did it make a sound? If we have good news to share, but tell no one, is it really good news, gospel? Mary had received an unprecedented announcement, and it had to be shared. Based on what Gabriel had told her, Mary realized that more than anyone, Elizabeth would understand and appreciate what she had to say. She went because the news was too good to keep to herself, and because the good news required, even as it created, community and solidarity.

I am as fond of the wonderful encouragement to evangelism attributed to St. Francis of Assisi as anyone: "Proclaim the Gospel at all times. If necessary, use words." Absolutely! Trying to live out our faith in all that we do, in keeping with the exhortation of the epistle readings for the day, is our call. And our call is to do so in community, not as soloists but as members of a holy choir of believers. But sometimes, both in and from that community, it *is* necessary to use words. "But how are they to call on one in whom they have not believed? And how are they to believe in one of whom they have never heard? And how are they to hear without someone to proclaim him? And how are they to proclaim him unless they are sent? As it is written, 'How beautiful are the feet of those who bring good news!'" (Rom. 10:14-15).

Our community, the church, gives us the words, the good news, and calls us to share and study them together, and together share them with the world. In the "Great Commission" (Matt. 28:19-20) Jesus does not say, "Go, find a quiet place by yourself, and think about everything I have said to you and done for you, then go on with your life as if nothing had happened." Jesus said, "Go therefore and make disciples of all nations, baptizing them in the name of the Father and of the Son and of the Holy Spirit, and teaching them to obey everything that I have commanded you." Go. Make disciples. Baptize. Teach. For that we need community. Just as Mary needed Elizabeth to share her good news with, and to share support for each other, we need community. The church. It is, in its historical reality, as imperfect as the believers who make it up. But because Jesus also said, "I am with you always" (Matt. 28:20), it is enough. Go tell somebody.

> You moon and rising stars, pour on our
>   barns and houses
> Your gentle benedictions.
> Remind us how our Mother, with far
>   subtler and more holy influence,
> Blesses our rooves and eaves,
> Our shutters, lattices and sills,
> Our doors, and floors, and stairs, and
>   rooms, and bedrooms,
> Smiling by night upon her sleeping
>   children:
> O gentle Mary! Our lovely Mother in
>   heaven!
> —Thomas Merton[2]

FOR FURTHER COMMENT

Additional comments on these Scripture texts, in part or in full, may be found in the seasonal volumes of *New Proclamation* as follows:

- 1 Samuel 2:1-10—Year B, Proper 28
- Zephaniah 3:14-18a—Year C, Advent 3
- Psalm 113—Year C, Proper 20

- Isaiah 12:2-6—Year C, Advent 3, Proper 28; Years ABC, Easter Vigil
- Romans 12:9-16b—Year A, Proper 17
- Colossians 3:12-17—Year C, 1 Christmas
- Luke 1:39-57—Years A & B, Advent 3; Year C, Advent 4

Notes

1. Raymond Brown, *The Birth of the Messiah* (Garden City, N.Y.: Image Books, 1979), 342–44.

2. Thomas Merton, "The Evening of the Visitation," in *The Collected Poems of Thomas Merton* (New York: New Directions, 1977 [1957]), 43.

BARNABAS, APOSTLE

JUNE 11

CRAIG A. SATTERLEE

LUTHERAN (ELW)	EPISCOPAL (BCP)	ROMAN CATHOLIC (LFM)
Isa. 42:5–12	Isa. 42:5–12	1 Cor. 15:1–8
Psalm 112	Psalm 112	Ps. 19:2-3, 4-5
Acts 11:19–30;	Acts 11:19–30;	
13:1–3	13:1–3	
Matt. 10:7–16	Matt. 10:7–16	John 14:6–14

KEY THEMES

• Christ through the church sends new apostles in response to new situations.
• Apostles are appointed and authorized by Jesus to carry Jesus' own proclamation further and perform the same deeds that Jesus does.
• Communities to whom apostles are sent become the authority by which the church continues its mission.
• Christ calls congregations to be apostolic.
• Generosity is an expression of faith.

ST. BARNABAS

Joseph, whom the apostles called Barnabas, which means "son of encouragement," is mentioned repeatedly in the Acts of the Apostles and the letters of Paul. Barnabas was a Levite born on the island of Cyprus. Acts includes Barnabas among the first believers in Jerusalem, and reports that Barnabas gave the proceeds from the sale of some land to the apostles, suggesting that he was wealthy (4:36–37). Some find in Barnabas's voluntary poverty an indication of his solidarity with the poor in the Christian community. Acts describes Barnabas as "a good man, full of the Holy Spirit and of faith" (11:24). Tradition includes Barnabas among the seventy disciples that Jesus commissioned and sent out (Luke 10:1). Although Barnabas was not one of the original Twelve, he, like Paul, is called an apostle (Acts 14:4, 14: cf. 9:27). Tradition suggests that the apostles gave Barnabas the nickname, "son of encouragement," because of his ability as a preacher. The Prayer of the Day lifts up Barnabas's generosity as exemplary, thanking God that he gave his life and resources not for recognition, but for the relief of the poor, the spreading of the gospel, and the well-being of the church.

Barnabas was convinced that Paul's conversion was authentic, and vouched for him to the Christian community (Acts 9:27). The Jerusalem church sent Barnabas to the growing community of Gentile believers in Antioch, and Barnabas brought Paul from Tarsus to assist in the mission (Acts 11:19-22). When the church at Antioch grew and was established with its own leaders, Barnabas and Paul, after fasting and prayer and the laying on of hands from the faithful, began a missionary journey, accompanied by John Mark. They preached the gospel in Cyprus and Pamphylia, where Mark left the mission. Paul and Barnabas went on to the cities in Asia Minor, where they were particularly successful at bringing the gospel to Gentiles. While on the island of Cyprus, Paul appears to have assumed the leadership of the mission since, when they moved on to the mainland, the party was known as "Paul and his companions" (Acts 13:13).

Barnabas tended to side with Paul in the debate over the responsibilities of Jewish and Gentile Christians. On one occasion, however, Barnabas joined Peter in refraining from eating with Gentiles (Gal. 2:13). Paul and Barnabas split over their disagreement about whether to take John Mark with them on another missionary journey. Barnabas took Mark with him to Cyprus, while Paul went with Silas. Paul and Barnabas's break appears final, although Paul later praises Barnabas as a working apostle (1 Cor. 9:6). We know nothing more of the life of Barnabas. Legend claims that he was stoned to death in the city of Salamis on Cyprus.

Several writings bearing the name of Barnabas have circulated at various times in Christian history. One document, the *Epistle of Barnabas*, was widely read in the early church. Many regarded it as genuine and worthy of inclusion in the New Testament. Modern scholarship attributes the *Epistle of Barnabas* to the second century, and acknowledges it as a valuable document from the early church. The feast of St. Barnabas was celebrated in the East at least as early as the fifth century. The West began celebrating the Barnabas feast in the ninth century.

SECOND READING

ACTS 11:19–30; 13:1-3 (ELW, BCP)
1 CORINTHIANS 15:1-8 (LFM)

Acts 11:19-30; 13:1-3 relates the missionary work of Barnabas and establishes him as an apostle. A new situation was created by the persecution that occurred after Stephen. Believers "who were scattered" proclaimed the coming reign of God to Jews in Phoenicia, Cyprus, and Antioch. Some believers from

Cyprus and Cyrene also preached the Lord Jesus to the Greeks, not Greek-speaking Jews, in Antioch. According to Acts, the very power of God was at work in their proclamation, and "a great number [of Greeks] believed and turned to the Lord" (11:21). In response to this new situation, the church at Jerusalem asserted its leadership and apostled Barnabas; that is, the Jerusalem church sent this trusted emissary as its authoritative representative to investigate the situation.

We might expect that, as a Levite, Barnabas might be meticulous in attending to the details of cultic and ritualistic purity and the separation of Jew and Gentile. Perhaps this is part of the reason the Jerusalem church chose to send Barnabas as its representative. This Levite concluded that the situation in Antioch was "the grace of God" and was glad. Barnabas therefore encouraged these believers to remain faithful to the Lord (v. 23), rather than to regulations, laws, and customs. Barnabas's assessment of the situation certainly added credibility to the claim that Christ had come to the Gentiles.

Barnabas not only blessed the ministry in Antioch; Barnabas endeavored to promote it. Remembering Saul, and apparently considering him ideally suited for this work, Barnabas departed to seek Saul in Tarsus and bring him back to Antioch. Paul and Barnabas spent a year together in Antioch, meeting with the church and teaching many people (v. 26). "The use of the word church here indicates that in Luke's view the community of Antioch, formed of persons of uncircumcised, non-observant, pagan origin, is the church or people of God as much as the Jewish congregation in Jerusalem."[2] In fact, the members of the Antioch congregation were the first to be called Christians, persons devoted to the worship and service of Christ.

> Grant, O God, that we may follow the example of thy faithful servant Barnabas, who, seeking not his own renown but the well-being of thy Church, gave generously of his life and substance for the relief of the poor and the spread of the Gospel; through Jesus Christ our Lord, who liveth and reigneth with thee and the Holy Spirit, one God, for ever and ever. Amen.[1]

As further proof that they are church, Acts reports that the Antioch Christians seized the opportunity to share in Christ's mission. Sometime during Barnabas's ministry in Antioch, when Agabus prophesied by the Spirit of a great famine (v. 28), the church determined to "break bread at a distance and share their food [with the Jerusalem congregation] as a sign of spiritual oneness."[3] Everyone gave according to their ability, and sent the food to the elders by the hands of Barnabas and Saul.

Acts 13:1 indicates that the Antioch church's leadership circle of prophets and teachers expanded beyond Paul and Barnabas. The congregation was now firmly established as Christ's church and participating in his mission. Directed by the Holy Spirit, the congregation then set Saul and Barnabas apart as apostles and sent them away on its behalf through the laying on of hands. The Antioch congregation *apostled* those whom the Jerusalem congregation sent to them to extend the mission to others. Paul and Barnabas continued their apostleship on the authority of the church in Antioch. Under the leadership of Barnabas and Paul, the Antioch congregation was functioning like the Jerusalem congregation in every way.

Depending on the context, the preacher might retell this story in one of two ways. First, the preacher might emphasize the new situation brought about by persecution and celebrate both the continued proclamation of the gospel by unknown, unnamed saints, and God through the church continuing to send apostles like Barnabas, who respond with authority, the Holy Spirit, and grace. Alternatively, the preacher might retell this story emphasizing the relationship between Barnabas and the Antioch congregation. This sermon might celebrate how the community to whom this saint was sent becomes the authority that empowers his continued mission.

THE GOSPEL
MATTHEW 10:7-16 (ELW, BCP)
JOHN 14:6-14 (LFM)

We might describe Matt. 10:7-16 as the "job description" of an apostle. Apostles are appointed and authorized by Jesus. They act in response to Jesus' command. Apostles carry Jesus' own proclamation further and perform the same deeds that Jesus does. In other words, apostles are to preach the nearness of the reign of heaven and to heal. The combination of proclamation and healing prevents the mission from getting reduced to ethical exhortation by demonstrating that God's extraordinary power to save is at work. Jesus' imperatives also indicate that poverty and defenselessness are characteristics of apostles. Here, too, apostles extend the lifestyle and ministry of Jesus. In addition to preaching and healing, apostles represent Jesus through their homelessness, defenselessness, and poverty.

> Great are the riches of charity, dearly beloved; without it, the rich are poor, while a beggar with it is rich. If a rich person does not possess charity, what has he? Earthly substance of size without charity is useless and vain; charity is full and overflows even though it possesses nothing of material wealth.
> —Caesarius of Arles[4]

In this passage, Jesus commands the apostles to go only to the lost sheep of the house of Israel (10:6). When we compare these instructions to the commission that Jesus gave the apostles after the resurrection, "to make disciples of all nations" (28:19), we are confronted by two possibilities. The apostles either expand Jesus' ministry or the "great commission" replaces the commission that Jesus gives in the appointed reading. On this saint's day, the first interpretation is more helpful. Centered in Jesus' own ministry to Israel, the apostles continue and then expand Jesus' mission so that it encompasses all the nations of the world. Barnabas's ministry to the Christian community at Antioch provides a concrete example of an apostle expanding Jesus' ministry.

How does this job description for an apostle, with imperatives to travel without money, a bag, and even a change of clothes, apply to churches that are established institutions and individuals that draw salaries, own homes, and accumulate pensions? Have changes in historical circumstance rendered this job description obsolete? How do apostles act with Jesus' authority when they do not share his lifestyle? Perhaps we find help in recalling that Matthew's Gospel is addressed to a community and not to an individual. Jesus sends a community of apostles and Matthew calls faith communities, also known as congregations, to be apostolic. How, in the freedom of the gospel, can Christian congregations proclaim the nearness of the reign of God, heal, and share in the itinerancy, poverty and defenselessness that characterized Jesus' way of life? What small and significant steps can congregations take to participate more fully in the way of life exemplified and commanded by Jesus? The voluntary poverty of Barnabas and the generosity of the Antioch church provide powerful examples for congregations to ponder. How might congregations becoming more apostolic influence the lives of their individual members, the greater community, and the world?

> How might your congregation become more apostolic? What new situation is your congregation facing that calls for renewed, apostolic leadership?

First Reading
ISAIAH 42:5-12 (ELW, BCP)

Isaiah 42:5-12 introduces an unspecified servant of God and charges this servant with a particular task. Read and heard on St. Barnabas Day, this passage provides strong allusions to three themes previously discussed, which are important to the commemoration of Barnabas: (1) apostles are called by God; (2) apostles continue the very mission and ministry of Jesus; and (3) God is doing a new thing.

On the feast day of St. Barnabas, we hear God's declaration (v. 6) as addressed to this apostle and, in fact, to all apostles. None other than the Lord calls Barnabas and apostles of all times and places in righteousness, holds those apostles' hands, and keeps them.

God calls Barnabas and all apostles to share in the very ministry of Christ. We cannot hear Isaiah's talk of opening eyes that are blind, and bringing out prisoners from the darkness of the prison (v. 7), without recalling Jesus' declaration in the synagogue at Nazareth that "today this scripture has been fulfilled in your hearing" (Luke 4:21). God calls Barnabas and the apostles to *extend* the ministry of Jesus.

God also calls apostles to *expand* the ministry of Christ, because "the former things have come to pass, and [God declares] new things" (v. 9). Isaiah provides a clue to these new things as God declares, "I will . . . give you as a covenant to the people, and a light to the Gentiles" (v. 6). Barnabas was part of God's covenant with Israel; he was a Levite. As a member of the Christian community in Jerusalem, Barnabas participated in the new covenant in Christ. Barnabas's mission and ministry to Christians in Antioch made him a light to the Gentiles. Barnabas and the apostles participate in the new thing God is doing in Christ. Together, the readings from Isaiah and Matthew, which describe the apostle's vocation, invite all followers of Christ to reflect on their responsibility and call.

FOR FURTHER COMMENT

Further comments on these Scripture texts, in part or in full, may be found in the seasonal volumes of *New Proclamation* as follows:

- Isaiah 42:5-12—Year A, Baptism; ABC, Monday in Holy Week
- Psalm 19:2-5—Year A, Proper 22; Year B, Lent 3, Proper 19; Year C, Epiphany 3; Years ABC, Easter Vigil
- Psalm 112—Year A, Epiphany 5; Year C, Proper 17
- 1 Corinthians 15:1-8—Year B, Easter; Year C, Epiphany 5; see also Philip and James, above
- Matthew 10:7-16—Year A, Proper 6
- John 14:6-14—Year B, Easter 5; Year C, Pentecost; see also Philip and James, above

Notes

1. Ibid., 184.

2. Traditional collect for St. Barnabas, *The Book of Common Prayer*, 189.

3. Robert Smith, *Acts*, Concordia Commentary (St. Louis: Concordia, 1970), 183.

4. Caesarius of Arles (470–542), Sermon 29. Cited in Frederick J. Schumacher (ed.), For *All the Saints: A Prayer Book For and By the Whole Church* (Delhi, NY: American Lutheran Publicity Bureau, 1966), Vol. IV, pp. 1310-11.

JOHN THE BAPTIST (ELW) / NATIVITY OF JOHN THE BAPTIST (BCP/LFM)

JUNE 24

RUTH A. MEYERS

LUTHERAN (ELW)	EPISCOPAL (BCP)	ROMAN CATHOLIC (LFM)
Mal. 3:1-4	Isa. 40:1-11	Isa. 49:1-6
Psalm 141	Psalm 85 or 85:7-13	Ps. 139:1-3, 13-15
Acts 13:13-26	Acts 13:14b-26	Acts 13:22-26
Luke 1:57-67	Luke 1:57-80	Luke 1:57-66, 80
(1:68-80)		

KEY THEMES

• The birth of John the Baptist reveals God's overflowing mercy.

• John's role will be to prepare the way and point to the one who is far greater than he.

• In what places do you see the world today yearning for God's salvation?

THE SAINT AND THE DAY

Saint Augustine's sermon on this feast day is perhaps the first witness to a commemoration of the birth of John the Baptist on June 24. By the fifth century, the celebration of John's nativity on June 24 was widespread in Western Christianity. There is some earlier evidence in the East for a feast honoring the Baptist on the day after Epiphany, reflecting a custom of honoring saints closely connected with a feast of our Lord on the day following that celebration. Since in the East Epiphany celebrated the baptism of Jesus, a commemoration of John the Baptist was in order.

The selection of June 24 as the date of John's nativity is based in part upon the chronology of Luke's Gospel. Gabriel appeared to Mary during the sixth month of Elizabeth's pregnancy, putting John's birth three months later and six months earlier than Jesus' birth. By the fourth century, the Nativity of our Lord was being observed on December 25. In the Roman calendrical system, dates were counted backwards from certain days of the month: the kalends on the first day of the month, the ides on the thirteenth or fifteenth, and the nones on the ninth day before the ides. December 25 was thus VIII Kalends January, and the comparable date six months earlier, VIII Kalends July, fell on June 24 (June having only thirty days).

Support for such a calculation of the date of John's birth appears in an anonymous fourth-century document entitled "Of Solstices and Equinoxes." The document begins by dating the conception of John the Baptist. According to Luke's Gospel, the angel Gabriel appeared to John's father, Zechariah, and announced John's birth while Zechariah was offering sacrifice for a religious festival. "Of Solstices and Equinoxes" identifies this festival as the Jewish high holy days occurring at the autumn equinox and claims that the conception of John the Baptist occurred at this time, placing his birth nine months later, at the summer solstice. A Christmas sermon of John Chrysostom in the late fourth century gives a similar account of the Lukan chronology. A feast of the conception of John the Baptist is celebrated in some Eastern churches on September 24, although such a feast never took hold in the West.

Augustine's sermon on the feast day comments on the coincidence of the date with the summer solstice. John himself had said in reference to Jesus, "He must increase, but I must decrease" (John 3:30). So, Augustine says, it is fitting that the days after John's birth grow shorter, while after Jesus' birth the days lengthen.

The celebration of a major Christian festival near the summer solstice resulted in the incorporation of pagan solstice rituals, many of which continued for centuries. In the ancient world, light and darkness were powerful symbols, and the turning of the year at the solstices was commonly marked by various ritual practices. Customs associated with St. John's Vigil, that is, the eve of his Nativity, included distribution of spices; gathering ferns; decorating houses and doors with fennel, birch, and flowers; and lamps burning through the night. Fires of St. John were popular in France and Britain.

> John appears as the boundary between the two testaments, the old and the new. That he is a sort of boundary the Lord himself bears witness, when he speaks of "the law and the prophets up until John the Baptist." Thus he represents times past and is the herald of the new era to come. As a representative of the past, he is born of aged parents; as a herald of the new era, he is declared to be a prophet while still in his mother's womb. For when yet unborn, he leapt in his mother's womb at the arrival of blessed Mary. In that womb he had already been designated a prophet, even before he was born; it was revealed that he was to be Christ's precursor, before they ever saw one another. These are divine happenings, going beyond the limits of our human frailty.
> —St. Augustine[1]

It is unusual for the church to celebrate the nativity of a saint. Since the commemoration of martyrs began with the veneration of Polycarp, the Bishop of Smyrna who was burned at the stake in the mid-second century, saints have traditionally been commemorated on the date of their death as their "birthday." Christian tradition, however, as taught by such luminaries as Origen, Ambrose, Jerome, and Leo the Great, has held that John the Baptist received special grace while still in the womb, bestowed when Mary visited his mother Elizabeth.

Hence the feast of John's nativity has traditionally been given greater weight than the commemoration of his death.

Beginning in the fifth century, the death (or "decollation") of John the Baptist was celebrated on August 29. The date is probably that of the dedication of a church at Sebaste (Samaria), where John's disciples were thought to have buried him. The tomb was discovered in the fourth century and probably desecrated in 362 by Julian the Apostate, who is said to have had John's relics disinterred and publicly burned in order to discourage veneration of the Baptist. Nonetheless, many churches claim to have some of his relics, particularly his head.

THE GOSPEL

LUKE 1:57-80 (BCP)
LUKE 1:57-67 (68-80) (ELW)
LUKE 1:57-66, 80 (LFM)

The Gospel tells of the birth, circumcision, and naming of John the Baptist. Elizabeth's neighbors and relatives rejoice with her because she had been childless and now had given birth at an old age. The text, literally "the Lord magnified his mercy upon her" (Luke 1:57), emphasizes the abundance of God's mercy. Circumcision is mentioned only in passing; in accord with Jewish law, the child was to be circumcised on the eighth day after birth (Gen. 17:12; Lev. 12:3). As God is faithful and merciful, the people live in obedience to God's law.

Participation of relatives and neighbors in naming a child was common (Ruth 4:17), although the custom of naming the child at the time of circumcision appears to have emerged later in the history of Israel. The determination of the child's name brings some surprises to the neighbors and relatives who had gathered. First, Elizabeth knows that the child is to be named John, even though she was not present when the angel announced his birth to Zechariah and decreed the child's name (Luke 1:8-13). Then Zechariah, mute throughout Elizabeth's pregnancy, regains his speech, an occurrence that is deemed miraculous. To all in the neighborhood, God's hand was evident. Their question, "What then will this child become?" (Luke 1:66), sets an expectation for the events that will unfold when John the Baptist begins his preaching ministry.

John the Baptist . . . is called prophet, friend of the bridegroom, lamp, angel, voice, Elijah, baptizer of the Savior, herald of the judge, and forerunner of the King. Each of these titles denotes a particular prerogative of John: the title of prophet, his prerogative of foreknowledge; the title of friend of the bridegroom, his prerogative of loving and being loved; burning light, his prerogative of sanctity; angel, his prerogative of virginity; voice, his prerogative of humility; Elijah, his prerogative of fervor; baptizer, the wonderful honor of baptizing the Lord; herald, the prerogative of preaching; and forerunner, the prerogative of preparation.
—Jacobus de Voragine[2]

The Gospel continues with what has become known as the Song of Zechariah, or *Benedictus*, the first word in the Latin translation of the hymn. Here the lectionaries diverge: the Roman lectionary omits the *Benedictus* altogether (although the Gospel Acclamation provides one verse of the hymn, Luke 1:76), the Lutheran lectionary requires the narrative introduction (Luke 1:67) and makes the remaining verses optional, while the Episcopal lectionary requires the *Benedictus* in its entirety.

The first part of the hymn (Luke 1:68-75) uses a characteristically Jewish prayer form, a *berakah* ("blessing"), in which God is blessed for particular actions. The text is filled with allusions to hymns of praise in the Hebrew Scriptures. The phrase "a mighty savior" (Luke 1:69), literally "horn of salvation" (Pss. 18:2, 92:10-11, 132:17), emphasizes God's saving power. God will deliver Israel "from the hand of all who hate us" (Ps. 106:10) and "has remembered his holy covenant" (Pss. 105:8-10, 106:45-46). Some scholars suggest that this part of the hymn originated in a community of John's followers, while the second half (Luke 1:76-79) was a Christian addition. The hymn shifts from thanksgiving for God's deliverance to a proclamation of the child's future. Using imagery from the prophet Malachi (Mal. 3:1-2), the hymn describes John as the forerunner of Jesus. With John's proclamation, the messianic age would dawn (Mal. 4:2; Isa. 9:2, 42:7, 58:8, 60:1-2).

> The great forerunner of the morn,
> the herald of the Word, is born;
> and faithful hearts shall never fail
> with thanks and praise his light to hail.
>
> With heavenly message Gabriel came,
> that John should be that herald's name,
> and with prophetic ut'trance told
> his actions great and manifold.
>
> His mighty deeds exalt his fame
> to greater than a prophet's name;
> of woman born shall never be
> a greater prophet than was he.
> —The Venerable Bede[3]

The story of John's birth draws to a close with a summary statement about his growth that echoes the experience of Samson (Judg. 13:24) and Samuel (1 Sam. 2:26) and anticipates the statement about Jesus' growth (Luke 2:52). This passage is included in the Episcopal and Roman lectionaries, but in the Lutheran lectionary it will only be read if the optional verses are included.

THE READINGS

ACTS 13:13-26 (ELW)
ACTS 13:14B-26 (BCP)
ACTS 13:22-26 (LFM)

This passage recounts Paul's first major sermon in Acts. Only the Lutheran lectionary includes verses 13–14a and so provides the geographic context: Paul has journeyed to Antioch in Pisidia, an inland region of Asia Minor. The Episcopal lectionary begins with the introduction of the immediate context: the synagogue service on the Sabbath, at which the officials invite Paul to speak. The first part of his sermon lays out the history of Israel, from the exodus to the reign of David. The Roman lectionary picks up the sermon as David is introduced. Paul's sermon emphasizes continuity, particularly Jesus' lineage in the house of David. John with his baptism of repentance is an important turning point, marking the end of one period of the history of Israel. John's assertion that he is "not worthy to untie the thong of the sandals on his feet" appears in all four Gospels (Matt. 3:11; Mark 1:7; Luke 3:16; John 1:27). Emphasizing his relationship to Jesus, it is particularly appropriate at this feast celebrated at the summer solstice, when the daylight begins to decrease. The appointed reading, ending well before the conclusion of the sermon, finishes as Paul introduces Jesus' ministry of salvation.

MALACHI 3:1-4 (ELW)
ISAIAH 40:1-11 (BCP)
ISAIAH 49:1-6 (LFM)

The Lutheran and Episcopal lectionaries appoint prophecies that describe the role of a forerunner or messenger. The prophecy from Malachi is echoed in the *Benedictus* (Luke 1:76) that concludes John's birth story, while Isaiah 40 is used by the evangelists to describe the arrival of John the Baptist as a preacher in the wilderness (Matt. 3:1-3; Mark 1:2-3; Luke 3:4-6; John 1:23).

In contrast, the Roman lectionary calls for one of the "servant songs" from Isaiah. This, the second of the four songs, emphasizes God's call to the servant from before birth. The lectionary thus calls attention to John's dedication to God while still in the womb, rather than his ministry as the messenger who points to one greater than himself. The responsorial psalm (Ps. 139:1-3, 13-15) further highlights God's activity from the time of the annunciation to Zechariah and subsequent conception of the child.

PREACHING APPROACHES

The readings for this feast direct our attention to God's abundant mercy. Elizabeth, childless in her old age, now bears a son. His father is speechless throughout the pregnancy, recovering his voice only when the child is named. This is not an intimate family event, but a cause for wonder throughout the neighborhood. Casting our gaze even wider, we are reminded of God's promises of salvation, deliverance from enemies, light in the darkness, a pathway of peace. With the birth of John, the stage is set for these to be fulfilled.

A different note is struck, particularly in the passage from Acts that cites John's recognition that he is but a messenger who prepares the way for the one yet to come. Popular images of John the Baptist depict him as a fiery preacher, calling for repentance. Yet for all the power such preaching suggests, John also shows humility, a willingness to play a supporting role as he points away from himself.

For Further Comment

Additional comments on these Scripture texts, in part or in full, may be found in the seasonal volumes of *New Proclamation* as follows:

- Malachi 3:1-4—Year C, Advent 2
- Isaiah 40:1-11—Year B, Advent 2
- Isaiah 49:1-6—Year A, Epiphany 2; Years ABC, Tuesday of Holy Week
- Psalm 85—Year A, Proper 14; Year B, Advent 2, Proper 10; Year C, Proper 12
- Luke 1:57-80—Year C, Advent 2, Reign of Christ

Notes

1. From a sermon by Saint Augustine on the birth of John the Baptist, http://www.catholic-forum.com/saints/saintj02.htm (accessed June 21, 2007).

2. Jacobus de Voragine, *The Golden Legend: Readings on the Saints*, trans. William Granger Ryan (Princeton: Princeton University Press, 1993), 1:328.

3. The Venerable Bede, "The Great Forerunner of the Morn," trans. John Mason Neale, in *The Hymnal 1982* (New York: Church Hymnal, 1985), no. 271/272.

PETER AND PAUL, APOSTLES

JUNE 29

BILL DOGGETT

LUTHERAN (ELW)	EPISCOPAL (BCP)	ROMAN CATHOLIC (LFM)
Ezek. 34:11-16	Ezek. 34:11-16	2 Tim. 4:6-8, 16-18
Ps. 87:4-6	Ps. 87:1-7	Ps. 34: 2-3, 4-5, 6-7, 8-9
1 Cor. 3:16-23	2 Tim. 4:1-8	
Mark 8:27-35	John 21:15-19	Matt. 16:13-19

KEY THEMES

• Evangelism: Who are the Gentiles?
• Conversion experiences.
• What is church?

Saints Peter and Paul share this feast day because tradition holds they were both martyred in Rome on this day c. 64 C.E., although the time and place of their deaths and burials is an unsettled question. There is so much biblical and extrabiblical material about their lives as to defy summary. As they each have another feast day in the calendar, the Confession of Peter on January 18 and the Conversion of Paul on January 25 (since 1908 these two feasts have marked the beginning and end of the ecumenical Week of Prayer for Christian Unity), for this feast they share we will note only the strong similarities and differences in their stories.

In temperament, Peter and Paul could not have been much more different. Peter was a laborer, brash, cheerful, and enthusiastic, given to strong feelings and quick action that he sometimes came to regret. Paul was educated, deliberate, dour, and introspective, and although he was also a man of action, he could not be called rash. Their temperaments are exposed in the stories of their faith journeys: Peter follows Jesus at a word, and continually vacillates throughout his time as a disciple between error and insight. Paul, in contrast, is a zealous and violent persecutor of Christians until he is finally and violently persuaded that Jesus is the Messiah and has personally called him to spread the good news. Thereafter he is as steadfast a friend of Jesus as he had been an enemy. Interestingly, both Peter's and Paul's new vocations are associated with a name change. *Peter*, meaning "rock," is a nickname given to Simon by Jesus, while the Hebraic *Saul* becomes the Hellenic *Paul* as he pursues his mission to the Gentiles.

The mission to the Gentiles is something else they have in common. Paul is instructed by Jesus in a vision to bring the gospel to the Gentiles (Acts 26:17-18), while Peter has his own vision, in Acts 10, of every kind of animal in a vast sheet, and God telling him to call nothing God has made unclean. This vision Peter understands to mean that he is not to withhold the good news from the Gentiles (Acts 10:28). Peter and Paul become the two greatest evangelists outside of the Jewish communities, and their mission eventually brings them both to Rome, the seat of secular authority, where they are both martyred for their faith. Because Paul is a Roman citizen, he is beheaded with a sword, while Peter is crucified upside down at his own request. The instruments of their death, the sword and the upside-down cross, became iconographic symbols for them in the Western church. In the Eastern church, which does not use symbols of death in its icons, Peter is shown with the keys to the kingdom and Paul is depicted carrying a book, symbols also used in Western iconography.

> Both apostles share the same feast day, for these two were one; and even though they suffered on different days, they were as one. Peter went first, and Paul followed. And so we celebrate this day made holy for us by the apostles' blood. Let us embrace what they believed, their life, their labors, their sufferings, their preaching, and their confession of faith.—St. Augustine of Hippo[1]

The Festival

The Feast of Peter and Paul has been observed on this day since at least the third century, although in the sixth century and continuing until the Second Vatican Council the Roman Church divided the festival, moving Paul's commemoration to the following day. It was found to be too difficult for the Pope and his retinue to travel from St. Peter's in the Vatican to St. Paul's outside the walls of Rome on the same day in order to celebrate both high masses. As so-called Princes of the Apostles and founders of the church, their feast day is celebrated widely, and many cathedral churches are dedicated to them, either singly or together.

Various festival traditions recognize their histories and their patronages. Northern European Christians seem to have transferred some of the aspects of the old gods Odin and Thor to the pair, especially power over weather, so prayers and ritual actions seeking clement weather have been associated with the day in the North. In Hungary on this day, crowns, crosses, and other symbolic objects are woven from straw and paraded around the church, blessed, and brought home to be hung over the table as a sign of good weather and bountiful harvest, since Peter is patron of harvesters. Because Peter is the patron of fishermen and shipwrights, in coastal areas celebrations of fisheries and the blessing of boats and the sea are common. Paul is patron of writers, whose work might be honored in congregations on this day.

THE READINGS

The great variation in readings between the lectionaries reflects a variety of ways to understand this festival. The narrative in the Acts of the Apostles doesn't include the martyrdom of Peter and Paul, and the Gospels don't make mention of Paul at all, which makes the choice of readings not at all obvious, and perhaps a little polemical. And unlike most apostles' day celebrations, there is so much about these two in Scripture that a preacher will probably want to draw on stories beyond the lectionary readings in illustrating a sermon.

The Roman lectionary, reflecting both the importance of Peter as patron of the church and the vestiges of the pre–Vatican II calendar, which commemorated Paul on June 30, focuses on Peter, choosing a reading from Acts of the Apostles that makes no mention of Paul, and using the version of Peter's confession found in Matthew 16, in which Jesus declares that Peter is the rock on which he will build his church, and that he will give the keys to the kingdom of heaven into Peter's care.

The Lutheran lectionary uses Mark's version of the confession of St. Peter that shows Peter having one of his many foolish moments, as he rebukes Jesus for predicting his death and resurrection. Peter's rash moments are so integral to his character that one can hardly preach about Peter without mentioning them, but this is the only reading for the day in any of the lectionaries that includes one. This may relate thematically to the ELW's reading from 1 Corinthians, which elevates the foolishness of God over the wisdom of the world (1 Cor. 3:18-20), but 1 Cor. 3:22 also mentions Paul and Peter in the same sentence, as being among the possessions of the faithful and not leaders to boast in.

Aurea Luce

With golden light and roseate beauty,
light of lights, you poured forth over all the world,
adorning the heavens with glorious martyrdom
on this holy day which grants pardon to the guilty.

Gatekeeper of heaven; his equal, teacher of the earth:
judges of the ages, true lights of the world, the one
triumphant on the cross, the other by the sword,
crowned with laurels, they occupy the council of life.

To the Trinity be eternal glory,
honor, power and jubilation,
by whose Unity may their authority endure,
from olden times and now and forever. Amen.
—Hymn for the Feast of Sts. Peter and Paul[2]

The Lutheran and the Episcopal lectionaries share the same reading from Ezekiel, about God gathering the lost sheep of his flock from the distant corners of the world. It both reminds us of and contrasts with Peter and Paul's evangelical missions, for while Ezekiel talks of the gathering of many from far and wide, he refers to the lost and strayed sheep of Israel, while Paul and Peter understood Jesus' mission to be to gather the Gentiles as well. The Episcopal lectionary makes this connection specific in choosing as its Gospel reading John's account of Jesus telling Peter, "if you love me, feed my sheep." The Episcopal and Roman lectionaries have overlapping readings from 2 Timothy. The passage they have in common is Paul's prediction of his own death, declaring that he has fought the good fight and finished the race, and awaits the crown of righteousness from Jesus' hand.

Let us place before our eyes the good Apostles. Peter, through unjust envy, endured not one or two but many labours, and at last, having delivered his testimony, departed unto the place of glory due to him. Through envy Paul, too, showed by example the prize that is given to patience: seven times was he cast into chains; he was banished; he was stoned; having become a herald, both in the East and in the West, he obtained the noble renown due to his faith; and having preached righteousness to the whole world, and having come to the extremity of the West, and having borne witness before rulers, he departed at length out of the world, and went to the holy place, having become the greatest example of patience.
—Clement of Rome[3]

In preaching on this day, there are many directions to go. As noted above, it seems almost necessary to supplement the lectionary readings with other passages from Scripture to round out the pictures of the apostle's lives. The varieties of conversion experience, with Peter's easy assent at one end of the scale and Paul's painful and symbol-laden experience at the other, could be a subject, as could the varieties of post-conversion experience, with Peter's continued failings and recoveries contrasting with Paul's steady fighting of the good fight. The conviction both men had that the good news was for all begs the question of who are today's outsiders, and how the gospel might be brought to them. The account of the Council of Jerusalem in Acts 15 would be a good text to bring to this theme, for it shows both Peter and Paul arguing for the mission to the Gentiles. Finally, the biggest theme of the day may be the question, What is this thing called church of which Peter and Paul are foundation and founder? It has grown and changed in ways that would no doubt astonish them. But one cannot predict the shape of a building from looking at the cornerstone: How are our communities still engaged in the work that Peter and Paul began?

FOR FURTHER COMMENT

Additional comments on these texts, in full or in part, may be found in the seasonal volumes of *New Proclamation* as follows:

- Ezekiel 34:11-16—Year A, Reign of Christ
- Psalm 34—Year A, All Saints; Year B, Proper 14, Proper 25
- 1 Corinthians 3:16-23—Year A, Epiphany 7
- 2 Timothy 4:1-8 (17-18)—Year C, Proper 24, Proper 25
- Matthew 16:13-19—Year A, Proper 16
- Mark 8:27-35—Year B, Lent 2, Proper 19
- John 21:15-19—Year C, Easter 3

Notes

1. Augustine of Hippo, Sermon 295:7-8, in John Rotelle, ed., *The Works of St. Augustine: Sermons,* 11 vol. (New Rochelle, N.Y.: New City Press, 1993), 3:197–99.

2. Hymn for the Feast of Sts. Peter and Paul, attributed to Paulinus of Aquileia (c. 750 – c. 802), trans. Scott Metcalfe for Blue Heron concert program, Cambridge, Mass., 2006, http://www.blueheronchoir.org/programs/bh060302b.pdf (accessed July 9, 2007).

3. Clement of Rome, *First Epistle to the Corinthians,* chap. 5, from *The Apostolic Fathers: The Epistles of S. Clement, S. Ignatius, S. Barnabus and S. Polycarp,* trans. Charles H. Hoole (London: Rivington, 1872), 7.

THOMAS, APOSTLE

July 3 (ELW, LFM) / December 21 (BCP)

Ruth A. Meyers

Lutheran (ELW)	Episcopal (BCP)	Roman Catholic (LFM)
Judges 6:36-40	Hab. 2:1-4	Eph. 2:19-22
Ps. 136:1-4, 23-26	Psalm 126	Psalm 117
Eph. 4:11-16	Heb. 10:35—11:1	
John 14:1-7	John 20:24-29	John 20:24-29

KEY THEMES

• "Doubting Thomas" comes to belief through his encounter with Jesus.
• God's steadfast love endures forever.
• The church is built upon the foundation of the apostles.

THE SAINT

Most of what we know about Thomas comes from four narratives in the Gospel of John. His name is included among the twelve apostles in each of the lists in the Synoptic Gospels and Acts (Matt. 10:3; Mark 3:18; Luke 6:15; Acts 1:13), but Matthew, Mark, and Luke provide no further detail about him. In three places, John tells us that Thomas was called the Twin (John 11:16, 20:24, 21:2), and some writers refer to him by the Greek *Didymus*, meaning "twin." The Gospels give no indication of the identity of his twin.

When Thomas first appears in John's Gospel, he is fearless. While his fellow disciples were hesitant to go with Jesus to Bethany because Jesus had just been threatened with stoning, Thomas encourages them, "Let us also go, that we may die with him" (John 11:16). One could also understand this response as a kind of challenge, that is, that Thomas is letting everyone know that he thinks it will turn out badly, though he is willing to follow Jesus wherever he goes.

A few chapters later, Thomas, still willing to follow Jesus, is confused about Jesus' assurance that he is going to prepare a place for his followers. Thomas's question, "How can we know the way?" leads to Jesus' proclamation that he is "the way, and the truth, and the life" (John 14:5-6).

Thomas is perhaps best known, however, for his doubt after the resurrection. When Jesus first appears to the disciples in the upper room on the evening of the day of the resurrection, Thomas is not with them. He refuses to accept their testimony, insisting that he must "see the mark of the nails in his hands, and put my finger in the mark of the nails and my hand in his side" in order to believe (John 20:25). Eight days later, in the same place, Thomas's encounter with the risen Jesus leads to his profound exclamation of faith, "my Lord and my God!" (John 20:28).

Thomas makes his final appearance in John in another resurrection story. He is among the disciples who meet the risen Jesus on a beach and make a miraculous catch of fish after a futile night of fishing (John 21:1-14). This story offers no further insight into Thomas's character.

According to the fourth-century church historian Eusebius, Thomas was assigned to preach the Gospel in Parthia when the apostles divided the labor of evangelizing different parts of the world. (The Parthians, among those who heard the disciples speaking in their native language on the day of Pentecost, inhabited the region of Persia, what is today Iran.) However, Thomas is most frequently associated with the proclamation of the Gospel in India. Christians living on the Malabar Coast of southwestern India refer to themselves as "St. Thomas Christians" and claim that Thomas was the first to evangelize them. While some contemporary scholars doubt that this community dates to the first century, a number of early Christian writers mention that Thomas was martyred, reputedly by stabbing with a spear, and buried in Mylapore, a small village near Chennai in southeastern India. An ancient stone cross, dating from between the sixth and eighth centuries, is preserved in the church built over the place where Thomas is supposed to have been buried. Thomas's relics are said to have been translated to Edessa at the end of the fourth century. From there, they were moved during the Crusades to Italy, to Ortona in the Abruzzi. The Cathedral of St. Thomas in Mylapore also claims to have some of Thomas's relics.

Dearly beloved, what do you see in these events? Do you really believe that it was by chance that this chosen disciple was absent, then came and heard, heard and doubted, doubted and touched, touched and believed? It was not by chance but in God's providence. In a marvelous way God's mercy arranged that the disbelieving disciple, in touching the wounds of his master's body, should heal our wounds of disbelief. The disbelief of Thomas has done more for our faith than the faith of the other disciples. As he touches Christ and is won over to belief, every doubt is cast aside and our faith is strengthened. So the disciple who doubted, then felt Christ's wounds, becomes a witness to the reality of the resurrection.—Gregory the Great[1]

The third-century apocryphal *Acts of Judas Thomas* gives a colorful account of the apostle's missionary efforts in India. Hired to build a palace for King Gundaphor, Thomas instead spent the king's money to care for the poor. The king was enraged and had Thomas thrown into prison. That night the king's brother died and discovered that Thomas's generosity with the king's money had resulted in a palace built in heaven for Gundaphor. The brother was allowed to return to earth to attempt to purchase the palace for himself, whereupon Gundaphor had Thomas released from prison. Thomas then baptized Gundaphor and his brother. Although there is no factual basis for this story, Thomas is considered the patron saint of builders and is often depicted artistically holding a carpenter's T-square.

We walk by faith, and not by sight;
no gracious words we hear
from him who spoke as none e'er spoke;
but we believe him near.

We may not touch his hands and side,
nor follow where he trod;
but in his promise we rejoice;
and cry, "My Lord and God!"

Help then, O Lord, our unbelief;
and may our faith abound,
to call on you when you are near,
and seek where you are found:

that, when our life of faith is done,
in realms of clearer light
we may behold you as you are,
with full and endless sight.
—Henry Alford[2]

In addition to the *Acts of Thomas*, several other apocryphal writings are associated with Thomas. The *Gospel of Thomas* is a collection of sayings and parables of Jesus, while the *Infancy Gospel of Thomas* records miracles supposedly performed by Jesus during his childhood. The fourth-century *Apocalypse of Thomas* is an eschatological treatise. The *Book of Thomas*, discovered among the documents at Nag Hammadi, contains teachings on ethics and eschatology that Jesus purportedly said in secret to Thomas. The attribution of these texts to Thomas suggests the weight of the apostle's name in the early and medieval church, although none of these writings is actually the work of Thomas.

For many centuries, Western Christians commemorated Thomas on December 21, the supposed date of his death. The 1969 revision of the Roman calendar shifted the feast to July 3, traditionally the date of the translation of his relics, because of the importance of December 17–24 in the season of Advent. In 1972, Pope Paul VI declared Thomas to be the "apostle of India," acknowledging the traditional field of Thomas's missionary endeavors.

The Gospel
JOHN 20:24-29 (BCP, LFM)

The appointed reading begins abruptly, in the middle of a longer story. The disciples had gathered on Easter evening, enclosing themselves securely behind locked doors. The risen Jesus appears, his body transformed sufficiently that he could become manifest in a locked room, yet still showing the marks of his crucifixion. Jesus commissions the disciples who are present, bestowing the Holy Spirit and sending them forth in his name. We learn only after this first scene that Thomas, one of Jesus' inner circle of twelve, was not present. His stubborn insistence on actually touching the wounds before he will believe dramatizes the experience of doubt.

When the disciples meet one week later, again on the first day of the week, Thomas is with them. In the early Christian community, Sunday quickly came to be significant as the day of the resurrection and the day for Christians to assemble for worship. On this occasion, Jesus appears once more behind closed doors. This time he invites Thomas to touch the marks in his hands and his side. The text is ambiguous as to whether Thomas actually touches the risen Jesus. What is significant is Thomas's awed exclamation of belief, "my Lord and my God!" With Thomas's profession of faith, we return to the affirmation from the first verse of John's Gospel: "the Word was God" (John 1:1). Jesus' response, "Blessed are those who have not seen and yet have come to believe" (John 20:29), is a challenge and a promise to Christians of all times.

JOHN 14:1-7 (ELW)

The Lutheran lectionary presents Thomas questioning Jesus during the farewell discourse to the disciples at the Last Supper. Jesus is warning his disciples of his impending death, but in language so oblique that they do not understand. With Jesus, death leads to life. In his death, he will return to God the Father, and he will prepare a place for his disciples. At the same time, Jesus will continue to be present in the community of faith through the sending of the Spirit, a promise that he will make explicit later in this discourse.

Jesus intends his words to be reassuring. Indeed, this passage is often read at Christian funerals. But Thomas insists on knowing more. In speaking up, he may be giving voice to questions that others also have, just as his doubt at the resurrection makes concrete the challenge of belief: "How can we know the way?" (John 14:5). Thomas's question sets up Jesus' affirmation that he is the way and the truth and the life.

THE READINGS
JUDGES 6:36-40 (ELW)
HABUKKUK 2:1-4 (BCP)
HEBREWS 10:35—11:1 (BCP)

These readings from the Lutheran and Episcopal lectionaries draw our attention to the experience of doubt and faith. The story of Gideon's fleece is part of a larger narrative of a hesitant leader who demands considerable reassurance from God. Like many who are called, Gideon expresses doubt about his ability to lead the people as God directs (Judg. 6:11-18). The appointed narrative begins after Gideon has already received one sign from God and then successfully destroyed an altar to Baal. Now Gideon asks for yet another sign. The real test is not the fleece that accumulated dew while the ground remained dry, since it was common to use a fleece to collect water. Reversing the sign, however, assures Gideon that God is truly with him.

No signs are offered in the readings from Habakkuk and Hebrews. The prophet expresses confidence in God. He has complained, asking God why the wicked seem to prevail. Now, as the appointed passage begins, the prophet is alert for God's reply. God directs him to write the vision for all to see, creating a billboard of sorts: "the righteous live by their faith" (Hab. 2:4). The Hebrew word translated as "faith" conveys confidence, steadfastness, and trust. Thus the righteous trust in God, whose promises will be fulfilled even if it appears otherwise. Citing this passage from Habakkuk, the selection from Hebrews underscores the message of confidence and endurance in the face of trials and adversity. It introduces a chapter that enumerates heroes of the faith, women and men who held fast to God's promises.

PSALM 117 (LFM)
PSALM 126 (BCP)
PSALM 136:1-4, 23-26 (ELW)

Each of the appointed psalms calls our attention to God's steadfast love. Psalm 117 says simply that God is faithful for ever, while Psalms 126 and 136 speak of God's restoration after a time of trial. The refrain in Psalm 136 drives home the point: "God's steadfast love endures forever." Though we may doubt and seek signs, though we may undergo great suffering, God is always with us.

EPHESIANS 2:19-22 (LFM)
EPHESIANS 4:11-16 (ELW)

The readings from Ephesians introduce the role of apostles in the life of the church. The entire letter is addressed to Gentile Christians. At the conclusion of chapter 2, the author (scholars are divided as to whether Paul himself wrote this letter) reminds his audience that they are no longer "strangers and aliens" (Eph. 2:19), that is, separate from people of Israel with whom God had made a covenant. The metaphor of a building is dynamic, emphasizing growth and development. Both this passage and chapter 4 speak of the work of apostles, chapter 2 emphasizing that the apostles are part of the foundation of the church. Both passages emphasize the church's unity in Christ.

PREACHING APPROACHES

143

THOMAS,
APOSTLE

JULY 3 /
DECEMBER 21

The experience of doubt is common to many Christians, and the story of Thomas offers an opportunity to explore that experience. Thomas knew well what had happened to Jesus; his arrest, trial, and crucifixion loomed over much of the time Jesus had spent with the disciples. Believing that Jesus had risen from the dead was a difficult leap for Thomas to make; most of the resurrection stories in the Gospels report doubt as one response. We are likely to question God and to doubt God's presence or care for us at moments of crisis, for example, the death of a young adult in an auto accident or a mass murder by a crazed gunman. Jesus' response to Thomas, both his proclamation that he is the way and the truth and the life (John 14:7) and his invitation to Thomas to touch his wounds (John 20:27), suggests that God hears and understands our questions and will respond. Jesus' statement blessing those who have not seen and yet come to believe should probably be taken literally, as a blessing on those who have not actually seen the incarnate or risen Jesus. The verses that follow in John 20 imply that people come to believe by hearing the stories of Jesus.

A very different approach would build on Ephesians to talk about Thomas as an apostle, one called and sent by Jesus to proclaim the good news and so help lay the foundation of the church. Many Christians know the reality of disagreements within the church. Both selections from Ephesians offer lyrical images of the church growing into a unity.

FOR FURTHER COMMENT

Additional comments on these Scripture texts, in part or in full, may be found in the seasonal volumes of *New Proclamation* as follows:

- Habukkuk 2:1-4—Year C, Propers 22, 26
- Psalm 126—Year B, Advent 3, Proper 25, Thanksgiving; Year C, Lent 5
- Ephesians 2:19-22—Year B, Proper 11
- Ephesians 4:11-16—Year B, Proper 13
- John 14:1-7—Year A, Easter 5
- John 20:24-29—Years ABC, Easter 2

Notes

1. From a homily by Pope Saint Gregory the Great, http://www.catholic-forum.com/saints/saintt07.htm (accessed June 19, 2007).

2. Henry Alford, "We Walk by Faith," from *The Hymnal 1982* (New York: Church Hymnal Corp., 1985), no. 209.

MARY MAGDALENE, APOSTLE

JULY 22

RUTH A. MEYERS

LUTHERAN (ELW)	EPISCOPAL (BCP)	ROMAN CATHOLIC (LFM)
Ruth 1:6-18 or	Judith 9:1, 11-14	Song of Sol. 3:1-4a or
Exod. 2:1-10		2 Cor. 5:14-17
Ps. 73:23-29	Ps. 42:1-7	Ps. 63:2, 3-4, 5-6, 8-9
Acts 13:26-33a	2 Cor. 5:14-18	
John 20:1-2, 11-18	John 20:11-18	John 20:1-2, 11-18

KEY THEMES

- Mary Magdalene, apostle to the apostles, becomes a witness to the resurrection, commissioned to announce the good news to the disciples.
- God through Christ transforms us and makes us ministers of the reconciling love of God.
- What is the message of reconciliation that your congregation proclaims and enacts in its context?
- In what ways have you experienced God's reconciling love?

THE SAINT

Identified both as apostle to the apostles and as a redeemed prostitute, perhaps no other biblical saint has been the subject of as much interpretation and misinterpretation as Mary of Magdala. Although her commemoration was added to the Western church calendar only in the Middle Ages, a number of patristic writers comment on the biblical texts about her. Noncanonical Gospels and other literature discovered during the nineteenth and twentieth centuries, particularly material found at Nag Hammadi, Egypt, in 1945, have shed new light on her role. Scholarship since the 1980s has emphasized her authority and leadership in early Christianity, while literature, film, and other artistic expressions continue to focus on her sexuality.

In all four Gospels, Mary Magdalene has a prominent place at the cross and the empty tomb. With other women, she watched the crucifixion from afar and saw Jesus laid in the tomb (Matt. 27:56, 61; Mark 15:40, 47; John 19:25), and on Easter morning she went to the tomb to anoint his body (Matt. 28:1; Mark 16:1; Luke 24:10). In every group of women, except those listed in John 19, she is named first, indicating her preeminence. Of particular importance is her encounter with the risen Jesus and his command for her to announce the good news to the disciples (John 20:11-18). Accordingly, she became known as "apostle to the apostles," a title given by the third-century bishop Hippolytus as well as Augustine of Hippo and John Chrysostom.

Apart from the passion and resurrection narratives, Mary Magdalene receives only one brief mention in the New Testament. Luke introduces her as one of a group of women who traveled with Jesus and "the twelve" and "provided for them out of their resources" (Luke 8:1-3). Magdala was a prosperous town on the shores of the Sea of Galilee, known for its exports of salt fish and fish oil, and Mary's ability to provide material support for Jesus and the disciples suggests that she may have been involved in the fishing industry or some other trade.

What has captured Christian imagination, however, is Luke's description of Mary as one "from whom seven demons had gone out" (Luke 8:2; cf. Mark 16:9). In New Testament times, demonic possession was a sign of illness and not necessarily an indication of sinfulness. Western Christians, however, have identified Mary Magdalene with the unnamed "woman in the city, who was a sinner," who washes Jesus' feet with her tears and wipes them with her hair, then kisses and anoints his feet (Luke 7:36-50). The sensual nature of this scene and a tendency to identify women's sinfulness with their sexuality has resulted in the identification of this woman as

> Lift your voice rejoicing, Mary,
> Christ has risen from the tomb;
>   on the cross a suffering victim,
>   now as victor he is come.
> Whom your tears in death were mourning,
>   welcome with your smiles returning.
> Let your alleluias rise!
> —Peter the Venerable[1]

a prostitute. Moreover, this anointing story was conflated with two others: an unnamed woman of Bethany anoints Jesus' head in a prophetic gesture that Jesus interprets as preparation for his burial (Matt. 26:6-13; Mark 14:3-9), and Mary, the sister of Lazarus and Martha of Bethany, anoints Jesus' feet as a prophetic anointing for burial (John 12:1-8). In the sixth century, Pope Gregory I declared in a homily that Mary Magdalene, the sinner of Luke 7, and Mary of Bethany were the same person, an identification that has persisted for centuries. The image of the sinful woman, a prostitute forgiven through her penitential encounter with Jesus, has overshadowed the more subversive stories of the prophetic anointings.

New understandings of Mary began to emerge as manuscripts of noncanonical texts were discovered during the nineteenth and twentieth centuries. Documents such as the *Gospel of Thomas*, the *Sophia of Jesus Christ*, the *Gospel of Mary*, and the *Gospel of Philip* depict Mary Magdalene as prominent among early Christians.

She speaks boldly, sometimes questioning the earthly or risen Jesus. She comforts and encourages the disciples, correcting them and urging them to believe and to act. She experiences and interprets visions, and she is praised for her insight. She also meets opposition from the male disciples, especially Peter, who object to a woman's presence and leadership. Some scholars propose that these texts reflect a struggle in the ancient church over the authority and leadership of women. Further complicating the picture, several of the texts portray her as an intimate companion of Jesus and, in the *Gospel of Philip*, as one whom Jesus often kissed. While some commentators have interpreted these references to mean a sexual or even marital relationship between Jesus and Mary, the texts themselves are far more ambiguous. There is no factual basis for the claim that Mary bore Jesus' child and their lineage has been secretly continued for two millennia.

Life is yours for ever, Mary,
for your light is come once more
and the strength of death is broken;
now your songs of joy outpour.
Ended now the night of sorrow,
love has brought the blessed morrow.
Let your alleluias rise!
—Peter the Venerable[2]

Although these noncanonical texts were unknown during the Middle Ages, legends of Mary's missionary journeys circulated in both the East and the West. Eastern Christian tradition holds that she traveled to Ephesus with the evangelist John and died there, her body later taken to Constantinople where it was venerated for many centuries. A Western legend claims that unbelievers sent Mary, along with Lazarus, Martha, and other Christians, out to sea in a boat without pilot or rudder. Providentially, they landed in France, where Mary proclaimed the gospel and later lived as a hermit. Various sites in Provence have claimed to have her relics.

In iconography, Mary is often depicted holding a red egg. An ancient legend reports that Mary was speaking to the emperor about Jesus' resurrection. He ridiculed her witness and said, "A man could no more rise from the dead than the egg in your hand turn red." At the emperor's words, the egg turned deep crimson.

THE GOSPEL

JOHN 20:1-2, 11-18 (ELW, LFM)
JOHN 20:11-18 (BCP)

Unlike the Synoptic accounts of the women's trip to Jesus' tomb (Matt. 28:1; Mark 16:1-2; Luke 24:1), in John's Gospel Mary comes to the tomb alone. Surprised when she finds it empty, she runs to tell Peter and the beloved disciple. The Lutheran and Roman lectionaries include these initial verses of the narrative, while the Episcopal lectionary begins the story with Mary standing outside the tomb, weeping.

The appearance of the angels at the tomb is common to all four Gospels. In John, Mary's despair is obvious as she pours out her anguish over not finding Jesus' body in the tomb. She does not wait for the angels to reply, but turns away. As the story unfolds, the common Johannine device of misunderstanding advances the plot (see, for example, the stories of the woman at the well [John 4:15], and Martha at the grave of Lazarus [John 11:20-24]; as well as the discourses on the bread of life [John 6:52], and the good shepherd [John 10:6]). Other resurrection scenes also include an initial difficulty recognizing the risen Jesus (Luke 24:15-16; John 21:4). Perhaps his risen form was sufficiently different that he was not immediately recognizable. Perhaps the narratives are emphasizing the difficulty of coming to believe.

Mary recognizes Jesus when he speaks her name, recalling Jesus' pronouncement that the sheep will recognize the voice of their shepherd (John 10:3-5). She turns, suggesting perhaps her conversion as she comes to believe in Jesus as her Lord. She apparently attempts to hold or embrace Jesus, a gesture he spurns, explaining that he has not yet ascended to the Father, that is, that his transformation is not yet complete. The situation will change soon thereafter, when Jesus encounters Thomas and invites him to touch his wounds so that he may believe (John 20:27). For Mary, there is only the command to let Jesus go, to relinquish her relationship with Jesus as he was.

> *Jesus saith to her, Mary!* . . . That voice of the shepherd, therefore, enters into Mary's heart, opens her eyes, arouses all her senses, and affects her in such a manner, that she immediately surrenders herself to Christ. Thus in Mary we have a lively image of our calling; for the only way in which we are admitted to the true knowledge of Christ is, when he first knows us, and then familiarly invites us to himself, not by that ordinary voice which sounds indiscriminately in the ears of all, but by that voice with which he especially calls the sheep which the Father hath given to him.—John Calvin[3]

Jesus directs Mary to announce to the disciples (his "brothers") what she has seen and heard. Her obedience to his command makes her an apostle, one sent by Jesus. Other accounts report that the disciples did not believe her (Mark 16:11; Luke 24:10), but John is silent about the disciples' response. They will have their own encounter with the risen Jesus that evening (John 20:19-23).

THE READINGS
RUTH 1:6-18 (ELW)
EXODUS 2:1-10 (ELW)
JUDITH 9:1, 11-14 (BCP)

Each of these lessons from the Lutheran and Episcopal lectionaries presents a tale of a courageous woman who defies the world's expectations for her behavior. The story of Ruth weeping and clinging to her mother-in-law Naomi echoes many of the details of Mary's tearful encounter with the gardener/Jesus at the empty tomb. Likewise, Ruth's steadfast commitment to Naomi parallels Mary's devotion to Jesus.

Exodus 2, the alternative first reading in the Lutheran lectionary, does not have the same poignancy as the scene from Ruth. Yet there is tenderness here, too, as Pharaoh's daughter takes pity on the Hebrew child. Defying her father's edict, she adopts the child, whom she later names Moses. God's purposes are fulfilled in a most surprising way.

And said to him, Rabboni! The efficacy of the address is evident from this circumstance, that Mary immediately renders to Christ the honor which is due to him; for the word *Rabboni* is not only respectful, but involves a profession of obedience. Mary therefore declares that she is a disciple of Christ, and submits to him as her Master. This is a secret and wonderful change effected on the human understanding, when God, enlightening her by his Spirit, renders her clear-sighted, who formerly was slow of apprehension, and, indeed, altogether blind. Besides, the example of Mary ought to serve the purpose of exhortation, that all whom Christ invites to himself may reply to him without delay.—John Calvin[4]

The Episcopal lectionary offers the apocryphal story of Judith, a pious widow who saves her people by beheading Holofernes, the head of the Assyrian army. The first seven chapters of the book of Judith tell of Holofernes and his army as they lay siege to Palestine. As the Israelite leaders prepare to surrender, Judith challenges them (Judith 8:11-27). Given five days to deliver the city, Judith turns to God in prayer. In the passage for this feast day, Judith implores God to act once again as the savior of those without hope. Though Judith's situation is very different from that of Mary Magdalene, as women both would have been viewed as weak and of lesser significance than men, and yet both have surprising roles in the furtherance of God's designs. While Judith accomplishes her aims in part through seduction, the preacher should resist any comparison to Mary's supposed status as a prostitute.

SONG OF SOLOMON 3:1-4A (LFM)

This passage expresses a woman's yearning for her beloved, suggesting a comparison to Mary's search for Jesus. Yet Mary is not allowed to cling to Jesus. Instead he sends her forth to announce good news. In light of the gospel, the Song of Solomon might best be viewed as the search for mystical union with God, a search that leads to transformation.

2 CORINTHIANS 5:14-18 (BCP, LFM)

The Roman and Episcopal lectionaries offer a commentary on Mary's experience at the empty tomb. As Mary had to recognize Jesus in a new way, no longer "from a human point of view" (2 Cor. 5:16), so Christians must come to see Jesus from the perspective of new creation. In this new creation, we have a transformed relationship with God. From our experience of reconciliation with God through Christ, we become ministers of that reconciliation in the world.

ACTS 13:26-33A (ELW)

This passage is part of Paul's sermon at the synagogue in Antioch in Pisdia, a region in the interior of Asia Minor. This section of the sermon proclaims the story of Jesus' crucifixion and resurrection, events that fulfill God's promises of salvation to the people of Israel (Acts 13:17-23). Those to whom the risen Jesus appeared are now his witnesses; Mary Magdalene would be among those witnesses.

PREACHING APPROACHES

Whether or not the preacher directly addresses the popular understanding of Mary as a redeemed prostitute (recognizing that this is an erroneous conflation of different scriptural accounts), many in the congregation are likely to be familiar with this view. The lessons, however, present a courageous woman who undergoes a remarkable transformation in her faith. From a grieving friend clinging to a familiar relationship, she becomes an apostle commissioned to bear witness to wondrous good news. In the first-century world of the text, and perhaps in our world as well, it is surprising to find a woman entrusted with a message of God's new creation. Yet God works in unexpected ways, through unlikely people.

Kontakion
When God, who is transcendent in essence,
  Came with flesh into the world,
  O Myrrhbearer,
He received you as a true disciple, for you
  turned all your love toward Him;
Henceforth you would yourself work many
  healings.
Now that you have passed into heaven,
  never cease to intercede for the world![5]

FOR FURTHER COMMENT

Additional comments on these Scripture texts, in part or in full, may be found in the seasonal volumes of *New Proclamation* as follows:

- Ruth 1:6-18—Year B, Proper 26
- Exodus 2:1-10—Year A, Proper 16
- Psalm 42—Year C, Proper 7; Years ABC, Easter Vigil
- Psalm 63—Year C, Lent 3
- 2 Corinthians 5:14-18—Year B, Proper 6; Year C, Lent 4
- John 20:1-2, 11-18—Years ABC, Easter Morning

Notes

1. Peter the Venerable, "Lift Your Voice Rejoicing, Mary," trans. Elizabeth Rundle Charles, from *The Hymnal 1982* (New York: Church Hymnal Corp., 1985), no. 190.

2. Ibid.

3. John Calvin, *Commentary on John*, Christian Classics Ethereal Library, http://www.ccel.org/ccel/calvin/calcom35.x.iii.html (accessed June 22, 2007).

4. Ibid.

5. http://orthodoxwiki.org/Mary_Magdalene (accessed June 22, 2007).

JAMES THE ELDER, APOSTLE

JULY 25

BILL DOGGETT

LUTHERAN (ELW)	EPISCOPAL (BCP)	ROMAN CATHOLIC (LFM)
1 Kings 19:9-18	Jer. 45:1-5	2 Cor. 4:7-15
Ps. 7:1-10	Ps. 7:1-10	Ps. 126:1-2ab, 2cd-3, 4-5, 6
Acts 11:27—12:3a	Acts 11:27—12:3a	
Mark 10:35-45	Matt. 20:20-28	Matt. 20:20-28

KEY THEMES

• Servanthood and power.
• The downside of zeal.
• Persecution, suffering, and martyrdom.

Saint James, the apostle known as James the Elder or James the Greater, was the son of Zebedee and Salome, brother of St. John the Evangelist, and one of the first of Jesus' companions. The Synoptics report that James and John, along with the other pair of brothers, Peter and Andrew, were called away from their nets by Jesus. The notable humility of John's Gospel about the evangelist himself extends to his brother as well: John's Gospel never mentions James, but it may be inferred in that account that after being called by Jesus, John summoned James in the same way that Andrew summoned Peter. The epithets *greater* and *elder* distinguish him from James the son of Alpheus, also an apostle.

James, John, and Peter are the most prominent among the apostles: they are the only ones of the Twelve to be witnesses at the raising of Jairus's daughter, the Transfiguration, and Jesus' final agony in Gethsemane. Jesus gives James and John the nickname *Boanerges* (Sons of Thunder), apparently because of their eagerness to act decisively if not always thoughtfully. Jesus rebukes them for forbidding a man from casting out demons in Jesus' name because he was not one of their company (Luke 9:49-50) and they seek Jesus' permission to call down a rain of fire on the Samaritans who refuse to receive Jesus (Luke 9:54). Apparently John and James and their family don't yet understand that Jesus' kingdom will not be an earthly one when either they (Mark 10:35-45) or their mother (Matt. 20:20-28) ask Jesus for the places of honor at his side when he sits on his throne. This request angers the other apostles, and Jesus, in his response, predicts James and John's martyrdom while denying the request. James was beheaded by Herod Agrippa in 44 C.E. (Acts 12:1-2), the first martyr of Agrippa's suppression of Palestine Christians.

And concerning this James, Clement, in the seventh book of his Hypotyposes, relates a story which is worthy of mention; telling it as he received it from those who had lived before him. He says that the one who led James to the judgment-seat, when he saw him bearing his testimony, was moved, and confessed that he was himself also a Christian. They were both therefore, he says, led away together; and on the way he begged James to forgive him. And he, after considering a little, said, "Peace be with thee," and kissed him. And thus they were both beheaded at the same time.—Eusebius[1]

Later legend has James preaching in Spain before returning to Jerusalem and being martyred. Tradition holds that his relics are held at the Cathedral Church of Santiago de Compostela in Spain; it is said that James's disciples brought his body back to Spain by boat after his death, although a more elaborate tale holds that after his decapitation his body was taken up by angels and sailed on an unmanned and rudderless boat to Iria Flavia in Spain, where a rock sprung up and enclosed his relics, which were later found and carried to Compostela. Santiago de Compostela was one of the three most important medieval pilgrimage sites. A late-twentieth-century revival of the pilgrimage tradition brings over one hundred thousand pilgrims a year to Santiago. St. Saturnin in Toulouse, France, also claims to possess James's relics.

THE FEAST

Saint James's Day has been celebrated on July 25 since at least the ninth century, and there are many traditions associated with the celebration. The symbol of St. James is the cockleshell, and the eating of shellfish is associated with the feast in many places. The French dish *Coquilles Saint Jacques* is the best known of these dishes, but in England, oysters are the traditional dish of the day, and an English saying holds "He who eats oysters on St. James's Day will never want."

In the readings, the themes of the day are servanthood, zeal, and martyrdom. As noted, James and John's zeal and their tempers earned them the nickname "Sons of Thunder," and that spirit seems to have guided the choice of the non-Gospel readings. The serving of justice at God's hand in 1 Kings, Jeremiah, and Psalm 7 is echoed in James and John's desire to call down fire from the heavens on the unwelcoming Samaritans. Unfortunately, we don't know the content of Jesus' rebuke to them, but the rebuke is a reminder that zeal, however holy, doesn't necessarily lead to good.

The Gospel readings, in which Jesus speaks of both the imperative of servant-hood and its cost using eucharistic and baptismal imagery, provide an excellent opportunity to reflect on contemporary concerns related to power, justice, and human needs. If we can hear in our personal, community, and national lives any echo of the Sons of Thunder and their desire to act decisively against those who oppose them and to sit at the place of highest honor, then Jesus' response and the subsequent deaths of both Jesus and James show us that God's call is in another direction. And since few if any in our communities will ever face the kind of persecution that James suffered, what does it mean for us to drink from Jesus' cup and share in Jesus' baptism? This day is also an apt time to remember and reflect on those throughout the world who do continue to suffer persecution and be killed for their faith.

THE READINGS

The Gospel readings give two accounts of James and John seeking places of honor in Jesus' kingdom. The most notable difference between Mark's and Matthew's versions is in who does the asking. In Mark it is the apostles who ask, but in Matthew it is their mother Salome who asks on their behalf. While it grabs our attention, it is probably not worth making too much of the distinction. In both accounts, the other ten apostles direct their anger against the sons. Whoever is doing the asking, it is understood that James and John are responsible.

It is worth noting that in Mark's Gospel, Jesus refers to his cup and his baptism in the present tense. It seems that Jesus is speaking of more than his upcoming death when he asks the disciples to share in his cup and baptism. Jesus implies that his current work of teaching, healing, and liberating are, in Mark, a part of what the disciples will share in, not just his persecution and death.

Jesus' response to the request, that the one who wishes to be great must be servant, and the one who desires to be first must be slave of all, is sufficient fodder for many sermons, as it speaks to our all-too-human desires for power and honor. Jesus turns these worldly values on their head. Remember that in the end, at the moment when Jesus does come into his kingdom, it is none of the disciples, but rather a pair of criminals who are at his right and left hand. In contrasting his own

O God, who brought your servant Abraham out of the land of the Chaldeans, protecting him in his wanderings, who guided the Hebrew people across the desert, we ask that you watch over us, your servants, as we walk in the love of your name to *Santiago de Compostela.*

Be for us our companion on the walk,
Our guide at the crossroads,
Our breath in our weariness,
Our protection in danger,
Our inn on the way,
Our shade in the heat,
Our light in the darkness,
Our consolation in our discouragements,
And our strength in our intentions.

So that with your guidance we may arrive safe and sound at the end of the Road and enriched with grace and virtue we return safely to our homes filled with joy. In the name of Jesus Christ our Lord. Amen.
—Prayer from the Pilgrims' Mass

life and the ideal of servant ministry with the values of the world, Jesus makes a political claim as well as a personal one: the followers of Jesus are not to be like the rulers and tyrants of the world (like Herod and Caesar, that is). More subversive than a call to use power for good, Jesus directs his followers to turn their backs on power altogether.

The reading from 2 Corinthians in the Roman lectionary is a stark reflection on the paradoxical nature of servanthood. Perhaps the cup that Jesus says the disciples will drink is described when Paul says, "We are afflicted in every way, but not crushed; perplexed, but not driven to despair; persecuted, but not forsaken; struck down, but not destroyed" (2 Cor. 4:8-9). The idea that the death of Jesus living in us is life itself is somewhat metaphysical, but the hope that Paul intends to convey is very concrete. In preaching on this text, consider how those who don't feel afflicted, perplexed, persecuted, or struck down can grasp that hope, and also how a message of hope might be brought to those who feel themselves crushed, driven to despair, forsaken, or destroyed.

> Give me my scallop-shell of quiet,
> My staff of faith to walk upon,
> My scrip of joy, immortal diet,
> My bottle of salvation,
> My gown of glory, hope's true gage;
> And thus I'll take my pilgrimage.
> —Sir Walter Raleigh[2]

The litany of violence in Psalm 7 and the readings from Jeremiah and 1 Kings is disturbing, to say the least, and foreshadows James and John's eagerness to call down a rain of fire on the Samaritans when they refuse Jesus' hospitality because he has set his face for Jerusalem. While the image of God in the Hebrew Scriptures can be very violent, as it is in the Jeremiah reading, it is worth noting that in the 1 Kings reading the Lord is not in the destructive wind or in the earthquake, or in the fire, but in the silence that follows. God is most often found in the midst of violence not to instigate it but to quell it.

FOR FURTHER COMMENT

Additional comments on these Scripture texts, in part or in full, may be found in the seasonal volumes of *New Proclamation* as follows:

- 1 Kings 19:9-18—Year A, Proper 14; Year C, Proper 8
- Psalm 126—Year B, Advent 3, Proper 25, Thanksgiving; Year C, Lent 5
- 2 Corinthians 4:7-15—Year B, Epiphany 9/Proper 4, Proper 5
- Mark 10:35-45—Year B, Proper 24

Notes

1. *Eusebius Pamphilus: Church History,* in *A Select Library of the Nicene and Post Nicene Fathers of the Christian Church,* Second Series: Volume I, ed. Phillip Schaff (Edinburgh: T&T Clark, 1890), xi: 2,3.

2. Sir Walter Raleigh, "The Passionate Man's Pilgrimage," in *Daiphantus* (1604), from *A Book of Elizabethan Lyrics,* ed. Felix E. Schelling (Boston: Ginn, 1895), 129–31.

THE TRANSFIGURATION OF OUR LORD (BCP/LFM)

AUGUST 6

WILLIAM F. BROSEND II

EPISCOPAL (BCP)	ROMAN CATHOLIC (LFM)
Exod. 34:29–35	Dan. 7:9–10. 13–14
Psalm 99 or 99:5–9	Psalm 97:1–2, 5–6, 9
2 Peter 1:13–21	2 Peter 1:16–19
Luke 9:28–36	Matt. 17:1–9 (Year A)
	Mark 9:2–10 (Year B)
	Luke 9:28a–36 (Year C)

KEY THEMES

- Nothing quite like this ever happened to any other biblical figure, but all are approximations, anticipations, and reverberations.
- Four matters merit homiletical attention: biblical content, transformation, voice, and responses.
- Moses and Elijah are present to point forward not to the resurrection but to the second coming.

The Transfiguration, again? Didn't we just do that on the Last Sunday of Epiphany? Yes, and we will do it again on Last Epiphany next year too. The question is, Why? Why is the Transfiguration such an important event that it receives special consideration in the lectionary twice a year? In a way this question can be asked of many of the feasts celebrated in this volume, met in the course of the three-year lectionary cycle and annually on the feast day. The Transfiguration is unique in its annual double encounter, in part because all three Synoptic Gospels record the event, something that testifies to its importance in the life of Jesus. But what about in the life of the church? The answer must wait on consideration of transfiguration/transformation in religious and biblical context, and examination of the texts assigned for the feast.

Remember "comparative mythology"? I was first trained in the era when Rudolf Otto and G. van der Leeuw, then Joseph Campbell and Mircea Eliade, held sway. Parallels were everywhere, and the Transfiguration of Christ was toward the top of the list. In mythology the gods were often transformed into animal, even human, figures, in order to communicate with humans. "The belief that gods and spirits can transform themselves, and demonstrate this power on others, is widespread in religion. An inexhaustible fund of myths and sagas of change bear witness to this, esp[ecially] in the Hellenistic Roman world, in which metamorphoses produced a whole literary genre (Ovid, Apuleius, Pseudo-Lucian)."[1]

Except when one looked more closely, beyond common terminology (*metamorphōsis*, and the like) and historical and geographical proximities (give or take a few centuries and a few hundred miles, of course), what we meet in the Synoptic Gospels seems worlds away from the pages of Ovid. Instead of cuneiform tablets and Egyptian papyri, the interesting parallels and the important context proved once again to be biblical. This should not have been surprising, given that Jesus was Jewish, Greco-Roman by political-military subjugation, not religious faith or practice, and that the religious context for the evangelists was the Septuagint, not the *Greek Magical Papyri*. But it has taken us a while to remember this foundational truth.

> O God, who on the holy mount revealed to chosen witnesses your well-beloved Son, wonderfully transfigured, in raiment white and glistening: Mercifully grant that we, being delivered from the disquietude of this world, may by faith behold the King in his beauty; who with you, O Father, and you, O Holy Spirit, lives and reigns, one God, for ever and ever. Amen.
> –Collect for the Feast of the Transfiguration, *The Book of Common Prayer*

However, on closer examination of the biblical material we are in many ways not much better off. Outside of the Synoptic parallels there are really no parallels, just antecedents that clearly formed and fashioned the narrative, and echoes that show its influence in the tradition. Nothing quite like this ever happened to any other biblical figure. Yes, Moses' face shined, Elijah ascended, Enoch walked with God, someone "known" to Paul visited the third heaven, Phillip popped around Palestine like Ezekiel before him, clouds come and go, garments glow, but all are approximations, anticipations, and reverberations. Yet they are important background and reflection on the event itself, and should be noted in our own reflections if not finally in our homilies. Here is a short list of important passages:

• Enoch, the father of Methuselah, "walked with God." Whatever that meant, it eventually meant that "he was no more, because God took him" (Gen. 5:24).
• When Moses was summoned to the mountain to receive the tablets, "the cloud covered the mountain" for six days, and "the glory of the LORD settled on Mount Sinai" and "Moses entered the cloud" (Exod. 24:12-18).

• Elijah (2 Kings 2:1-12), Ezekiel ("Then the spirit lifted me up, and as the glory of the LORD rose from its place. . . . The spirit lifted me up and bore me away" [3:12, 14]), and the apostle Philip ("the Spirit of the Lord snatched Philip away, and the eunuch saw him no more" [Acts 8:39]) experienced some form of Spirit-induced transcendent locomotion, as did one "known" to the apostle Paul, "whether in the body or out of the body I do not know; God knows" (2 Cor. 12:2).

• Jesus, echoing Daniel and anticipating the eschaton, promises at his trial that "'you will see the Son of Man seated at the right hand of the Power,' and 'coming with the clouds of heaven'" (Mark 14:62), and later "two men in dazzling clothes" (Luke 24:4) or perhaps an "angel of the Lord," whose "appearance was like lightning and his clothes white as snow" (Matt. 28:2-3), announce his resurrection.

All of these point to or draw from the Transfiguration of Christ, but none of them begin to capture or exhaust its meaning.

THE READINGS

The texts from Hebrew Scripture, *Exodus 34:29-35* (BCP) and *Daniel 7:9-10, 13-14* (LFM) are important and true antecedents for the evangelists' and our understanding of the Transfiguration. When Moses comes down from the mountain with the second set of tablets he is this time transformed, so that "his face shone because he had been talking with God" (Exod. 34:29). The tradition-history is complex, and one can only speculate about the difference in Moses' encounter with God in Exodus 34, in which the "glory of the LORD" passes by, and all Moses' previous encounters with God. It was a difference Luke picks up on, as we will see. Daniel is important for a different reason, in this case a difference crucial for my interpretation of the significance of the Transfiguration. After all, as we saw in recalling the wider biblical context, there are clouds of heaven, fiery wheels, and clothing white as snow elsewhere in Scripture. But in Daniel we have them in an apocalyptic context, and that is suggestive for our reading of the Transfiguration.

The psalms appointed for this feast (*Psalms 97 and 99*) are traditional enthronement psalms celebrating God's dominion and glory, in part as it is reflected in the idealization of the king, and require no further comment. The epistle, *2 Peter 1:13-21*, is fascinating, however. Second Peter is in my estimation a late work, arguably the last book written in our New Testament, the second chapter dependent on the epistle of Jude.[2] I also believe the letter to be pseudonymous, with Peter executed c. 62 C.E. Our author provides in the first chapter a bit of apostolic nostalgia on Peter's behalf, remembering the words and deeds of Jesus, and encouraging his readers to do the same: "You will do well to be attentive to this as to a lamp shining in a dark place, until the day dawns and the morning star rises in your hearts" (2 Pet. 1:19). Central to this recollection is the Transfiguration, and central to this particular recollection is one of the seven (or eight, following Luke) features of the event itself, the voice, "This is my Son, my Beloved, with whom I am well pleased" (2 Pet. 1:17). We turn now to biblical accounts of the Transfiguration.

Most interpreters identify seven aspects of the event as common to the three accounts. Luke adds a distinctive and important eighth, that Jesus went up the mountain "to pray" (9:28).

1. The event takes place on a mountain (*oros*), a designated period of days (six in Matt. 17:1 and Mark 9:2, eight in Luke 9:28) after Peter's confession and the first passion prediction.

2. Jesus takes the "big three"—Peter, James and John—with him.

3. Jesus is "transfigured" (*metamorphōthē*) in Matt. 17:2/Mark 9:2; in Luke 9:29, "the appearance of his face changed" (*to eidos tou prosōpou autou heteron*—literary Luke's suspicion of the term *metamorphosis*?), changes emphasizing Jesus' face (so Luke, and Matt. 17:2, "his face shone like the sun") and his garments, "his clothes became dazzling white, such as no one on earth could bleach them" (Mark 9:3; also Matt. 17:2 and Luke 9:29).

4. Two men appeared with Jesus, identified as Moses and Elijah (Mark reverses the order), and are specifically said to be speaking with Jesus. Luke adds that they appeared "in glory" (*en doxēi*) and that they "were speaking of his departure [*exodus*], which he was about to accomplish at Jerusalem" (9:31).

5. Peter speaks, his motives and competency variously described, the title used for Jesus varying according to the evangelist's preference (Matthew: Lord; Mark: rabbi; Luke: master), in all accounts suggesting a spontaneous celebration echoing the Feast of Booths might be in order.

6. A cloud (*nephelē*) overshadows all (*episkiazousa* or variants, a nice alliteration with *skēnas*, "booth") and a voice is heard: "This is my Son, my Chosen; listen to him!" (Luke 9:35); "This is my Son, the Beloved; listen to him!" (Mark 9:7); "This is my Son, the Beloved; with him I am well pleased; listen to him!" (Matt. 17:5).

7. After the voice is heard the cloud, Moses, and Elijah are no longer visible. The four come down from the mountain; in Mark (9:9) and Matthew (17:9) Jesus tells the three not to share what they had seen until "the Son of Man has been raised from the dead."

Jesus' admonition to the disciples does not apply to us. On the contrary, our call is to proclaim the Transfiguration. How should we best do so?

PREACHING THE TRANSFIGURATION OF CHRIST

I think it is indeed a good thing that the Transfiguration is celebrated twice a year, because there is more to be said than can be squeezed into a single annual homily. Four foci (if that is possible) certainly merit homiletical attention: contexts, transformations, voice, and responses.

Multiple contexts go with most all biblical territory, so no surprise here. Some notice was given to many of the relevant biblical passages, but no conclusion was reached. While the presence of Moses and Elijah certainly invites a look back to Old Testament antecedents, I think that is a misreading. Moses and Elijah, via Malachi and Zechariah, are present to point forward—forward not to the resurrection ("until after the Son of Man is raised from the dead") but to the second coming. I take the primary soteriological context to be eschatological, making the Daniel passages (LFM) particularly significant.

Jesus, then, is transformed or transfigured into the appearance of the returning Christ, "coming with the clouds of heaven." This is not the Jesus of the resurrection appearances (or nonappearance in Mark), mistaken for the gardener in John 20, about whom some doubted in Matthew 28, not recognized on the road to Emmaus in Luke 24. His appearance here is unmistakable, as it will be at the last day.

All the more reason to listen to the voice from the cloud, is it not? Bruce Chilton[3] reminds us to attend to this voice in the tradition of the *bat qol* ("daughter of a voice") in Hebrew Scripture and tradition. This voice, in the very center of the Synoptic Gospels, echoes the voice after Jesus' baptism (Mark 1:11 and parallels), and it also echoes into the silence in the garden and at the cross. In fact it must do so, carrying forward the baptismal affirmation powerfully enough to carry through the devastating silence at Gethsemane and Calvary.

Our responses will be as multiple as the contexts. Surely we cannot ignore the stammering response of Peter while on the mountain, nor the stumbling responses of the three when they come down, James and John lobbying for the best seats (Mark 10:37), Peter denying any and all connection to the one he had seen transfigured (Mark 14:66-72). How, we may ask, could something so awesome in its impression be so fleeting in its impact? Better yet, we may ask this of ourselves, since this is so demonstrably so, not only of the apostles but of disciples throughout the ages, present company included. What shall we make of the event?

The voice speaks for itself, of course. Listen to him! For my sake and for your sake and for the sake of the church and the world, listen to him! What had he

It is doubtful that we should understand the transfiguration as an event simply staged for the three apostles. Probably it had meaning for Jesus as well. . . . A process of preparation and planning is taking place, a search for God's will disclosed in Scripture, and this process emerges out of prayer (Luke 9:28-29).
—Robert C. Tannehill[4]

just said? "The Son of Man must undergo great suffering, and be rejected by the elders, chief priests, and scribes, and be killed, and on the third day be raised." Then he said to them all, "If any want to become my followers, let them deny themselves and take up their cross daily and follow me. For those who want to save their life will lose it, and those who lose their life for my sake will save it. What does it profit them if they gain the whole world, but lose or forfeit themselves?" (Luke 9:22-25).

The Transfiguration affirms the baptismal voice, and validates the voice of the One to whom we are commanded, "Listen to him!" Not just in the promise of the resurrection, but in the promise of the final fulfillment in glory. Somewhere between *Elmer Gantry* and *Left Behind* we lost sight of the fact that the promise of the end is a promise of hope and fulfillment, substituting neoapocalyptic for biblical assurance. The Transfiguration, interpreted eschatologically, is a reminder that Christ's return will be as triumphant and gracious as it will be unmistakable.

FOR FURTHER COMMENTARY

Additional comments on these Scripture texts, in full or in part, may be found in the seasonal volumes of *New Proclamation* as follows:

- Exodus 34:29-35—Year C, Last Epiphany/Transfiguration Sunday
- Daniel 7:9-10, 13-14—Year B, Reign of Christ
- Psalm 97—Year C, Easter 7; Years ABC, Christmas Day 2
- Psalm 99—Year A, Proper 24; Years A & C, Last Epiphany/Transfiguration Sunday
- 2 Peter 1:13-21—Year A, Last Epiphany/Transfiguration Sunday
- Luke 9:28-36—Year C, Last Epiphany/Transfiguration Sunday
- Matthew 17:1-9—Year A, Last Epiphany/Transfiguration Sunday
- Mark 9:2-10—Year B, Last Epiphany/Transfiguration Sunday; Lent 2

Notes

1. *Theological Dictionary of the New Testament,* ed. Gerhard Kittel, trans. Geoffrey Bromiley (Grand Rapids: Eerdmans, 1964), 4:756.

2. See my commentary *James and Jude,* New Cambridge Bible Commentary (Cambridge: Cambridge University Press, 2004).

3. Bruce Chilton, "Transfiguration," in *The Anchor Bible Dictionary,* ed. D. N. Freedman (New York: Doubleday, 1992), 6:640–42.

4. Robert C. Tannehill, *The Narrative Unity of Luke-Acts,* vol. 1 (Philadelphia: Fortress Press, 1986), 225.

MARY, MOTHER OF OUR LORD (ELW/BCP) / THE ASSUMPTION OF THE BLESSED VIRGIN MARY (LFM)

AUGUST 15

WILLIAM F. BROSEND II

LUTHERAN (ELW)	EPISCOPAL (BCP)	ROMAN CATHOLIC (LFM)
Isa. 61:7–11	Isa. 61:10–11	Rev. 11:19a, 12:1–6a, 10ab
Ps. 34:1–9	Psalm 34 or 34:1–9	Ps. 45:10bc, 11, 12ab, 16
Gal. 4:4–7	Gal. 4:4–7	1 Cor. 15:20–27
Luke 1:46–55	Luke 1:46–55	Luke 1:39–56

KEY THEMES

• The Magnificat is Mary's song in praise of God, not our song in praise of Mary.
• The assumption of Mary is not discontinuous from God's promise to all the faithful, but a symbol of the same.
• Mary is a historical figure who voluntarily joined God on the path God invited her to walk, was thoroughly connected to her own Jewish heritage, and invites and meets us in community.

The Assumption of the Blessed Virgin Mary—for Anglicans and others the Feast of Mary, the Mother of Our Lord—comes at the midpoint between the Annunciation and the Nativity, and so provides a wonderful opportunity to bring together devotion, adoration, and learning centered on the Holy Mother of God. The biblical text, while of course important, has in one significant instance (the Gospel) already been commented on, and the other texts are somewhat tangential to the focus of this feast. My efforts will therefore move quickly through consideration of the texts to questions about preaching on this day, and to further developing my "homiletical Marian theology."

The material from *Second Isaiah* resounds with the praise of God, "I will greatly rejoice in the LORD, my whole being shall exult in my God" (Isa. 61:10), the verses for the ELW appropriately including God's commitment to justice and righteousness ("I the LORD love justice"; Isa. 61:8). The appointed psalms, 34 or 45, are distinctive, and quite varied. *Psalm 34* is a song of praise with Magnificat-like phrasing and concerns ("My soul makes its boast in the LORD; let the humble hear and be glad. O magnify the LORD with me, and let us exalt his name together"; vv. 2-3). It also includes a favorite verse, "O taste and see that the LORD is good" (v. 8), that echoes the prophet's "my whole being shall exult." Praise, on this day, needs all the body, soul, and senses. *Psalm 45*, by contrast, is a royal hymn, likely in celebration of a royal wedding, and in anticipation of a royal birth, a fitting tribute to the *theotokos*.

> O God, you have taken to yourself the blessed Virgin Mary, mother of your incarnate Son: Grant that we, who have been redeemed by his blood, may share with her the glory of your eternal kingdom; through Jesus Christ our Lord, who lives and reigns with you, in the unity of the Holy Spirit, one God, now and for ever. Amen.
> —Collect for the Feast of Mary, the Mother of Our Lord, *The Book of Common Prayer*

The New Testament material is equally varied. *Galatians 4:4-7* is part of Paul's working through of what might be called his theology of adoption, understanding the incarnation as God's plan to adopt us as God's children by making us brothers and sisters of God's son. The Marian emphasis is found in verse 4, "when the fullness of time had come, God sent his Son, born of a woman." The Roman Catholic reading is, shall we say, a little more dramatic.

> A great portent appeared in heaven: a woman clothed with the sun, with the moon under her feet, and on her head a crown of twelve stars. She was pregnant and was crying out in birth pangs, in the agony of giving birth. Then another portent appeared in heaven: a great red dragon, with seven heads and ten horns, and seven diadems on his heads. His tail swept down a third of the stars of heaven and threw them to the earth. Then the dragon stood before the woman who was about to bear a child, so that he might devour her child as soon as it was born. And she gave birth to a son, a male child, who is to rule all the nations with a rod of iron. But her child was snatched away and taken to God and to his throne. (Rev. 12:1-5)

Wow! That will liven up a service—a seven-headed, ten-horned dragon laying waste to heaven and earth and laying in wait for the birth of the Messiah. Mary here is depicted as Queen of Heaven, in full apocalyptic glory, the "enemy" as a sort of heavenly Leviathan (who let him in there anyway?). It is not possible to interpret the apocalypse adequately for or on this occasion, and commentaries abound. The essential thing, of course, is that the dragon's efforts were unsuccessful.

The Magnificat was addressed in part in my treatment of the Visitation, May 31. Attention was given to parallels between Mary's song and Hannah's song (1 Sam. 2:1-10), not only as a literary and liturgical phenomenon, but as evidence of Luke's strategy for showing Mary, and later Jesus, as fully participating in the Judaism in which they lived and from which they emerged. The crucial themes of the Magnificat, praise of God, distrust of power, reversal of order, and God's care for the poor and oppressed, and the role the canticle played in introducing those themes in Luke/Acts, were duly noted.

Much more could and probably should be said, but about one thing in particular we may need to be reminded on this wonderful feast day. The Magnificat is Mary's song in praise of God, not our song in praise of Mary—that is Elizabeth's song, "Blessed are you among women, and blessed is the fruit of your womb. And why has this happened to me, that the mother of my Lord comes to me? . . . And blessed is she who believed that there would be a fulfillment of what was spoken to her by the Lord" (Luke 1:42-43, 45). The actions Mary praises—scattering the proud, bringing down the mighty, lifting up the lowly, and feeding the hungry—are God's acts, acts that Mary's words implicitly invite us to emulate.

Preaching the Feast of Mary / Feast of the Assumption

Finally, when blessed Mary, having completed the course of her earthly life, was about to be called from this world, all the apostles, coming from their different regions, gathered together in her house. . . . And behold, the Lord Jesus came with his angels and, taking her soul, handed it over to the archangel Michael, and withdrew. At dawn, the apostles lifted up her body on a pallet, laid it in a tomb, and kept watch over it. . . . And behold, the Lord presented himself to them and ordered that her holy body be taken and carried up to heaven.
–Gregory of Tours[1]

I am not a dogmatic theologian, in both senses of the adjective. Nor, as an Anglican, is the Assumption of Mary a binding doctrine of my faith. But I get it, just as I "get" what the *Protevangelium of James* intends by postulating the immaculate conception of Mary. On a very simple and basic level there is no claim too great for the mother of our Lord. From her conception until after her death, she was unique among women, the *theotokos*.

The doctrine of the Assumption of Mary, and the feast in its celebration, along with the Immaculate Conception, provide theological and liturgical frames around all that we want to say about Blessed Mary. Perhaps the insights of a Roman Catholic theologian, Edward Schillebeeckx, will be helpful: "Her assumption into heaven was not merely a privilege bestowed on her without relation to the rest of her life. It formed the summit of her sublime redemption. Salvation, after all, embraces the *whole* human being, not only his soul but also his body."[2] Schillebeeckx's reading, like most others, recognizes the assumption of Mary's body, after death, as a type of the resurrection. So also Karl Rahner: "The Church looks on high and greets in Mary her own type and model, her own future in the resurrection of the body."[3] In other words, the assumption of Mary is not discontinuous from God's promise to all the faithful, but a symbol of the same. It is another first fruit for all who confess, at the end of baptismal creed, "I believe in . . . the resurrection of the body."

This is particularly important for readings of Mary like that of Elizabeth Johnson, who does not discuss the Assumption in *Truly Our Sister*, perhaps because the doctrine tends to highlight Mary's uniqueness in ways that set her apart from human experience so that her own historicity is lost. But if we understand the Assumption's importance not for Marian ideology, but as a symbolic foretaste of the resurrection promised to all faithful departed, this concern is appropriately ameliorated.

For Protestants, and I expect for Catholics as well, August 15 will be about much more than disputations over the fate of Mary's body at her death. It will be a celebration of all that Mary was and is. Some of this is captured in the incredibly rich vocabulary we use to express our devotions, from "BVM" ("Blessed Virgin Mary") to *theotokos*, from Miriam of Nazareth to "Queen of Heaven." My own evolving homiletical Marian theology joins Johnson in focusing on Mary as historical figure, who voluntarily chose to join God on the path God invited her to walk, was thoroughly connected to her own Jewish heritage, and invites us, and meets us, in community.

> Our Lady continues to be alluring, calling all the hurting, disfigured, and disinherited to herself. It is like the call of Jesus: "Come to me all of you who are tired and weary, and I will refresh you." Her gentleness, evident concern, and compassionate love are the source of her re-creating power.
> —Virgil Elizondo[4]

The blessings of Mary are indescribable, but we try. However theologians try to express it, the faithful will, in the particularity of their devotion, transcend what language fails to capture, and will do so in a vast array of culturally specific ways. It is not just Mary, it is the "Black Madonna" ("Our Lady of Czestochowa, Poland") and a long list of other country and culture-specific appropriations. I confess that *La Virgen de Guadalupe* holds a special place in my heart, and I remind us of her by way of example and homiletical suggestion.

Guadalupe is important for a host of reasons, her story empowering indigenous peoples in the Americas, immigrants in the United States, and the faithful around the world for centuries since her appearance to Juan Diego at Tepeyac in 1531. Like most culturally specific apparitions and stories, *La Virgen* transcends her own story. In the briefest possible sketch, recall that in the age of the *conquistadores* Mary appeared to an Indian man, and asked him to go to the bishop in nearby Mexico City and tell him that Mary desired a shrine be built on Mt. Tepeyac.

Juan Diego, meeting great resistance because he was indigenous, persevered, and eventually, through a miraculous flowering, was able to convince the recalcitrant bishop. The story is itself important as a document of liberation,[5] but it is the appropriation and the particular identification of the Guadalupe with the aspirations and needs of oppressed persons that matters most.

"The Guadalupe vision is not something totally new, " writes Virgil Elizondo, "for it is simply the ideal of the kingdom of God as lived and proclaimed by Jesus. This is the lifestyle and ideal that he died for. . . . What is uniquely new in Guadalupe is that it advances our understanding of Christianity in some very refreshing and stimulating ways."[6] Elizondo goes on to identify five advances in our understanding:

• It is about truth itself. "Guadalupe is the truth about truth itself. . . . According to the Guadalupan vision, truth exists in the relational, the interconnected, the beautiful, and the melodic" (116).

• It is about evangelization and faith. "We might summarize the evangelizing method, expression, and fervor of the Guadalupe process by stating that it proceeded by the way of beauty, initiated a gradual dialogue, was most respectful of the evangelized, and empowered them with new life" (119).

• It is about God. "The most fascinating aspect of Guadalupe is that it introduces us to a more comprehensive and open-ended concept of God—a mestizo God. In Our Lady, the Spanish and Nahuatl concepts of God are beautifully combined to present us with an understanding of God that is fuller than either one of them had suspected" (124).

• It is about Christ and the new humanity. "The redemption of the New World begins at Tepeyac . . . not a 'new' world that would simply rebuild the old ways . . . but a new world that would be authentically new because of its inclusion of all the peoples of all the Americas as children of the one Mother" (128–29).

• It is about the triune God. "Our Lady of Guadalupe does not suggest a new doctrine. Rather, she offers alternative basic imagery for this doctrine so that it might be better understood, appreciated and loved . . . she illumines the indwelling of the Blessed Trinity—the mystery of God—through the image of the Mother who sends the child to call the Father so that together they may create a new home for everyone" (130–31).

The Holy Trinity, God, Jesus, evangelism, and truth itself. Not bad. And not just Guadalupe. Mary in her many appearances throughout history and culture has done what Mary in the New Testament did: served as an exemplar by the model of her own faith, bringing God into history through her own body. The call for preaching on this feast day is to join Mary in your own particularity, and that of your community.

Additional comments on these Scripture texts, in part or in full, may be found in the seasonal volumes of *New Proclamation* as follows:

- Isaiah 61:7-11—Year B, Advent 3
- Psalm 34—Year A, All Saints; Year B, Proper 14, Proper 15, Proper 16, Proper 25
- Psalm 45—Year A, Proper 9; Year B, Proper 17
- Galatians 4:4-7—Year B, Christmas 1
- Luke 1:39-57—Year C, Advent 4; Years A & B, Advent 3

Notes

1. Gregory of Tours, *Libri Miraculorum,* cited in *Mary and the Fathers of the Church,* ed. Luigi Gambero, S.M., trans. Thomas Buffer (San Francisco: Ignatius, 1999).

2. Edward Schillebeeckx, *Mary, Mother of the Redemption,* trans. N. D. Smith (New York: Sheed and Ward, 1964), 76. Emphasis in original.

3. Karl Rahner, *Mary Mother of the Lord* (New York: Herder and Herder, 1963), 92.

4. Perhaps the best English text of the story of La Virgen and Juan Diego (*Nican Mopohua*) is found in Virgil Elizondo, *Guadalupe: Mother of the New Creation* (Maryknoll, N.Y.: Orbis, 1997), 122.

5. Elizondo, *Guadalupe,* 5–22.

6. Elizondo, *Guadalupe,* 115.

BARTHOLOMEW, APOSTLE

August 24

Ruth A. Meyers

Lutheran (ELW)	Episcopal (BCP)	Roman Catholic (LFM)
Exod. 19:1–6	Deut. 18:15–18	Rev. 21:9b–14
Psalm 12	Psalm 91 or 91:1–4	Ps. 145:10–13, 17–18
1 Cor. 12:27–31a	1 Cor. 4:9–15	
John 1:43–51	Luke 22:24–30	John 1:45–51

KEY THEMES

- In his encounter with Jesus, Bartholomew, also known as Nathanael, recognizes him as the one who fulfills the Old Testament prophecies.
- As an apostle, Bartholomew had a central role in building the church, even though little is known of his life and ministry.
- The ministry of the apostles comes from God.

The Saint

Bartholomew ranks among the more obscure of the twelve apostles. In the New Testament, his name appears only in the lists of the Twelve (Matt. 10:3; Mark 3:18; Luke 6:14; Acts 1:13). Despite the absence of scriptural detail, stories of Bartholomew's apostolic ministry and his death circulated during the Middle Ages.

By the ninth century, Christians began to speculate that Bartholomew is to be identified with the Nathanael who appears in the first chapter of John's Gospel. The Synoptic Gospels all list the name Bartholomew in conjunction with that of Philip, while according to John, Philip brought Nathanael to Jesus (John 1:45ff.). Not only is Philip thus closely associated with Bartholomew in the Synoptics and with Nathanael in John, the Synoptics never mention Nathanael, while John never mentions Bartholomew. The discrepancy in the name can be explained as a difference in systems of naming: "Bartholomew" is a patronymic meaning "son of Tolmai," and it is possible that the same person could have been known by the personal name "Nathanael."

Identifying Bartholomew with Nathanael adds a scrap of scripturally based bio-graphical detail to this otherwise unknown apostle. The stories of Bartholomew's ministry and martyrdom, however, show no trace of this identification.

Bartholomew is most commonly said to have preached the gospel first in India and then in Armenia, although other accounts place him in Mesopotamia, Persia, Egypt, and Ethiopia, or in Bosporus, Phrygia, and Lycaonia, all regions of modern-day Turkey. According to the fourth-century church historian Euse-bius, when the evangelist Pantaenus traveled to India in the second century, he found people who already knew of Christ. They showed Pantaenus a copy of the Gospel of Matthew in the Hebrew language, which they said Bartholomew had left with them. In the seventh century, stories about Bartholomew began to circulate in Armenia. According to one account, Bartholomew baptized the cousin of the king of Persia along with three thousand others and founded a church dedicated to the *Theotokos* (Mary the God-bearer). This and other stories of Bartholomew's ministry in Armenia supported a claim to apostolicity for the church in Armenia. Some accounts report that Bartholomew first preached in India, then went to Armenia, where he was martyred.

Various stories are told regarding the manner of Bar-tholomew's death. He is often said to have been flayed alive by King Astyages in the city of Albanopolis in Arme-nia. Most scholars suggest that this story is based upon the mythical story of Marsyas, the flute player who lost a contest with the god Apollo and was flayed alive. Other stories, however, report that Bartholomew was crucified head down, and still others, that he was beheaded. Some combine these, saying that Bartholomew was first cruci-fied, then taken down and flayed to increase his suffering, and finally beheaded. The story of his flaying captured medieval imaginations. Bartholomew is custom-arily depicted carrying a large knife and wearing his own skin over his arm, as, for example, in Michaelangelo's *Last Judgment* in the Sistine Chapel. He is considered the patron saint of tanners.

Hail, O blessed of the blessed, thrice blessed Bartholomew! You are the splen-dor of Divine light, the fisherman of holy church, expert catcher of fish endowed with reason, sweet fruit of the bloom-ing palm tree! You wound the devil who wounds the world by his crimes! May you rejoice, O sun illumining the whole earth, mouth of God, tongue of fire that speaks wisdom, fountain ever flowing with health! You have sanctified the sea by your passage over it, you have purpled the earth with your gore, you have mounted to heaven, where you shine in the midst of the heav-enly host, resplendent in the splendor of undimmable glory! Rejoice in the enjoy-ment of inexhaustible happiness!
—Theodore the Studite[1]

In death as in life Bartholomew is reputed to have traveled widely. First buried in Armenia, where he is thought to have been martyred, his relics became the site of many miracles. Dismayed by the veneration of his body occasioned by these miracles, non-Christian Armenians placed Bartholomew's remains in a lead coffin and cast them into the sea. They reached the island of Lipari, off the coast of Sic-ily, and Bartholomew's remains were enshrined there. After the Saracens invaded

Sicily in the ninth century, Bartholomew's bones were scattered, then gathered by a faithful monk and sent to Benevento in southern Italy. Later, his relics were translated to Rome for safekeeping. In the eleventh century, Queen Emma, wife of King Canute, presented one of Bartholomew's arms to Canterbury Cathedral. The cathedral in Frankfurt, Germany, is said to possess Bartholomew's skull.

THE GOSPEL
JOHN 1:43-51 (ELW, LFM)

By appointing this Gospel, the Roman Catholic and Lutheran lectionaries adopt the tradition that identifies Bartholomew as Nathanael, son of Tolmai. The preacher who draws upon this text will probably want to make explicit that identification, without belaboring the explanation. The Gospel can then be interpreted as the story of this apostle's call to follow Christ.

The first chapter of John's Gospel concludes with the call of the first disciples: Andrew, who brings his brother Simon Peter (John 1:35-42), and, the next day, Philip, who finds Nathanael and leads him to Jesus. Philip's introduction—"we have found him about whom Moses in the law and also the prophets wrote" (John 1:44)—emphasizes that Jesus fulfills the Old Testament prophecies. Jesus describes Nathanael as "an Israelite in whom there is no deceit" (v. 47), linking Nathanael to the patriarch Jacob. Whereas Jacob deceived his aged father Isaac and cheated his brother Esau out of their father's blessing (Genesis 27), Jesus proclaims Nathanael to be free of deceit. Moreover, while Jacob had a vision in which angels were ascending and descending a ladder reaching to heaven (Gen. 28:11-12), Jesus promises that Nathanael will actually see the angels ascend and descend upon the Son of man, that is, on Jesus himself, who becomes the place of God's revelation. In this final verse of the chapter, the Greek shifts to plural forms of "you"; others besides Nathanael will witness this sight. Nathanael thus represents Israel's coming to God.

> O Christ, you have deigned wondrously to show your majesty to your disciples who preach to the world your trinity in the one divinity! Among those preachers your benign foresight directed blessed Bartholomew, whom you honored with a special gift of virtues, to a far distant people, and that people, remote from you as they had been in their human affairs, he merited, by his increased preaching, to bring close to you. Oh, with what praises this wonderful apostle should be celebrated!
> —St. Ambrose[2]

Nathanael also embodies the movement from doubt to faith. When Philip first introduces Jesus as the "son of Joseph from Nazareth," Nathanael questions whether anything good can come from Nazareth. Yet he accepts Philip's invitation to see for himself, and upon meeting Jesus, affirms his identity as Son of God and King of Israel.

LUKE 22:24-30 (BCP)

The medieval Sarum missal appointed Luke 22:24-30 for the feast of Bartholomew, and subsequent Anglican liturgical revisions have maintained this traditional Gospel. Although the passage does not refer specifically to Bartholomew, as one of the Twelve he would have been among those whom Jesus addresses here.

Matthew, Mark, and Luke all tell of the disciples' disputes about which of them was the greatest; only Luke places this narrative in the context of the Last Supper. This setting underscores the contrast between the disciples' worldly ambitions and Jesus' impending self-offering on the cross. As is often the case in the Gospels, the disciples fail to understand the true nature of Jesus' life and ministry, even after Jesus tells them that his body is given for them. His reference to the manner in which the Gentiles exercised authority would have resonated deeply with the disciples, who would have had significant experience of the harsh manner of Roman oversight in ancient Palestine.

Lest the preacher leap too quickly to a call to servant ministry, Jesus' exhortation that the disciples imitate his example of servanthood leads immediately to his promise to confer a kingdom on them. True exaltation is a gift of God, bestowed not according to the world's standards but as a reward for enduring trials with Jesus. The disciples will be granted a place at the heavenly banquet and moreover will reign with Christ. The reference to the twelve tribes of Israel hints at the restoration of the people of Israel. In this context, "judging" the tribes of Israel might best be understood as leading or ruling rather than as passing judgment.

Kontakion

You have appeared to the universe as a
    great sun,
shining with the radiance of your
teachings and awesome miracles.
You enlighten those who honor you,
    apostle of the Lord, Bartholomew.
—Translation of the Relics of the Holy
Apostle Bartholomew[3]

THE READINGS

EXODUS 19:1-6 (ELW)
1 CORINTHIANS 12:27-31A (ELW)
DEUTERONOMY 18:15-18(BCP)
1 CORINTHIANS 4:9-15 (BCP)
REVELATION 21:9B-14 (LFM)

In various ways, each of the non-Gospel readings for this feast speaks of God's call or of the work of apostles. The passage from Exodus introduces the theophany at Sinai, in which God appears in thunder, lightening, and thick clouds, then gives the Ten Commandments to Moses. Throughout, Moses acts as intermediary between God and the people. In the appointed selection, God speaks in lyrical language, promising a unique covenant relationship with the people of Israel if they will obey God. This offer of a covenant begins and ends with God's command for Moses to speak these words to the people of Israel.

While Exodus refers to God's appointment of Moses, the selection from Deuteronomy speaks of prophets who will follow in the tradition of Moses. Just as God spoke through Moses, so too God will raise up other prophets who will speak in God's name. The passage is part of a larger segment of Deuteronomy that introduces regulations for many aspects of Israel's life. Prophets were an integral part, serving as intermediaries who like Moses helped discern and convey God's word.

The selections from the New Testament introduce aspects of apostolic leadership. In 1 Corinthians, Paul is addressing a fractious Christian community whose members claimed allegiance to different leaders and so had different understandings of the implications of the Gospel. The passage appointed from chapter 4 utilizes irony and exaggeration to rebuke the Corinthians, although Paul assures them that he does not want to shame them but rather to admonish them. By pairing this reading with the Lukan passage on servanthood, the Episcopal lectionary emphasizes the costly character of apostolic life.

Troparion

O wise Bartholomew
　　thy holy relics appeared like the dawn
　　shining in the East and coming to the West.
They shine with the gifts
　　of the Daystar of life
　　and dispel the darkness of diseases
　　from those who approach them with
　　faith and hope.
—Translation of the Relics of the Holy
Apostle Bartholomew[4]

In contrast, the Lutheran lectionary appoints the concluding verses of chapter 12, Paul's teaching on spiritual gifts. The rhetorical questions in these verses underscore Paul's metaphor of the body of Christ, in which God bestows a diversity of gifts and ministries that work together for the common good. Among those whom God appoints are apostles.

Earlier versions of the Roman lectionary also appointed 1 Corinthians 12, but the 1969 lectionary introduced a passage from Revelation that describes the heavenly Jerusalem. The vision of splendor is a promise of restoration for Israel and for the church. Inscribed on the twelve foundations of the city are the names of the twelve apostles, highlighting their importance for the church.

PREACHING APPROACHES

The lectionaries that appoint John 1 as the Gospel draw our attention to call and response to Jesus. Nathanael Bartholomew—Nathanael son of Tolmai—is not named or presented here as an apostle, sent to proclaim the message of Jesus. Rather, this is a story of his movement from doubt to faith. Jesus appears from a surprising place, the small village of Nazareth, and yet he is the one promised by

Moses and the prophets. Nathanael responds to Jesus' insight, and he joins Philip, Andrew, and Peter in the circle of disciples, followers of Jesus. To Nathanael Jesus promises revelation of God's greatness.

The readings from 1 Corinthians and Revelation introduce the term *apostle*, and a preacher may find it profitable to reflect upon the importance of the apostles even when, as with Bartholomew, we know nothing certain of their ministry or field of missionary endeavor. The church is "apostolic," in continuity with Christ and the apostles, faithful to the teaching of the apostles, proclaiming the gospel in word and deed, carrying out Christ's commands to baptize and to share in the Eucharist.

The Episcopal lectionary nudges a preacher to ponder the meaning of service. Though Bartholomew's name is preserved among the apostles listed in the Gospels, he is largely anonymous, a reminder that most Christians minister in relative obscurity. What is important is not any worldly standard of greatness, but faithfulness to Christ even in times of suffering. This is not a call to eschew any exercise of authority, nor a glamorization of suffering. Rather, true authority comes from God, who enables Christians to withstand their trials.

FOR FURTHER COMMENT

Additional comments on these Scripture texts, in part or in full, may be found in the seasonal volumes of *New Proclamation* as follows:

- Exodus 19:1-6—Year A, Proper 6
- Deuteronomy 18:15-18—Year B, Epiphany 4
- Psalm 91—Year B, Proper 24; Year C, Lent 1, Proper 21
- Psalm 145—Year A, Propers 9, 13; Year B, Proper 12; Year C, Proper 27
- 1 Corinthians 12:27-31a—Year C, Epiphany 3
- John 1:43-51—Year B, Epiphany 2
- Luke 22:24-30—Year C, Passion/Palm Sunday

Notes

1. Attributed to Theodore the Studite, as reported by Jacobus de Voragine, *The Golden Legend: Readings on the Saints*, trans. William Granger Ryan (Princeton: Princeton University Press, 1993), 2:116.

2. Attributed to Ambrose, as reported by Jacobus de Voragine, *The Golden Legend*, 2:114.

3. http://orthodoxwiki.org/Apostle_Bartholomew#Hymns (accessed June 19, 2007).

4. http://users.netmatters.co.uk/davidbryant/C/TropKon/Aug.htm#Aug25 (accessed June 19, 2007).

THE NATIVITY OF THE
BLESSED VIRGIN MARY (LFM)

SEPTEMBER 8

GERARD S. SLOYAN

ROMAN CATHOLIC (LFM)
Mic. 5:1-4a or Rom. 8:28-30
Ps. 12:6ab, 6cd
Matt. 1:1-16, 18-23 or 1:18-23

KEY THEMES

- The only story of Mary's coming to birth is apocryphal.
- This is a Christ feast, like all the Mary feasts.
- The Temple stood and was in daily cultic use while Jesus was being experienced as the Risen One by his friends.

Only three feasts in the calendar of East and West mark the person's day of birth. All other feasts of sainted persons are the date of their departure to the life everlasting. The nativity feasts of exception are the Christ Mass, December 25; the birth of John the Baptist on June 24; and of Mary, the mother of Jesus, on this day, September 8. The first documents testifying to a celebration of the Birth of the Blessed Virgin Mary, obviously nine months after the feast of her conception on December 8 (paralleled by the Annunciation–Christmas interval of the same length) are sermons by Andrew of Crete (ca. 660–740), a native of Damascus. The better-known St. John of that city who outlived him by some fifteen years also left a homily preached on today's feast. The birth of the Baptist may have played its part in introducing an observance of our Lady's birthday. Previous to any known eucharistic celebration on this day Pope Sergius I (689–701), Palermo-born but of Greek parents, had ordered solemn processions to the Church of Santa Maria Maggiore on the Mary feasts of her Nativity, Annunciation, Falling Asleep (Dormition) on August 15, and Purification on February 2, much later denominated the Presentation of Jesus in the Temple. The mention of Pope Sergius's introducing the festal observances occurs in the *Liber Pontificalis*, short biographies of bishops of Rome begun in 354 and successively edited down to 1431 and beyond.

MATTHEW 1:1-16, 18-23 OR 1:18-23

The *Roman Missal* of 1570 chose the first sixteen verses of Matthew's chapter 1, as above, for its Gospel reading. Its culmination with Joseph's father Jacob and his wife Mary is the evident reason. The modern lectionary proposes the lector's continuing the story of "how the birth of Jesus came about" (v. 18) through verse 23 or favoring that shorter pericope over the preceding genealogical table of thirteen names with Jesus the fourteenth. It is well known that the source of neither Matthew nor Luke's list of names from the exile down to Joseph is discoverable. The names of the ancestors before the exile appear in 1 Chronicles 1–2, Ruth 4:18-22, and a few other places in the four Books of Kingdoms. As to whether Jesus should be accounted in David's royal line if he were not of Joseph's blood, the fact that Jewish family lines were reckoned through the males does not alone do it. It is Joseph's taking Mary into his house and naming the child, according to the angel's instruction in a dream (Matt. 1:20-21), that makes him Jesus' father at Mosaic Law. As to the familiar difficulty of this evangelist's citing Isaiah in the Greek of the Septuagint, which speaks of a virgin as *parthenos* (v. 23), the normal word for a young woman of marriageable age, whereas the prophet's word in the Hebrew text is, *almah* (Isa. 7:14), not the *bethûlah* of physical virginity, it is the Septuagint translators of another than the Masoretic text who are to be faulted for speaking *koinē*, that is, everyday Greek. Matthew's intention is the same as Luke's here, to specify that Joseph is not the child's natural father.

The only story of Mary's coming to birth is totally apocryphal, that is, spurious. It is from the First (or Original) Gospel of James, thought by nineteenth-century scholarship to come from the third century but, on the evidence of more recently discovered papyri, to come from the fourth.[1] In it Joachim, a very rich man, and his wife Anna are elderly and childless. She bemoans her inability to bear a child until two messengers come to tell her that an angel has come to Joachim, out with his flocks in the field, to say that she will conceive and bear. The child Mary's growth and progress is recorded as at the ages of six months and one year. The whole tale is built on the Samuel story more than any biblical narrative, with snatches of Mary's own conceiving of Jesus, while her virginity is described as retained throughout. This "Gospel" is more sober in its telling than many that came later and is entirely committed to glorifying Mary, especially against what may have been slanders of her at the age of the writing.

THE READINGS

MICAH 5:1–4A OR ROMANS 8:28–30
PSALM 12:6AB, 6CD

The 1570 *Missal* ordered by the Council of Trent had employed the Wisdom [of Solomon] 8:22–35 as its only other reading. This means that it had had a place on the feast day going back to the Middle Ages. *Lectionary for Mass* of 1969 was doubtless sensitive to the fact that God's wisdom who was "with him before the mountains were brought forth, . . . playing with him . . ." all the while the earth and sea and sky were being formed, was better applied as a type to Christ than to Mary. LFM replaced it with an option of the Micah or the Romans reading. *Micah 5:1–4a* predicts a mother of David's city, Bethlehem-Ephrathah, who will give birth to a ruler in Israel who shall "shepherd his flock by the strength of the LORD" (v. 4). This establishes, as do all the Mary feasts in the Roman calendar, that this is a Christ feast. She begins in her canticle of wonderment with the words "My soul magnifies the Lord," in the Vulgate *Magnificat anima mea Dominum* (Luke 1:46). There is nothing of herself in her role of motherhood of her divine human Son.

This radiant and manifest coming of God to men most certainly needed a joyful prelude to introduce the great gift of salvation to us. The present festival, the birth of the Mother of God, is the prelude, while the final act is the fore-ordained union of the Word with flesh. Today the Virgin is born, tended and formed and prepared for her role as Mother of God, who is the universal King of the ages. —St. Andrew of Crete[2]

Romans 8:28–30 is by all means a less cryptic lection than Micah as it speaks of God's "predestining of some to be in the image of his Son." The *Psalm* snatch *(12:6)* in response to either is beyond comprehension in any English translation from the Hebrew but is thoroughly *Magnificat*-like in the Septuagint or Jerome's Latin from another Hebrew text of this book, namely that Christ acted as high priest and unblemished victim in offering his blood in redemptive sacrifice. An important question for Christianity is how the apostolic church arrived so soon and so sure-footedly at the conviction that Jesus crucified and risen did for all humanity, Jew and non-Jew alike, what God had appointed to be done for Israel in Jerusalem's temple. If its structure had been reduced to ruin immediately following Jesus' uprising from the dead the apostolic company might well have conceived his self-offering as the beginning of a new phase in the life of his people. Once it was learned that death could not hold him, that could have been their conclusion. The Temple was down, he was up. But we have no assurance that the Temple had been leveled by Roman power before a small band of unlettered men from the north concluded that a thoroughly new age had been inaugurated with his uprising from the dead. Rather, the opposite is true: It stood and was in daily cultic use while Jesus was being experienced as the Risen One by his friends.

We can date Jesus' death and resurrection fairly accurately in the year 30. Even if that were sure, it would not contribute much to the dating of any New Testament writing. Two mistakes we should avoid that generations of the learned before us have not avoided are that it took several decades for the early church in Galilee and Jerusalem to arrive at the meaning of the events that they had recently been through. A second pitfall is that the Jews who had experienced the remarkable, brief public life, death, and resurrection of one of their number needed Greek categories of philosophy and pagan religions to arrive at a satisfactory interpretation of the events. A thoroughgoing familiarity with Israel's history as conveyed in its holy books was sufficient. And the interpreters need not have resided in the land of Israel to come to some correct conclusions. Diaspora Judaism was well equal to this task as the writings called Gospels and Paul, a native of a Gentile-majority city and of probable long Damascus residence, showed. None of the four Gospels was written by a native of 'eretz Yisrael but this did not hinder any of the four from mastering the life of their Jewish people in their native place, whatever their travels might have been in the spread of the gospel. That the four knew their people's Scriptures primarily in the Greek version known as the Septuagint is clear, with apparent knowledge by one or another of a passage from a Hebrew version or an Aramaic *targum*.

> Thy birth, O Virgin Mother of God, heralded joy to all the world. For from thee hast risen the Sun of justice, Christ our God. Destroying the curse, He gave blessing; and damning death, He bestowed on us life everlasting. Blessed art thou among women and blessed is the fruit of thy womb. For from thee hast risen Sun of justice, Christ our God.
> —From *The Divine Office–Matins* (Morning Prayer)[3]

FOR FURTHER COMMENT

Additional comments on these Scripture texts, in part or in full, may be found in the seasonal volumes of *New Proclamation* as follows:

- Micah 5:1-4a—Year C, Advent 4
- Romans 8:28-30—Year A, Proper 12
- Matthew 1:1-16, 18-23—Year A, Advent 4

Notes

1. For the full text in translation, see Bart D. Ehrman, *Lost Scriptures* (Oxford: Oxford University Press, 2003), 63–72; based principally on Émile de Stryker, *Forme la plus ancienne du Protoévangelium de Jacques* (Brussels: Bollandistes, 1961).

2. Living Water Community, The Nativity of the Blessed Virgin Mary, http://www.livingwatercommunity.com/virgin/nativity_of_the_virgin.htm (accessed May 24, 2007).

3. Ibid.

HOLY CROSS DAY (ELW/BCP)/ THE EXALTATION OF THE CROSS (LFM)

SEPTEMBER 14

GAIL RAMSHAW

REVISED COMMON	EPISCOPAL (BCP)	ROMAN CATHOLIC (LFM)
Num. 21:4b–9	Isa. 45:21–25	Num. 21:4b–9
Ps. 98:1-5 or 78:1-2, 34-38	Psalm 98 or 98:1-4	Ps. 78:1-2, 34-35, 36-37, 38
1 Cor. 1:18-24	Phil. 2:5-11 or Gal. 6:14-18	Phil. 2:6-11
John 3:13-17	John 12:31-36a	John 3:13-17

KEY THEMES

• Holy Cross Day commemorates the dedication in 335 of the Basilica of the Holy Sepulchre in Jerusalem.
• The cross we revere is on the forehead of every baptized person.
• Holy Cross Day reminds us of the paradox of Christ, the everlasting surprise of God.

THE DAY

In the fourth century, Emperor Constantine, having established Christianity as an approved religion in the Roman Empire, set about to build magnificent churches for public worship. Holy Cross Day, September 14, which the Eastern churches call the Exaltation of the Holy Cross, commemorates the dedication in 335 of the Basilica of the Holy Sepulchre in Jerusalem, one of the edifices that Constantine commissioned. The basilica was constructed on land that was purported to be the hill of Calvary and the place of Christ's tomb, thus a most sacred site for Christians. To recall this day of dedication is to thank God for also our own church edifices and for the cross of Christ we can praise therein.

The day has a second layer to its story. A decade before the basilica was constructed, Constantine's mother, Queen Helena, had traveled to the Holy Land for a kind of archaeological dig, and in the excavations she found what she believed

178

to be the True Cross. The story goes that she knew which one of the three crosses that had been exhumed was Christ's, because it raised to life a corpse upon which it was laid. This cross was then regularly displayed in Jerusalem during Holy Week. A pilgrim named Egeria wrote some decades later that guards were stationed on both sides of the cross to keep the faithful from biting off a piece of the cross and taking it home with them. For already there had begun a relic trade in what were called "fragments of the True Cross." When in the sixth century the nun Radegund acquired for her convent in Poitiers, France, one such fragment of the True Cross, she asked a poet whom we call Fortunatus, who lived at the convent, to compose a hymn in honor of the cross. His hymns "*Vexilla Regis*" ("The royal banners forward go") and "*Pange, lingua*" ("Sing, my tongue"), which praise the cross as a life-giving tree, are still sung by many Christians, especially during Holy Week.

Each year many churches repeat the ancient ritual described by Egeria when on Good Friday they observe some version of the veneration of the cross. Although it is now common for the youth group to construct the cross from raw timbers, in medieval times it was believed that the cross that was venerated had affixed to it one of these fragments of the True Cross. To recall this history and its legend on this day is to realize that Christianity is not in fact a pilgrimage religion. We are not obligated to walk to Jerusalem to kiss a cross, for Christ himself is in our midst each time we gather, wherever we are. The cross we revere is on the forehead of every baptized person.

The day has yet a third layer to its story. A medieval legend narrated a charming tale of how the cross of Christ could have raised the dead to life. The story goes that when Adam died, an angel ordered his son, Seth, to plant a sprig from Eden's tree of life in Adam's grave. Over the centuries there grew up a tree that was able to perform miracles. Finally—you guessed it—the tree was cut down and its wood was used to make the cross of Calvary.

> This cross is the tree of my eternal salvation, my nourishment when I am hungry, my fountain when I am thirsty. . . . It is the ladder of Jacob, the pillar of the universe, the support of the whole world. —Anonymous third-century homily[1]

Thus the cross was both figuratively and literally praised as the tree of life. You might want to read to the children this legend, most easily found in the beautifully illustrated picture book by Brian Wildsmith, *The True Cross*.[2] Rehearsing this legend in our day superimposes in our minds the image of the tree of life onto the cross of Christ. Many medieval churches depicted the cross as a verdant tree, and we are seeing this very layering of images becoming popular once again. At ecclesiastical goods shops, one can now purchase a cross on which is a corpus of a dying man, or one entwined with leafy branches, flowers, and fruits. Both crosses mean to proclaim the same truth: the cross is our tree of life.

THE GOSPEL

JOHN 3:13-17 (RCL, LFM)
JOHN 12:31-36A (BCP)

A paradox is a claim that seems to be wrong, but we discover it to be true. All the various readings suggested by the three lectionary systems seek to proclaim the paradox that the cross is the tree of life. What we assumed was an instrument for the death of one man is lauded as the source of life for the whole world.

The Gospel choice from John 3 is part of the Johannine narrative of Jesus' conversation with Nicodemus. The Son of God will indeed be lifted up, Jesus tells Nicodemus, but not in the mythic manner of a Son of man, a mystical figure positioned in the sky halfway between earth and heaven, from there to judge us all. No, says Jesus, the Son will be lifted up onto the cross, from there to save us all.

The Gospel choice from John 12 employs the same image: Christ will be lifted up to draw all people to himself. The darkness that we associate with Christ's death on the cross is actually the light of the world. It is not surprising that we read from John on Holy Cross Day, for John's Gospel more than the other three develops the paradoxes of Christian faith. Classic religion is used to speaking as if God is up. Yes, writes John, Christ is up, but we need look no higher than the cross. Yes, Jesus dies, but in that death is life for us all.

THE READINGS

NUMBERS 21:4B-9 (RCL, LFM)
ISAIAH 45:21-45 (BCP)

For those who read from John 3, the first reading is from Numbers 21. One of the ways that first readings are chosen is to cite the Old Testament passage that the Gospel itself quotes. That John 3 comments on this passage from the Pentateuch reminds us that all Christian reading of the New Testament is dependent on the Old Testament. We use the Hebrew Scriptures in a different way than do the various groups of contemporary Jews; we hope to use these Scriptures respectfully of their other interpretations; but we must use the Old Testament in order to make any sense of Christian proclamation. John's Gospel cites the story of the serpent in the wilderness as a picture of healing that comes from the most unlikely of places, just as our life comes, most surprisingly, from the cross of Jesus' death.

The story in Numbers 21 seems to have enshrined a reinterpretation of a pre-Yahwist, or perhaps even anti-Yahwist, practice of goddess worship. Asherah, a popular Canaanite goddess of life, was commonly depicted as a tree, a pole, or a serpent on a tree or pole. Recall this same memory of Asherah behind the Eden story in Genesis 3. Even for us a serpent on a pole has become an icon for healing: think of our symbol for the medical profession. But the author of Numbers wants to praise the power of the Lord. Thus Asherah is forgotten. The plague from which the Israelites are suffering comes from God as punishment for the people's ingratitude. The healing also was credited to the Lord God. For the believing Israelite, a symbol of death has paradoxically brought life to God's people. For the fervent monotheist, what looked like the might of the Canaanite goddess is really the mercy of the Lord.

Probably the Johannine author did not know this history of goddess worship. Rather, he uses the ancient tale of the serpent that can heal us from serpents as a parallel to Jesus' cross, which as an instrument of death can save us from death. Divine death can swallow up our human

Behold the life-giving cross, on which
  was hung the Savior of the world.
Oh, come, let us worship him.
—The liturgy of Good Friday[3]

deaths. For Christians, there is nowhere that can grant us life but our God. "Turn to me and be saved," says *The Book of Common Prayer's* first reading from Isaiah 45. Only in Christ is our righteousness and strength. It is interesting that in Hinduism, Krishna, an incarnation of the god Vishnu, is always depicted as having bluish skin. One explanation for this tradition is that humans were dying of poison, and Krishna drank the poison. It turned him blue, but he lived, and so did the people. What is divine can eat death and live. So God takes our death onto the cross so that we can live.

PSALM 98 (BCP); 98:1-4 (RCL, BCP ALT.)
PSALM 78:1-2, 34-38 (RCL ALT., LFM)

The psalm appointed as the response to Numbers 21 sets us in yet another paradox. Psalm 98 is the psalm of Christmas Day, praising God as the victorious sovereign. We superimpose onto our image of Christ on the cross the picture of a king on a throne. The alternate selection from Psalm 78 reiterates the outline of Numbers 21, praising God for forgiving the people who were untrue to the covenant. God has every right to punish us, but, surprisingly, instead forgives. Lifted up on the cross, healing the people via a serpent, reigning from his execution, forgiving rather than snuffing us out: we Christians can use the ancient psalm as a song to proclaim Christ as the life of the world.

1 CORINTHIANS 1:18-24 (RCL)
PHILIPPIANS 2:5-11 (BCP); 2:6-11 (LFM)
GALATIANS 6:14-18 (BCP ALT.)

Because September 14 falls near the beginning of the Western academic year, Holy Cross Day has sometimes served as the inspiration for the start of school. Students are in school presumably to gain wisdom. Yet one of the second readings appointed for the day is vintage Paul describing the power of the cross. Not the Jewish expectation of miracles, and not the Greek preference for rational thought, but something surprising is the life of our religion: Christ is the power of God, the wisdom of God. To preach Christ crucified, the cross as the tree of life, is a stumbling block now as then, and judged as foolishness by countless people now as then. Although the epistles include much material that seems tangential to our lives, the text from 1 Corinthians is as pertinent to the twenty-first century as any text contained in the Bible.

The first-century hymn quoted in Philippians 2 is an alternate epistle reading. Yet again we encounter biblical texts proclaiming the paradox of our faith in Christ. The hymn praises God for giving up divine prerogatives; the sovereign for becoming a slave; God who exalted his Son on the cross. In response, we kneel before this Christ on his holy cross. Episcopalians have the option of a passage from Galatians 6. Our boasting is only in the cross of Christ: God is making all things new. Here is Christian paradox once more: for as we believe that God is speaking always newly to us in the assembly, we do well to wonder what will be new in our midst, surprising even Paul, the author of Galatians.

> Holy God, holy and only wise,
>   wisdom of great price,
>   you choose the way of folly:
> God the crucified:
>   yet we behold your wisdom.
> –Susan Briehl[4]

Christians did not depict the cross on walls or in sculpture or on pages until sometime in the fourth century, after Constantine had outlawed crucifixions and the memory of how disgusting and degrading was this method of execution had faded somewhat from people's minds. We who are accustomed to splendid artistic versions of the cross do well to recall the horror of the cross so that we can hold in the same picture with our Redeemer every suffering criminal, every bleeding victim, every one abandoned by respectable folk. For these suffering ones are perhaps better images of Christ than the gorgeous one hanging on our wall. Holy Cross Day is that reminder of the paradox of Christ, not what we thought, not what we prefer, not what we construct, but the everlasting surprise of God.

Yet we need for our crosses to suggest also the tree of life. In "The Dream of the Rood," a poem written over a thousand years ago in Anglo-Saxon, the poet dreams of the cross speaking. The dreamer sees the cross—the "rood"—as a brilliantly bejeweled processional cross in a church. But then the dreamer sees that the rubies are really drops of Christ's blood, and the cross tells of Christ climbing up onto it, from there to be the Ruler of the whole world. If our crosses are too pained, we need to turn the blood into rubies, or perhaps roses.[5]

FOR FURTHER COMMENT

Additional comments on these Scripture texts, in part or in full, may be found in the seasonal volumes of *New Proclamation* as follows:

- Numbers 21:4b-9—Year B, Lent 4
- Psalm 78—Year A, Proper 21, Proper 27
- Psalm 98—Year B, Easter 6; Year C, Proper 27, Proper 28; Years ABC, Christmas 3, Easter Vigil
- 1 Corinthians 1:18-24—Year A, Epiphany 4; Year B, Lent 3; Years ABC, Tuesday of Holy Week
- Philippians 2:5-11—Year A, Proper 21; Years ABC, Passion/Palm Sunday
- Galatians 6:14-18—Year C, Proper 9
- John 3:13-17—Year A, Lent 2; Year B, Lent 4, Trinity Sunday
- John 12:31-36a—Year B, Lent 5; Years ABC, Tuesday of Holy Week

Notes

1. Anonymous paschal homily, *The Paschal Mystery: Ancient Liturgies and Patristic Texts*, ed. A. Hamman (Staten Island, N.Y.: Alba House, 1969), 64–65.

2. Brian Wildsmith, *The True Cross* (New York: Oxford University Press, 1977).

3. "Behold the life-giving cross," liturgy for Good Friday, *Evangelical Lutheran Worship* (Minneapolis: Augsburg Fortress, 2006), 264.

4. Susan Briehl, "Holy God, Holy and Glorious," *Evangelical Lutheran Worship* (Minneapolis: Augsburg Fortress, 2006), 637.

5. "The Dream of the Rood," *The Earliest English Poems*, trans. and ed. Michael Alexander (Baltimore: Penguin Books, 1966), 103–10.

MATTHEW, APOSTLE AND EVANGELIST

SEPTEMBER 21

CRAIG A. SATTERLEE

LUTHERAN (ELW)	EPISCOPAL (BCP)	ROMAN CATHOLIC (LFM)
Ezek. 2:8—3:11	Prov. 3:1-6	Eph. 4:1-7, 11-13
Ps. 119:33-40	Ps. 119:33-40	Ps. 19:2-3, 4-5
Eph. 2:4-10	2 Tim. 3:14-17	
Matt. 9:9-13	Matt. 9:9-13	Matt. 9:9-13

KEY THEMES

• The vast mercy of God in Christ.
• Jesus not only eats with those the righteous consider outcasts and sinners; Jesus calls them to leadership in his church.
• The Gospel of Matthew's portrait of Jesus as the fulfillment of God's covenant with Israel.

ST. MATTHEW

The name Matthew appears in every list of the twelve apostles recorded in Scripture. In the Gospel that bears his name, Matthew was a tax collector for the Roman government in the city of Capernaum. In all likelihood, Matthew was born in Galilee and belonged to a Jewish family. Yet, as a tax collector, Matthew was despised by and excluded from Jewish community.

In Mark and Luke's Gospels, Levi is the tax collector whom Jesus calls to discipleship, not Matthew. In these Gospels, Matthew and Levi do not appear to be the same person, and Origen and other early Christian writers distinguished between these two characters. Nonetheless, some traditions conflate these two tax collectors by proposing that Levi was this disciple's original name, and the other disciples gave him the name Matthew, which in Hebrew means "gift from God," after he became one of Jesus' followers. Mark calls Levi the son of Alphaeus. Matthew, Mark, Luke, and Acts all identify Alphaeus as the father of the apostle James; otherwise Alphaeus is unknown.

We know little of Matthew's life after Jesus called him to be a disciple. Tradition suggests that Matthew was the eldest disciple, that he preached in Ethiopia and Persia, and died a martyr's death. Legend dramatizes Matthew's death as occurring either by fire or by sword.

Since the second century, Matthew has been identified as the author of the Gospel that bears his name. Yet, that Matthew the apostle is also the evangelist is open to debate. The Gospel according to Matthew itself offers no clues as to who wrote it, though the designation "according to Matthew" is quite old. Those supporting the apostle Matthew as the author of this Gospel point to routine touches of modesty that Matthew would include. For example, while Mark and Luke give the fourth pair of apostles as "Matthew and Thomas," the Gospel of Matthew gives them as "Thomas and Matthew." Assuming that Matthew and Levi are the same person, those who support Matthean authorship also note that, while Luke 5:29 explicitly states, and Mark 2:15 suggests, that Levi (Matthew) gave a banquet for Jesus, Matthew's description of the same banquet modestly does not indicate who the host was. On the other hand, Matthew's Gospel does not read like an eyewitness account. In fact, Matthew is thought by many scholars to contain material borrowed from Mark, something one would not expect an eyewitness to do, particularly since Mark's Gospel is not an eyewitness account either. Early Christian readers, hearing the Gospel ascribed to "Matthew," would naturally associate it with the apostle of that name. Thus the assumption that the apostle Matthew is also the evangelist becomes common very early in the church's life.

St. Matthew's Day is observed on November 16 in most Eastern churches, but the West has always observed it on September 21. Luther's German translation of the New Testament was published on St. Matthew's Day in 1522. Matthew's symbol as an evangelist is an angel; in art he is often depicted with sword and moneybag.

THE GOSPEL
MATTHEW 9:9-13 (ELW, BCP, LFM)

Matthew 9:9-13 recounts Matthew's call to discipleship and the dispute that arises during the dinner party at Matthew's house. The pattern of the story is common. Jesus forgives, accepts, heals, or, in this case, calls to discipleship. Someone considered righteous objects. Then Jesus makes a pronouncement. Perhaps this pattern can provide the movement of the sermon on this saint's day.

Passing by the tax booth, Jesus sees Matthew and commands him to follow. In response to Jesus' command, Matthew immediately leaves the tax office and follows. The point is that Jesus' authoritative word makes disciples, and it was this, not any supposed previous contact between the two, that readied Matthew to repent and follow. Afterward, at a dinner party at Matthew's house, where many sinners and tax collectors joined Jesus at table, a dispute arises when the Pharisees object to Jesus eating with these people. This Gospel reading celebrates more than Jesus' keeping company with those to whom God's people object and exclude; it celebrates the truth that Jesus calls to leadership people whom the righteous find objectionable and even reject. Regrettably, the Prayer of the Day emphasizes Matthew's response more than Jesus' call.

In Jesus' day, tax collectors were social outcasts for several reasons. First, they were usually dishonest. The job carried no salary, and so tax collectors were expected to make their living by cheating the people from whom they collected taxes. Devout Jews therefore avoided tax collectors because they did not observe the law. Moreover, patriotic and nationalistic Jews hated tax collectors generally because they were agents of the Roman government, the occupying power. Their hatred compounded when tax collectors, including Matthew, were also Jews, because these tax collectors collaborated with the enemy and betrayed their own people for money. Thus, throughout the Gospels, tax collectors are presented as a standard type of sinful and despised outcast. Jesus calling Matthew to discipleship was truly scandalous.

The coming of the reign of God was sometimes pictured as a great feast (compare Matt. 8:11).[1] The dinner party at Matthew's house, therefore, has overtones of the eschatological fellowship of the messianic banquet. We know that with whom one chose to eat was a very serious matter in first-century Judaism. Since the Pharisees raise their objection with Jesus' disciples and not directly to Jesus, this scene is intended to address both Jesus' practice of extending table fellowship to those considered outcasts, and the continuing practice of accepting "sinners" into the church.[2]

Employing a proverb commonly used in Hellenistic literature, and adding a quotation from Hosea 6:6, Jesus responds that the mercy of God, which Jesus extends to all humanity, takes precedence over everything else. While the law is not rejected outright, Jesus declares that the law must be understood in light of God's mercy in Christ.

SECOND READING

EPHESIANS 2:4-10 (ELW)
2 TIMOTHY 3:14-17 (BCP)
EPHESIANS 4:1-7, 11-13 (LFM)

Ephesians 2:4-10 (RCL) is a celebration of God's rich mercy and great love, with which God has loved humanity (v. 4). The phrase "rich in mercy" is an

Old Testament description of God's character, used to offset God's wrath. God's "great love," which never leaves humanity to perish, is evident in two of God's actions. First, God makes those who are dead alive again (v. 5). Second, God raised us so that, rather than being held down by our alienation from God, we are together in the heavenly places in Christ (v. 7). In other words, God does for Christians what God did for Christ in the resurrection and ascension. Unlike Christ, God raised us while we were dead to sin. God raised us "so that in the ages to come he might show the immeasurable riches of his grace in kindness toward us in Christ Jesus" (v. 7). In great mercy God raised us so that God could show us God's immeasurable grace. God raises us to give us more life. God loves us to give us more love. God brings us into a future in which God will reveal more and more of God's grace. God does all of this as God's free gift, and not because of anything humanity has done. Yet God will only raise the Christian and the church completely out of sin and into Christ's heavenly presence "in the coming ages." In the meantime, we are to live a way of life marked by good works, not in any way to contribute to our salvation, but because of what God has made us, created us to be in Christ Jesus. This grand pronouncement of God's mercy in Jesus Christ provides a powerful response to objections to "sinners" whom Christ may be calling to discipleship.

> O Glorious Saint Matthew, in your Gospel you portray Jesus as the longed-for Messiah who fulfilled the Prophets of the Old Covenant and as the new Lawgiver who founded a Church of the New Covenant. Obtain for us the grace to see Jesus living in his Church and to follow his teachings in our lives on earth so that we may live forever with him in heaven. Amen.[3]

As an alternative approach to preaching on this day, 2 Tim. 3:14–17 (BCP) celebrates Scripture as formative for Christian life and teaching: "All scripture is inspired by God and is useful for teaching, for reproof, for correction, and for training in righteousness" (v. 16). Like Timothy, the church is reminded that, when the situation is chaotic and the course is unclear, we are to remember and turn to holy teachers and sacred Scripture for sound instruction and help to remain faithful. We can trust and rely on what was received from the earliest Christian witnesses to the resurrected Christ.

On this day, the sacred Scripture that the church remembers and turns to for sound instruction is Matthew's Gospel. The church celebrates this apostle and evangelist as one of the holy teachers through whom God gave us the gift of Christian Scripture. In keeping with Paul's exhortation to Timothy, the preacher might celebrate the good news and themes of the Gospel according to Matthew as an instance of where we might turn for formation in Christian life. Matthew's Gospel presents a predominantly Jewish-Christian

> Casting aside the bonds of the custom house for the yoke of justice,
> you were revealed as an excellent merchant, rich in wisdom from on high.
> You proclaimed the word of truth and roused the souls of the slothful by writing of the hour of Judgment.
> —*Kontakion* (Tone 4)[4]

perspective that is open to the Gentile mission. Jesus is the fulfiller and the fulfillment of God's will as it is described in the Old Testament. Matthew's Gospel extensively cites the Old Testament prophets to prove that Jesus fulfilled all that was spoken about the Messiah who would come to establish God's reign. This Gospel writer faithfully and creatively shapes early church teachings about Jesus and the Christian life to portray Jesus as the new Moses and the new Solomon, and to emphasize that Jesus is the royal Son of God and Immanuel, God with us.

Matthew emphasizes Jesus' divine authority on earth and in heaven (cf. 16:19; 28:18-19). Matthew also demonstrates Jesus' authority over nature through miracles, his authority over sin through forgiveness, and his authority over death by the resurrection. Through Jesus, all believers, the true Israel, receive forgiveness and eternal life. Thus Matthew expands Jesus' mission, and that of his followers, to include all nations. Once again, God's grace and mercy overflow in Christ Jesus!

Who among those we reject might Christ be calling to discipleship, even leadership?

FIRST READING

EZEKIEL 2:8—3:11 (RCL)
PROVERBS 3:1-6 (BCP)

The call story in Ezekiel 2:8-3:11 predicts the ministry of Jesus and the apostles presented in Matthew's Gospel. In fact, we might imagine the prophet to be Jesus and, after Jesus, the apostles and the church. The prophet is given the sweet scroll of God's word to eat. The scroll indicates that, in addition to direct address, God gives God's word in a book. We are reminded of a time when such a claim would be revolutionary and of the special claim that Matthew's Gospel and all the books of the Bible have on us.

God commands the prophet to eat the scroll twice. The first command is preparation for preaching; the second command, in which the prophet fills his stomach with the scroll, is so that the prophet goes away filled with God's word. In contrast to rebellious Israel (2:8), the prophet experiences God's word as sweet. He knows himself to be entrusted with God's word and is obedient.

God then sends the prophet to speak God's word to the house of Israel. In Matthew, Jesus claims that he was sent to the house of Israel and sends the disciples to the house of Israel (15:24, 26). God then predicts the thick-headed and hard-hearted response of God's people, who will not listen. In Matthew, Jesus laments, "Jerusalem, Jerusalem, the city that kills the prophets and stones those who are sent to it! How often have I desired to gather your children together as a hen gathers her brood under her wings, and you were not willing!" (23:37).

When the house of Israel is not willing, God sends Ezekiel to the exiles and sends Jesus, and after him the apostles, to the Gentiles.

FOR FURTHER COMMENT

Additional comments on these Scripture texts, in part or in full, may be found in the seasonal volumes of *New Proclamation* as follows:

- Psalm 19:2-4—Year A, Proper 22; Year B, Lent 3, Proper 19; Year C, Epiphany 3; Years ABC, Easter Vigil
- Psalm 119:33-40—Year A, Epiphany 7, Proper 18
- Ephesians 2:4-10—Year B, Lent 4
- Ephesians 4:1-7, 11-13—Year B, Proper 13
- 2 Timothy 3:14-17—Year C, Proper 24
- Matthew 9:9-13—Year A, Proper 5

Notes

1. M. Eugene Boring, *Matthew*, New Interpreter's Bible, vol. 8 (Nashville: Abingdon, 1995), 235.

2. Ibid.

3. Catholic Community Forum, Patron Saints Index; http://www.catholic-forum.com/saints/pray0152.htm (accessed May 23, 2007).

4. http://orthodoxwiki.org/Apostle_Matthew#Hymns (accessed June 28, 2007).

MICHAEL AND ALL ANGELS

GAIL RAMSHAW

LUTHERAN (ELW)	EPISCOPAL (BCP)	ROMAN CATHOLIC (LFM)
Dan. 10:10-14; 12:1-3	Gen. 28:10-17	Dan. 7:9-10, 13-14 or Rev. 12:7-12a
Ps. 103:1-5, 20-22	Psalm 103 or 103:19-22	Ps. 138:1-2a, 2bc-3, 4-5
Rev. 12:7-12	Rev. 12:7-12	
Luke 10:17-20	John 1:47-51	John 1:47-51

KEY THEMES

• In the New Testament, only Jude and the book of Revelation specifically mention Michael, the warrior of God battling against Lucifer.
• Angels have functioned as personal guardians or as spirits of the dead far more in popular piety than they have in theology and liturgy.
• The point of the Gospel readings is not angels, but the revelation of God in Christ.

THE DAY

The day of Michael and All Angels begins back in the ancient Near East, in a worldview populated by an array of powerful yet unseen beings. Many deities, many spirits, some beneficent, some maleficent, filled the religious consciousness of the peoples who were neighbors of the Israelites. Contemporary scholarship suggests that, despite the monotheistic emphasis of the editors of the Hebrew Bible, also the Israelites over the centuries more or less shared this belief in invisible spirits. In the Jewish version of these crowded skies, such beings were messengers of God, servants of the one Eternal One. So although Genesis makes no mention of God creating angels, the Pentateuch does involve angels in some beloved narratives. Unless by extremely rare exception, humans do not see God, but they can see angels. Often the Scriptures say that it is an angel of the Lord, not the very being of God, who speaks with humans. Angels carry out the will of God. They are the mouth, the face, the arms of the Divine.

Especially during the intertestamental times, Jews systematized an elaborate hierarchy of angels. We might see this practice as a kind of cultural adaptation of their orthodox monotheism, and we recognize the stories about good and evil spirits as commonplace in world religions. It is during these centuries that the myth of the war in heaven became popular. No longer could the sin of Adam and Eve sufficiently explain the pervasive evil in the world. A greater, more cosmic story was needed. The situation and the adventure of the first humans were thrown back in time, writ larger. Before human time, it was angels, who had been created to live in community with God, who decided to wrest for themselves a higher status, to be like gods, thus precipitating the battle between the good and the evil angels and the exile of the evil angels to the nether regions. The continuing power of these evil spirits helped account for the horrific experience of the faithful people. Lucifer, "bearer of light," is the name given to the angel who attempted to take over the rule of heaven, and Michael, "who is like God," is the name given to the angel who drove the evil spirits down into the depths.

> Ye watchers and ye holy ones,
> bright seraphs, cherubim, and thrones,
> raise the glad strain: Alleluia!
> Cry out, dominions, princedoms, powers,
> archangels, virtues, angel choirs: Alleluia!
> —Athelstan Riley[1]

According to the angelology of postexilic Judaism, there were four archangels who held up the four legs of the throne of God. Michael was the warrior against Satan; Gabriel announced the end of time—thus Luke's designation of Gabriel as the one who announces Mary's pregnancy; Raphael, known best in the charming story of Tobit, is the healer; and Uriel, who never made it into Christian imagination, was the angel of death, the harbinger of plague and punishment. These archangels were part of a hierarchy of nine ranks of angels, usually termed angels, archangels, principalities, powers, virtues, dominions, thrones, cherubim, and seraphim. Many Christians recognize these titles from the well-known hymn "Ye Watchers and Ye Holy Ones." In the sixth century after Christ, the mystic Christian whom we call Pseudo-Dionysius developed this "celestial hierarchy" into a neo-Platonic cosmos that, while gorgeous and inventive, is perhaps relatively useless for contemporary theology.

Thus angels wing their way through intertestamental times into the New Testament. But specific mention of Michael, the warrior of God battling against Lucifer, we find only in Jude and the book of Revelation. Not surprisingly, it is the highly apocalyptic writings in which a prehistoric story of the cosmic battle between good and evil is especially useful. For beleaguered and oppressed peoples, looking forward to the end of evil, anticipating God's final battle at the end of time, the story of a divine messenger who once before overcame evil and finally once again will lead the troops to battle is particularly comforting. God will appoint Michael to lead the last battle against evil: in God and God's warrior Michael we can place our hope.

Despite the biblical and apocryphal stories that link Michael with battle, the earliest Christian veneration of Michael occurred in the Eastern churches and praised Michael for powers of healing. In the Western church, the first recorded church dedicated to Michael's honor was consecrated on September 29 in a town near Rome, and from the sixth century the day honoring Michael as a warrior angel appears on the Roman calendar. During the Reformation times, Lutherans and Anglicans added "and all angels" to the medieval festival honoring Michael. The old practice of calling Michael "saint" led to considerable confusion of who or what Michael is, and some contemporary church calendars omit the title *saint* in their designation.

Michael the warrior won out over the healer, especially in church iconography. Countless medieval churches depict on their walls the warrior slaying the dragon. Often dressed in armor contemporaneous to the painting, Michael fit well into a society rife with warfare and within a Christianity that assumed it was meant to destroy not only the forces of evil, but also dangerous religions. Michael battling evil resonated in a church that took the power of evil quite seriously: evil was a ferocious dragon, and we needed divine power to escape being devoured by Satan. This understanding of Michael stands in radical contrast to the popular imagery of angels in contemporary America, where angels are depicted as sweet young girls with curly hair who protect individuals from personal harm. It is striking how the centuries have redefined the task of angels, from battling against cosmic evil to holding children's hands as they cross the street.

> "Fear not" is what [the angels of Scripture] always urge of the humans they encounter. But the angels populating the card, gift, and hobby shops of American malls suggest that there is nothing at all to fear. . . . What were once God's angels have become our own, fulfilling roles that other people might have taken, as confident, friend, or therapist.
> —Kathleen Norris[2]

While the understanding of the angels as extensions of divine providence does have scriptural basis, a common contemporary understanding of angels is wholly nonbiblical, even non-Christian. More and more one hears that dead humans become angels. One theory as to the popularization of this idea suggests that the Baroque depictions of toddler angels were cited to console parents after the death of their children. Even at a contemporary Christian funeral, one might hear the preacher saying that the deceased is now the guardian angel newly assigned to watch over the family. Such a depiction of angels misunderstands what the Bible means by angel, trivializes the reality of death, and ignores the Christian proclamation of the resurrection, and we ought to do whatever we can to curb this strand of popular religion in Christian proclamation. The idea that my dead aunt becomes an angel is only another illustration of the pattern that angels have functioned far more in popular piety than they have in theology and liturgy, that while many people claim not to believe in God, they affirm their belief in angels as personal guardians or as spirits of the dead.

LUKE 10:17–20 (ELW)
JOHN 1:47–51 (BCP, LFM)

Current lectionaries propose two different Gospel readings for Michael and All Angels. In the passage from *Luke 10*, the disciples are keen on conquering demons, but Jesus relativizes this task with the gospel message that God has saved them. So not only through the twenty centuries of the church, but even in its primary texts, although people are fascinated with demons, battles, and angels, the creedal focus is on the saving action of God. The authority to preach the gospel is seen as more important than the power to exorcise demons. In this reading, Jesus speaks with the voice of God: Jesus was in heaven to witness the war before the creation of the world. But when the Gospel reading is concluded, we might smile: it is almost as if this Gospel reading on Michael and All Angels Day is an anti-angel gospel. Angels? Demons? Scary movies about devil possession? Whatever—but the real message is God.

> Of what use is it to speak of angelic spirits unless we seek to derive some profit from them for ourselves? We should draw something from our earthly contemplation of these heavenly citizens to perfect the manner of our own life and by zealous devotion excite ourselves to increased virtue.
> —Gregory the Great[3]

According to another lectionary system, the Gospel is the conclusion of *John 1*, the magisterial opening chapter of John in which Jesus is introduced as Word, God, light, life, enfleshment of the Divine, Son of the Father, Lamb of God, rabbi, Messiah, son of Joseph, king of Israel, and Son of man. John relies on his readers to know the story of Jacob's dream, in which God's angels ascend and descend to and from heaven over the chosen son of Israel. As well, intertestamental apocalyptic imagery popularized the idea of the people of Israel, symbolized by one man standing midway between earth and heaven, mediating the relationship between people and God. Like the Luke reading, the point of this Gospel reading is not angels, but the revelation of God in Christ.

THE READINGS

DANIEL 10:10–14; 12:1–3 (ELW)
DANIEL 7:9–10, 13–14 (LFM)
REVELATION 12:7–12 (ELW, BCP, LFM)

Both Gospel choices, then, bring the focus to Christ. Most of the other readings are selected from the few biblical references to Michael. The book of Daniel, probably written in the second century before Christ, records the apocalyptic vision that a prophet had after three weeks of fasting and prayer. According to the angelic message in *Daniel 10*, the contemporaneous evil ruler, "the prince of the kingdom of Persia," will eventually meet his doom at the hands of the prince Michael. Although one might look forward to a horrendous battle against evil and good, the promise in Daniel 12 is inspiring: God will send Michael to protect the people. Here is the gospel: God will save us. In *Daniel 7*, the people are comforted by a vision of the throne of God surrounded by all the angels. We are not to fear, for God will come to save us, and the angels are even now serving the Almighty.

One reading appointed for this day is the short account in *Revelation 12*, so important in some Christian circles, nearly ignored in some others. It is the biblical report of the prehistoric war in heaven between Michael and the dragon. In this passage, the terms *dragon, devil,* and *Satan* are made synonymous. Like the passages from Daniel, this apocalyptic text provided both an adequate explanation for the relentless power of evil and communal comfort in the promise for God's final victory over the forces of the devil. Like the popular attraction to angels, fascination with the apocalyptic end of all things is again alive in the church. The readings make this speculation less significant than the continuous salvation of God.

> The angels embrace God in their ardor, for they are living light; and they are winged, not in the sense that they have wings like the flying creatures, but in the sense that they circle burningly in their spheres through the power of God.
> —Hildegard of Bingen[4]

PSALM 103 (BCP); 103:1-5, 20-22 (ELW); 103:19-22 (BCP ALT.)
PSALM 138:1-2A, 2BC-3, 4-5 (LFM)

Perhaps the psalms say the day best. In the words of *Psalm 103*, we praise God for endless divine gifts, and we affirm that God's "ministers," who do God's will, join us in our praises. In the words of *Psalm 138*, it is not angels, but God whom we bless for steadfast love and faithfulness. The glory, not of Michael, but of God, is great.

With all festivals and commemorations that focus on something other than Christ, the church uses the announced topic as an arrow to point to Christ. Michael may be a much-appreciated fruit on the tree, but the tree is Christ. For a worship service that uses these readings to celebrate Michael and All Angels, it is easier to say what the day ought not to be than what it ought to be. It ought not baptize sentimental popular piety; it ought not trivialize angels into personal talismans against trouble; it ought to affirm the potency of evil; it ought to praise God for the many ways that we are protected from harm and saved from evil; and it ought to proclaim Christ as our hope for the final victory over death and the devil.

Some communities that do not keep the specific date September 29 and that wish to keep the Sunday lectionary in place may want to incorporate Michael and All Angels into the nearest Sunday proclamation. For example, in the Revised Common Lectionary, the Sunday between September 25 and October 1 inclusive presents the following Gospel readings: Matt. 21:23-32, which deals with divine authority and obedience to the will of God; Mark 9:38-50, warnings to those who obstruct rather than assist the faith of others; and Luke 16:19-31, the parable of the rich man and Lazarus. Each of these Gospel readings provide openings for reference to the angels, for they serve with divine authority, obey the will of God, assist the faithful; yet even were they to testify to Christ, they could do no more than can the saving gospel of Jesus Christ.

FOR FURTHER COMMENT

Additional comments on these Scripture texts, in part or in full, may be found in the seasonal volumes of New Proclamation as follows:

- Genesis 28:10-17—Year A, Proper 11
- Daniel 7:9-10, 13-14—Year B, Reign of Christ
- Psalm 103—Year A, Proper 19; Year B, Epiphany 8/Proper 3; Year C, Proper 16
- Psalm 138—Year A, Proper 16; Year B, Proper 5; Year C, Epiphany 5, Proper 12
- Luke 10:17-20—Year C, Proper 9
- John 1:47-51—Year B, Epiphany 2

Notes

1. Athelstan Riley, "Ye Watchers and Ye Holy Ones," *Evangelical Lutheran Worship* (Minneapolis: Augsburg Fortress, 2006), no. 424.

2. Kathleen Norris, *Amazing Grace: A Vocabulary of Faith* (New York: Riverhead, 19998), 328.

3. Gregory the Great, *The Sunday Sermons of the Great Fathers*, vol. 3, ed. M. F. Toal (Chicago: Henry Regnery, 1959), 205–06.

4. Hildegard of Bingen, *Scivias*, trans. Mother Columba Hart and Jane Bishop (New York: Paulist, 1990), 364.

LUKE, EVANGELIST

OCTOBER 18

CRAIG A. SATTERLEE

LUTHERAN (ELW)	EPISCOPAL (BCP)	Roman Catholic (LFM)
Isa. 43:8-13 or	Bar. 38:1-4, 6-10,	2 Tim. 4:10-17b
35:5-8	12-14	
Psalm 124	Psalm 147 or	Ps. 145:10-11,
	147:1-7	12-13ab, 17-18
2 Tim. 4:5-11	2 Tim. 4:5-13	
Luke 1:1-4; 24:	Luke 4:14-21	Luke 10:1-9
44-53		

KEY THEMES

• The relationship of the promises of the Old Testament and their fulfillment in Christ.
• The healing power of the gospel, the healing ministry of the church, and the ministry of health professionals and institutions.
• The gospel is good news for the poor.
• The ministry of women.

ST. LUKE

Luke is believed to be "Lucius of Cyrene" and "Lucius my fellow countryman" (Acts 13:1; Rom. 16:21), a disciple of Paul and coworker with him. The special sensitivity Luke's Gospel shows to evangelizing Gentiles leads to the tradition that Luke was himself a Gentile. The parable of the Good Samaritan, and stories of Jesus praising the faith of Gentiles, such as the widow of Zarephath, Naaman the Syrian, and the one grateful leper who is a Samaritan (4:25-27; 17:11-19), are only found in Luke. Luke is believed to be a Greek from either Antioch or Philippi.

We know little about Luke's life, beyond that he was a physician (Col. 4:14). While tradition holds that Luke was among the seventy disciples commissioned by Jesus, Luke's Gospel indicates that he was not an eyewitness to the life and ministry of Jesus (1:2).

Luke accompanied Paul on some of his missionary journeys. Assuming that Luke wrote Acts, and using this book as a guide, we can reconstruct the itinerary of Luke's ministry. Acts is written in the third person, as a historian recording facts, up until the sixteenth chapter. Then in Acts 16:10, the pronoun *they*, which the author uses to refer to Paul and his companions, becomes *we*. Assuming that Luke is the author, and now counts himself as a member of Paul's party, we can conclude that Luke first joined Paul's company at Troas and accompanied him into Macedonia, where they traveled to Samothrace, Neapolis, and Philippi. Luke then switches back to the third-person pronoun, which seems to indicate he was not thrown into prison with Paul and that, when Paul left Philippi, Luke stayed behind to take charge of the church between the apostle's visits. Seven years passed before Paul returned to the area on his third missionary journey. In Acts 20:5, the return to the pronoun *we* indicates that Luke left Philippi to rejoin Paul in Troas. They traveled together through Miletus, Tyre, and Caesarea, to Jerusalem.

Luke is believed to have been with Paul during Paul's two imprisonments. During his first imprisonment, Paul writes, "Epaphras, my fellow prisoner in Christ Jesus, sends greetings to you, and so do Mark, Aristarchus, Demas, and Luke, my fellow workers" (Philemon 23-24). Then, when everyone else either deserts Paul in his final imprisonment, or is sent away, Luke remains with Paul to the end. Paul writes, "Only Luke is with me" (2 Tim. 4:11, from the epistle reading appointed for this day).

According to early tradition, Luke wrote the Gospel that bears his name in Greece and preached the faith there and in Bithynia, an important province in Asia Minor. Luke's inspiration and information for his Gospel and Acts is said to have come from his close association with Paul and his companions.

The reports of Luke's life after Paul's death are conflicting. Some say he preached in Greece, others in Gaul. Some early writers claim Luke was martyred, others say he lived a long life. The earliest tradition we have says that Luke died in Boeoria at the age of eighty-four, without ever marrying. Luke is often portrayed with an ox or a calf because these are the symbols of sacrifice and refer to the sacrifice Jesus made for all the world.

Emperor Constantinus II removed Luke's supposed relics from Thebes in Boeoria and had them taken to Constantinople and placed in the Church of the Holy Apostles with the relics of St. Andrew on March 3, 357. The date of Luke's commemoration, October 18, may reflect the date of his death. This saint's date appears on the Western calendar in the eighth century, but the commemoration is considerably older in the East. St. Luke's Day is a particularly fitting time to celebrate the church's ministries of healing, through liturgies that include the laying on of hands and anointing of the sick, as well as prayers for and recognition of the ministry of physicians and nurses, hospitals, and senior living centers. St. Luke's Day is also an appropriate time to celebrate the Gospel according to Luke and the Acts of the Apostles as the single, unified story of God's saving activity in Jesus Christ.

THE GOSPEL
LUKE 1:1-4; 24:44-53 (ELW)
LUKE 4:14-21 (BCP)
LUKE 10:1-9 (LFM)

Evangelical Lutheran Worship appoints the beginning and end of Luke's Gospel. Considering these bookends in turn invites us to first look ahead in Luke's Gospel, and then to look back. Together, these bookends point to everything that comes between them. The phrase "set down an orderly account" in Luke's Prologue (1:1-4) suggests that, rather than new material, this Gospel recasts tradition for a new context and a new audience. Luke's reference to "the events that have been fulfilled among us" (1:1) indicates that a major theme of this recasting is the relation between the Old Testament as promise and the life and ministry of Jesus as fulfillment. The events handed on are the birth, life, death, resurrection, and ascension of Jesus; in other words, they are the content of Luke's Gospel. The phrase "eyewitnesses and ministers of the word" refers to the same group, and describes this role first before and then after the resurrection and Pentecost.[1] In Luke's Gospel, this group functions as eyewitnesses; in Acts they are ministers of the word. What follows is the tradition of the apostles, and Luke is qualified to write it, after "investigating everything carefully from the very first" (v. 3). Luke undertakes to write an "orderly account," suggesting that this Gospel's structure is intended to persuade the reader of its message, so that the one beloved of God may "come to recognize completely"[2] that Jesus is the crucified and risen Messiah (cf. 24:30-31).

Luke's Gospel concludes with the risen Christ's final teaching and ascension (24:44-53). The words that Jesus spoke to the Eleven while he was still with them (v. 44) are the three passion predictions in Luke's Gospel (9:22, 44; 18:33). Jesus invites us to remember these words as well, to look back into Luke's Gospel, and to see how these words developed. But more than remembering, Jesus opens the Eleven's minds to comprehend that Jesus' words and deeds are the fulfillment of Scripture (24:45). Jesus interprets the Old Testament christologically; Jesus fulfilled God's promises via a cross and empty tomb. On their own, neither Jesus' first followers nor disciples today can grasp that Jesus accomplished salvation through his death and resurrection. Both salvation and faith are God's gifts in Jesus

Christ. Jesus also opens the Christian community's mind to grasp that its work of preaching repentance and forgiveness of sins in Christ's name to all nations is also the fulfillment of Scripture, in that it is an extension of Christ's own ministry. The commission is an expansion of the mission of the seventy (Luke 10:1-9, appointed by LFM). By calling the eleven witnesses of his suffering, death, and resurrection, opening their minds to the necessity of their proclamation, and promising them power from on high, Jesus commissions the Eleven for their mission, which Luke recounts in Acts. Jesus then ascends to God and is worshiped as God by the disciples. Acts begins with the fuller account of Jesus' ascension (1:1-11), linking these two works attributed to Luke.

Between these two bookends, Luke presents the Gospel as good news for the poor and the reign of God as social justice. Luke is the only Gospel writer to include the parable of the rich man and Lazarus. Luke transforms "Blessed are the poor in spirit" in the Beatitudes to "Blessed are the poor." We hear the purpose of Jesus' ministry in both Mary's Magnificat and in Jesus' inaugural sermon in Nazareth (Luke 4:14-21, appointed by BCP). Luke also has a special connection with the women in Jesus' life, particularly Mary. Luke's Gospel includes the annunciation, Mary's visit to Elizabeth and the Magnificat, the presentation, and the story of Jesus' disappearance in Jerusalem. Finally, throughout Luke's Gospel, Jesus takes the side of sinners who want to return to God's mercy. Luke gives us the parable of the Forgiving Father or Prodigal Son. Luke also presents the story of Jesus being anointed in terms of a forgiven woman disrupting the feast by washing Jesus' feet with her tears. St. Luke's Day invites us to preach on any of these themes.

> How can your congregation participate in God's work of healing all creation? Visit http://www.webofcreation.org for ideas.

First Reading
ISAIAH 43:8-13 or 35:5-8 (ELW)
BARUCH 38:1-4, 6-10, 12-14 (BCP)

Isaiah 35:5-8 provides a vivid portrait of God's healing intent. The beauty of this passage is the prophet's declaration that God will bring wholeness to creation, as well as to humanity. Those who are blind will see; those who are deaf will hear. Those unable to walk and speak will do so. The earth will become lush and green as it is renewed by God's gift of water. The challenge is that the sermon ought to do more than talk about healing. The sermon should itself be an act of Christian healing.

I am legally blind and find myself concerned by much of the preaching I hear on passages like this one, which address persons with disabilities.[3] Many of the sermons I have heard I have experienced as anything but healing. When possible, modify prejudice or offensive language both in Scripture and in preaching. For example, speak of the person rather than the disability. Isaiah might have spoken of *people who are* lame, and the tongue of *the person who is* speechless (35:6). This sort of editing is itself an act of healing, because it proclaims that people who live with disabilities are first and foremost *people*.

Scripture overwhelmingly presents disabilities as negative. They are the manifestation or consequence of sin, which often gets translated into an individual's personal, moral failure. Once we make this theological move, it becomes easy to sidestep the issue altogether by spiritualizing disability. For example, our spiritual blindness prevents us from comprehending the faith and responding to our neighbor in love. This kind of preaching only reinforces the unspoken notion that physical blindness is a sign or consequence of sin. This perception is further reinforced when Jesus cures those who are blind or uses the term to slam the Pharisees. Thank goodness that, in John, Jesus makes it clear that the man was not born blind because of either his sin or that of his parents. The homiletic challenge is to preach about embodiment as more than a metaphor and proclaim the good news that Jesus is concerned with our bodies as well as our spirits.

Yet, receiving 20/20 vision is not the chief concern of my life, nor is finding a cure a preoccupation of most of the people I know who live with disabilities. Many of us believe that there is nothing wrong in being disabled. There is no tragedy or pity in disability. The myths, fears, and stereotypes about disability, which still operate in society, make living with a disability difficult. We do not seek a cure or sympathy as much as equality, independence, dignity, and inclusion. We welcome sermons that speak to the need for this kind of healing.

St. Luke's Day might also provide an occasion to preach about God's will for the healing and wholeness of all creation. God does not save humanity and abandon the world and its creatures. The healing that Jesus brings is for all of creation. As an extension and expansion of Christ's ministry, the church works for the preservation and healing of all life.

Most charming and saintly Physician, you were animated by the heavenly Spirit of love. In faithfully detailing the humanity of Jesus, you also showed his divinity and his genuine compassion for all human beings. Inspire our physicians with your professionalism and with the divine compassion for their patients. Enable them to cure the ills of both body and spirit that afflict so many in our day. Amen.[4]

How might you preach the gospel as good news for the poor in your community?

Additional comments on these Scripture texts, in part or in full, may be found in the seasonal volumes of *New Proclamation* as follows:

- Isaiah 35:5-8—Year A, Advent 3; Year B, Proper 18
- Psalm 124—Year A, Proper 16; Year B, Proper 21
- Psalm 145:10-18—Year A, Proper 9, Proper 13; Year B, Proper 12
- Psalm 147—Year B, Epiphany 5; Years ABC, Christmas 2
- 2 Timothy 4:5-13 (10-17)—Year C, Proper 25
- Luke 24:44-53—Years ABC, Ascension
- Luke 4:14-21—Year C, Epiphany 3
- Luke 10:1-9—Year C, Proper 9

Notes

1. Arthur Just, *Luke,* Concordia Commentary (St. Louis: Concordia, 1996), 36.

2. Ibid.

3. Craig A. Satterlee, "Insights of a Man Born Blind," *The Lutheran* 16, no. 10 (October 2003): 30–31.

4. From Catholic Community Forum, Patron Saints Index; http://www.catholic-forum.com/saints/pray0242.htm (accessed May 23, 2007).

SIMON AND JUDE, APOSTLES

OCTOBER 28

RUTH A. MEYERS

LUTHERAN (ELW)	EPISCOPAL (BCP)	ROMAN CATHOLIC (LFM)
Jer. 26:(1–6) 7–16	Deut. 32:1–4	Eph. 2:19–22
Psalm 11	Ps. 119:89–96	Ps. 19:1–4
1 John 4:1–6	Eph. 2:13–22	
John 14:21–27	John 15:17–27	Luke 6:12–19

KEY THEMES

• The apostles Simon and Jude are thought to have ministered together to proclaim the gospel, incorporating diverse peoples into the household of faith.

• The church is built on the foundation of the apostles.

• In what ways have you worked with another to proclaim the gospel or enact Christian discipleship? How has God sustained you in your Christian ministry?

THE SAINTS

In Western Christianity, the apostles Simon and Jude are traditionally commemorated together on October 28, which may be the date of the translation of their relics to an altar in St. Peter's Basilica in Rome. In the East, they have had separate feast days. Little is known of either saint, and variant texts have resulted in different understandings of their names and identities.

Simon appears near the end of the list of apostles in all three Synoptic Gospels and in Acts (Matt. 10:4; Mark 3:18; Luke 6:15; Acts 1:13). Matthew and Mark identify him as "the Cananaean," while in Luke and Acts he is nicknamed "the Zealot." These titles effectively distinguish him from the better known Simon Peter. Some manuscripts of Matthew and Mark call Simon the "Cananite" instead of "Cananaean," leading some early Christians to identify Simon as the unnamed bridegroom in the wedding at Cana described in John 2. The seventeenth-century translators of the Authorized (King James) Version of the Bible rendered the word as "Canaanite," suggesting that Simon's birthplace was in the region known in the Old Testament as Canaan. Contemporary scholars, however, reject an identification of "Cananaean" as a place name and instead understand it to be the transliteration of an Aramaic word meaning "zealot." Thus all four New Testament lists of the apostles give Simon the nickname "Zealot." The Zealots were a fanatical Jewish sect who inspired the revolt against the Romans that led to the destruction of Jerusalem in 70. Simon may have been a member of this party, although scholars disagree as to whether it already existed at the time of Jesus. Alternatively, Simon may simply have been especially zealous in his religious belief.

While Simon is named on all four lists of the apostles, Jude is included only on the lists in Luke and Acts, where he is identified as "Judas of James" (Luke 6:16; Acts 1:13). In Matthew and Mark, his name is replaced by Thaddeus (Matt. 10:3; Mark 3:18), who in some ancient manuscripts is named "Lebbaeus," or "Lebbaeus called Thaddeus." Most commentators identify Thaddeus with Jude and suggest that Matthew and Mark have used the name to avoid confusion of the apostle with the traitor Judas Iscariot.

The appellation "of James" has been variously interpreted to mean "son of James" (as in the New Revised Standard Version) or "brother of James" (as in the King James Version). "Son of James" would be the more common construction in Greek and would parallel Luke's description of the apostle James as "[son] of Alphaeus" (Luke 6:15). However, the author of the epistle of Jude identifies himself as the "brother of James" (Jude 1:1), leading some to suggest that Jude the apostle was the brother, not the son, of James. Contemporary scholars point out that the letter refers to apostolic times as being in the past and that the author distinguishes himself from the apostles (Jude 1:17-18). Thus it is unlikely that the apostle Jude wrote the epistle bearing the same name, also calling into question an identification of the apostle as the brother of James. Others have proposed that Simon as well as Jude and James are relatives of Jesus, based on the list of Jesus' brothers in Matt. 13:55 and Mark 6:3. This, too, is most unlikely.

Kontakion
Let us all bless the eloquent Simon in praise,
who sowed the doctrines of wisdom in the hearts of the faithful;
for he now stands before the throne of glory
and rejoices with the angels,
as he prays for us all unceasingly.[1]

Outside of the lists of apostles, only Jude and not Simon appears anywhere in the Gospels and then only in one brief mention. In the midst of Jesus' discourse after the Last Supper, Judas, whom John describes as "not Iscariot," asks why Jesus will reveal himself to the disciples and not to the whole world. Jesus responds that he and the Father will come to all who love him (John 14:22-23). The episode offers little insight into the character of Jude.

Various traditions circulated about the missionary activity of Simon and Jude. Some report that the apostle Thomas sent Jude to Edessa. From there, Jude is reputed to have preached the Gospel in Mesopotamia and Pontus, while Simon first went to Egypt. Later in their missionary journeys, the two traveled together to Persia, where they taught and baptized many converts and eventually were martyred. In art Jude is sometimes represented with a club, perhaps the instrument of his martyrdom, while Simon was supposedly sawn in two and so is sometimes depicted with a saw. However, the *Monology* of Basil reports that Simon died peacefully at Edessa. Jude (Judas Thaddeus) is sometimes confused with another Thaddeus who also died peacefully in Edessa.

For reasons not entirely clear, Jude has become known as the patron saint of desperate or lost causes. Some have suggested that Christians were reluctant to pray to Jude because of the similarity of his name to that of the traitor Judas Iscariot. Hence they turned to him only when their invocations of other saints were futile, that is, only when they were truly desperate.

THE GOSPEL

JOHN 14:21-27 (ELW)

The Lutheran lectionary appoints the only text in which either Simon or Jude appears in the Gospels apart from the lists of apostles. The passage is part of Jesus' farewell discourse, his words to the disciples at the Last Supper in John's Gospel. At several points in the discourse, one of Jesus' disciples interrupts him with a question. Here, Judas asks for clarification: Jesus says he is to be revealed only to believers, yet other teaching about the end of time held that he would be manifest to the whole world (for instance, Mark 13:26; 1 Thess. 4:16-17). How can this be?

In his response, Jesus speaks not of the second coming, but rather of an ongoing spiritual presence. Just as God sent Jesus, now God will send another, the *parakletos*, a word sometimes transliterated as "Paraclete" and sometimes translated "Counselor," "Advocate," or "Comforter." The emphasis here is on God's sustaining love for those who love and obey God. Jesus will not abandon his disciples but rather through the sending of the Spirit will continue to guide them. The passage concludes with Jesus' assurance that he will bestow upon them his peace, a term that means well-being, harmony with God and with the community.

Kontakion

You were chosen as a disciple for your firmness of mind:
An unshakable pillar of the Church of Christ,
You proclaimed His word to the Gentiles,
Telling them to believe in one Godhead.
You were glorified by Him, receiving the grace of healing,
Healing the ills of all who came to you,
O most praised Apostle Jude![2]

JOHN 15:17-27 (BCP)

This passage is taken from a later portion of Jesus' farewell discourse. Jesus has been telling the disciples that they will share his life, a life lived in union with God. But they must share all of Christ's life, including the world's hatred. Jesus sketches a sharp contrast between the life of discipleship and the world. The world has hated and rejected Jesus. Likewise, Jesus warns, the world will hate the disciples and will persecute them.

At the conclusion of this section, Jesus again promises the disciples that he will not leave them defenseless but will send the Advocate ("Paraclete," "Counselor," "Comforter"), assuring the disciples of God's continuing presence. Here the emphasis is on bearing witness: the Advocate will bear witness to the truth of Jesus as God's Son. The disciples, too, are to testify to this truth. Of particular note on this feast of apostles, they have been with Jesus "from the beginning" and so have seen the signs that Jesus has done and know that Jesus is from the Father.

LUKE 6:12-19 (LFM)

Luke introduces the Twelve, whom Jesus chooses as "apostles" after a night in prayer. Both Simon the Zealot and Judas son of James are named. There is no indication of any responsibility assigned to the apostles, other than that implicit in the term *apostle*, which is derived from a verb meaning "sent out."

Just prior to the appointment of the Twelve, Jesus has been in conflict with the Pharisees, and Luke reports their hostility as they begin to plan "what they might do to Jesus" (Luke 6:11). After the naming of the apostles, the story proceeds with an account of Jesus' healing ministry that sets the stage for the Sermon on the Plain (Luke's version of the longer Sermon on the Mount reported in Matthew). The apostles have no particular role in this scene; they simply accompany Jesus as he responds to the crowd.

The context Luke provides for the naming of the apostles suggests their participation in Jesus' ministry, assisting him as he deals with large crowds and ensuring continuity when the plotting of the Pharisees results in Jesus' crucifixion. It is characteristic of Luke's Gospel for significant moments to be preceded by prayer.

THE READINGS

JEREMIAH 26:(1-6) 7-16 (ELW)
1 JOHN 4:1-6 (ELW)

Both of these texts introduce disputes in communities of faith. The passage from Jeremiah reports a controversy between the prophet and the people of Israel. The priests and prophets of the Temple are his chief accusers; they speak to the officials of Judah. The addition of "all the people" at several points in the narrative emphasizes that Jeremiah stands alone among the people. Jeremiah's offense is a sermon he preaches in the Temple, prophesying the destruction of the Temple if the people did not change their ways and obey God (Jer. 26:1-6; cf. Jer. 7:1-15). The Temple priests and prophets accuse Jeremiah of speaking words that did not come from God, an offense punishable by death (Deut. 18:20). In his defense, Jeremiah reiterates his prophecy as a word spoken by God and warns of dire consequences if the officials put him to death. Nonetheless, he is willing to accept death rather than refuse to speak the words God has commanded. The officials relent, citing the example of Hezekiah's decision about the prophet Micah a century earlier.

The background to 1 John is a division in the community. In the passage appointed for this feast, the author warns of false teaching. A true confession of faith will acknowledge that Jesus has come in the flesh, in contrast to some early Christian teachings that denied or minimized Jesus' humanity.

EPHESIANS 2:13-22 (BCP); 2:19-22 (LFM)

The Roman and Episcopal lectionaries appoint a passage that calls attention to the importance of apostles for the community of faith. The entire letter to the Ephesians is addressed to Gentiles who at one time did not share in the inheritance of Israel. Now, however, through Christ the Gentiles who had been "far off" are incorporated into the household of God. The predominant metaphor is a building in which Christ is the cornerstone and apostles and prophets are the foundation. Yet it is not static, as most structures are. The building is dynamic, growing into a holy temple where God dwells.

The Episcopal lectionary extends the selection, making more explicit the former division between Jew and Gentile and the reconciling work of Christ. The image of a "dividing wall" (Eph. 2:14) may be a reference to the wall in the Jewish Temple separating foreigners from the inner court. Through Christ, groups that had been divided are brought together in a new reality, reconciled not only to one another but also to God.

Because of the paucity of information about either Simon or Jude, the preacher might best consider the role of apostles more generally in the Christian community. According to Ephesians, the apostles are part of the foundation of the church. Faithfulness to the teaching of the apostles means continuity in Christian tradition. We have a rich inheritance, stretching through the centuries, and Simon and Jude are among those who first proclaimed the message of Jesus that has been handed on to us.

The teaching of Jesus has met resistance, however, and several of the appointed texts introduce this theme. Although we do not know for certain that either Simon or Jude suffered martyrdom, it is plausible that these apostles were persecuted, and a preacher might address the challenges of remaining faithful in the face of rejection. The gift of the Holy Spirit, whom Jesus introduces in his farewell discourse as the Advocate, offers faithful disciples the assurance of God's sustenance.

We remember Simon and Jude on the same day because of an ancient tradition that they worked together to preach the gospel in Persia. Engagement in God's mission is not a solitary endeavor. Rather, we are knit together in a community, sent into the world with the good news as God sent Jesus and sent the Spirit.

FOR FURTHER COMMENT

Additional comments on these Scripture texts, in part or in full, may be found in the seasonal volumes of *New Proclamation* as follows:

- Deuteronomy 32:1-4—Years ABC, Easter Vigil
- Ephesians 2:13-22—Year B, Proper 11
- John 14:21-27—Year C, Easter 6
- John 15:17-27—Year B, Pentecost
- Luke 6:12-19— Year C, Epiphany 6

Notes

1. http://orthodoxwiki.org/Apostle_Simon (accessed June 21, 2007).
2. http://orthodoxwiki.org/Apostle_Jude (accessed June 21, 2007).

REFORMATION DAY

OCTOBER 31

GAIL RAMSHAW

LUTHERAN (ELW)
Jer. 31:31-34
Psalm 46
Rom. 3:19-28
John 8:31-36

KEY THEMES

- Reformation Day was established in 1667 largely as an anti-Catholic effort designed to combat the Roman Catholic Church's anti-Protestant campaign.
- The themes of Reformation Day are about the perpetual need for the church to undergo reform.
- The prayer of the day offers specific petitions that pose questions for us toward the continuous reformation of our churches.

THE DAY

Even people who know only a little about the history of the Christian church are aware that on October 31, 1517, anticipating that many of the faithful would enter through the church doors the following day to observe All Saints Day, Martin Luther posted on the door a list of his grievances with contemporary Roman Catholic practices. Overly simplistic understandings of late medieval Europe lead some people to believe that this event began the Reformation. A more thorough reading of the decades prior to 1517 makes clear that many smaller beginnings of the Reformation preceded Luther. The list includes at least the rise of nationalism, the invention of the printing press, the mystics in their convents accessing God without recourse to priests and the sacraments, Roman Catholic reform movements especially within the religious orders, Wycliff's translation of the Bible, and Hus's Moravian movement. Thus, however we keep Reformation Day, we ought to avoid the suggestion that Luther arrived at the doors of the church in Wittenberg alone and by himself.

For some Lutheran churches, this day is celebrated as a kind of birthday of their denomination. Of course Luther had no intention in 1517 of starting another church body, and such an emphasis distorts history and the actions of Luther. Commemoration of the life and achievements of Luther belongs on the anniversary of his death day, February 18. Commemoration of the establishment of the Lutheran churches belongs on June 25, the anniversary of the presentation of the Augsburg Confession.

Yet many Lutherans are inheritors of what for some is a beloved tradition. The annual celebration of this day began in 1667, when a Lutheran festival was inaugurated in Saxony on October 31. Its establishment was in large part an anti-Catholic effort designed to combat the Roman Catholic Church's anti-Protestant campaign. Because many Christians find worship on a day other than Sunday to be beyond their ability or interest, recently some Lutherans have moved their Reformation celebration to the Sunday preceding October 31. They then celebrate All Saints Day, set on November 1, on the next Sunday. However, it needs to be carefully considered whether any such denominational self-congratulation is helpful in our time. Ecumenical concerns urge us to keep this day with a tone other than polemic.

> God's Word shall stand above the powers,
>   shall end all their thanksgiving.
> The Spirit and the gifts are ours,
>   for God with us is living.
> —Martin Luther[1]

Christian liturgy is never a look backward, but always a celebration in the present of something grounded in the past and coming to fruition in the future. Thus the themes of Reformation Day are not about 1517, but about the perpetual need, now in the twenty-first century, for the church to undergo reform. The church that needs reforming is, of course, not another denomination, but our own. The parish church door on which we post any suggestions or complaints is our own.

Rubrical suggestions in *Evangelical Lutheran Worship* suggest that the regular Sunday readings govern both Reformation Day and All Saints Day. Rather than use a specific set of readings that break the Sunday synoptic pattern, Reformation and All Saints can be included in, with, and under the regular in-course readings. Such an added emphasis can occur, for example, by the use of two prayers of the day, appropriate hymn choices, specific petitions in the intercessions, and brilliant preaching that weaves such anniversaries into the fabric of the sermon. Were it the case that on these two Sundays the regular Sunday readings get replaced, we would totally miss, for example, Jesus' teaching of the two commandments of the Law, the healing of blind Bartimaeus, the parable of the Pharisee and the tax collector, and the story of Zacchaeus. By incorporating a Reformation emphasis into the regular Sunday readings, we might speak of the sight that came to Bartimaeus and that needs to come also to the church; that the church should know itself to be the tax collector begging for mercy; that we in the church are too often

Zacchaeus, trying to catch a glimpse of Christ but defrauding our neighbor along the way. Mercifully, we are invited out of our tree to feast with Jesus.

THE PRAYER OF THE DAY

The first prayer of the day in *Evangelical Lutheran Worship* provides a worthy list of the themes of the day. First comes our gratitude to God for the gift of the church and our praise for the Spirit's continuous renewal of the assemblies of God's people. Second comes a plea for the outpouring of the Spirit. The prayer concludes with a trinitarian doxology, for only by our life within the triune God is there hope for the continuing reformation of our churches. The prayer then offers specific petitions that pose questions for us toward the continuous reformation of our churches:

1. "Keep us steadfast in your word." So: What is the shape of our congregation's study of the Bible? How faithful and intense is the biblical catechesis for our children, our confirmation classes, our adult catechumens, and our adult Sunday school? Is there a weekly opportunity for laypeople to study together next week's lectionary readings? Do we train lectors so that the proclamation of the Word is stunning for us all to hear?

2. "Protect and comfort us in times of trial." So: Are our church body and our congregation serving the call of the gospel to receive the protection and comfort God gives, then to extend it to a needy world? Are we finding our comfort in the gospel, or in our entertainment, our therapies, our inner selves?

3. "Defend them against all enemies of the gospel." So: Are we attending to the Christians around the world who suffer for their faith? Are we dealing with American cultural patterns, such as school sports scheduled on Sunday morning, that keep parishioners from hearing the gospel weekly? Is it right to think of sports schedules as enemies of the gospel?

4. "Bestow on the church your saving peace." So: Is our congregation gladly and humbly accepting the peace of the Lord? Are we living out the peace of the Lord in all our dealings? Do we understand our weekly greeting of peace to be, not a mere Good Morning, but an Easter Day sharing of the presence of the Risen Christ among us?

The genius of the two suggested prayers of the day lies in their insistence that the church that cries out for reformation is ours. We are always those who stand in need of Christ's Spirit of renewal. Even on his deathbed, Luther reminds us to beware of self-congratulation. "We are beggars: this is true," were the last words he wrote. Our church is the one needing reformation: this is most certainly true.

However, there will be some assemblies that choose the designated readings for Reformation Day. The Gospel reading of *John 8:31-36* proclaims the
central theme of the Fourth Gospel: that Christ himself is the way, truth, and life,
that Christ himself is the Son of the Father who will make us free. The passage
employs a metaphor common also in the parables of the New Testament: that
Christ is like the son in the house, and thus the heir who will receive the inheritance, and that humankind are like slaves, who are to work for the master and
might be sold away from the household. In this particular
use of the metaphor, John adds the idea that humankind is enslaved, not to God, but to sin. There is here no
Enlightenment notion that humans are free agents, in
charge of their own destiny, no American ideal that each
human by nature enjoys independence. Rather, powers
far greater than ourselves rule our hearts and minds, and
if it is not God who empowers us, it is sin.

The metaphor reflects the male dominance of the
century from which the writing comes: it is the son who
will inherit the house, for the daughter will be married
out, to become part of another man's house. The social
situation of sons and daughters in first-century Palestine opens the way for the New Testament's primary
descriptor of Jesus as the Son of God, the One who inherits the status, the One
who bears the promise of the future in himself. We can inherit the mercy of God
only by being permanently attached to the Son. The church has understood this
attaching to begin in baptism and to be continuously strengthened by hearing the
Word and partaking in the meal.

In the passage appointed, "the Jews"—John's shorthand terminology for des-
ignating those who do not accept Jesus as the Son of God and incarnation of the
Divine—claim the privilege of their status as descendents of Abraham, and thus
as bearers of the promise of divine blessing. On Sunday morning, the Christian
proclamation of the Scriptures means, however, always to be addressing us, not a
first-century audience of the Gospel. Our question is, then, How are we claiming
some status from our heritage? Unfortunately, a good deal of how Reformation
Day is observed places us precisely in the same boat at "the Jews," who are assuming that their membership in the most blessed group is their saving grace.

This reading is thus a call to refrain from the claim that as Lutherans, as descendents of any preferred group, we can find our comfort. It is all too easy in any
age for believers to take refuge in the status of their tradition. No, says this John
reading to us in the twenty-first century, our refuge is to be placed not in our

Almighty God, gracious Lord, we thank
you that your Holy Spirit renews the
church in every age. Pour out your Holy
Spirit on your faithful people. Keep them
steadfast in your Word, protect and comfort them in times of trial, defend them
against all enemies of the gospel, and
bestow on the church your saving peace,
through Jesus Christ, our Savior and Lord,
who lives and reigns with you and the Holy
Spirit, one God, now and forever. Amen.
—*Evangelical Lutheran Worship*[2]

church, not in our heritage, but only in Christ. We are to "continue" in the Word. In John, the Word is Christ, and Christ is the Word of God. We are to find our very life in Christ; we live in him and out of him. And since in Christ is all the beloved world of God, we will find our life in that Word to be a truly crowded existence.

The first reading from *Jeremiah 31* contains a summary of the prophet's proclamation. At some future time, God will establish a "new covenant." This passage is the only place in the Hebrew Scriptures that employs this phrase. and it finds its meaning for Christians only in light of the New Testament. Jeremiah had witnessed the Josiah reform, an attempt to reinvigorate the people by means of a renewed emphasis on the Mosaic Law, and he judged that it did not work. The reform of the people, their connection with God and their devotion to one another, must come some other way, some new covenant yet to be unfolded. The designation of this reading as a meditation on Reformation Day is an excellent example of why Christians continue to proclaim the Hebrew Scriptures: we have come to see our encounter with the risen Christ as at least one meaning of passages in the Old Testament. These passages illumine our understanding of who Jesus is and how he brings us life.

We believe that God's creative graciousness is offered to us and to everyone for healing and reconciliation so that through the Word made flesh, Jesus Christ, "who was put to death for our transgressions and raised for our justification" (Rom. 4:15), we are all called to pass from alienation and oppression of sin to freedom and fellowship with God in the Holy Spirit. —The Joint Declaration by Lutherans and Catholics on Justification by Faith[3]

The second reading from *Romans 3* brings to our consciousness the biblical studies of Martin Luther himself. It was especially in his study of Romans that he came to his conviction that we are justified by grace apart from the works of the law. The image behind this passage is of God as a judge whose demand for righteous living convicts every human of sin and before whom humankind can never justify itself. In the language of the medieval substitutionary theory of atonement, Christ bears our sins, takes on our punishment, and by placing our trust in him, we are justified before God. In a remarkable sixteenth-century painting by Franz Floris, Christ is on the cross, the beams of which become both the limbs of the tree of life and the wings of divine protection, under which huddle all of needy humanity.

Contemporary American English often uses the word *believe* to mean that we "think it happened" or "accept it as fact." We are aware of this usage when, for example, people speak of whether one "believes" in evolution. However, Paul means not "think it happened." He means "place our trust," rely on for our life and through our death, experience as the source and summit of the meaning in our lives. The call in Romans to life in faith is as pertinent today as ever, for it remains a perpetual temptation to trust in something other than our baptism into the death and resurrection of Christ. (Additional comments on Jer. 31:31–34, in part or in full, may be found in the seasonal volumes of *New Proclamation* as follows: Year B, Lent 5; Year C, Proper 24.)

Notes

1. Martin Luther, "A Mighty Fortress Is Our God," trans. Frederick H. Hedge, alt.; *Evangelical Lutheran Worship/*(Minneapolis: Augsburg Fortress, 2006), no. 505.

2. Prayer of the Day, Reformation Day, *Evangelical Lutheran Worship*, p.58.

3. "The Declaration," *Justification by Faith: Lutherans and Catholics in Dialogue VII*, ed. H. George Anderson, T. Austin Murphy, and Joseph A. Burgess (Minneapolis: Augsburg, 1985), 73.

# ALL SOULS DAY /
COMMEMORATION OF ALL
THE FAITHFUL DEPARTED

NOVEMBER 2

GAIL RAMSHAW

EPISCOPAL (BCP)
Wis. 3:1-9 or Isa. 25:6-9
Psalm 130 or 116:10-17

1 Thess. 4:13-18 or 1 Cor. 15:50-58

John 5:24-27

ROMAN CATHOLIC (LFM)
Wis. 3:1-9 or 4:7-15 or Isa. 25:6-9
Ps. 23:1-3a, 3b-4, 5, 6 or 25:6+7b,
    17-18, 20-21 or 27:1, 4, 7+8b+9a,
    13-14
Rom 5:5-11 or 5:17-21 or 6:3-9 or
    8:14-23 or 8:31b-35, 37-39 or
    14:7-9, 10c-12
    or 1 Cor. 15:20-28 or 15:51-57
    or 2 Cor. 4:14-5:1 or 5:1, 6-10
    or Phil. 3:20-21 or 1 Thess. 4:13-18
    or 2 Tim. 2:8-13
Matt. 5:1-12a or 11:25-30 or 25:31-46
    or Luke 7:11-17 or 23:44-46, 50,
    52-53; 24:1-6a or 24:13-16, 28-35
    or John 5:24-29 or 6:37-40 or
    6:51-59 or 11:17-27 or 14:1-6

KEY THEMES

- All Souls Day, as a time to pray for souls in purgatory, became a treasured observance in late medieval times among Roman Catholics.
- For most Anglicans and Protestants, this memorial of the beloved dead coincides with the parish celebration of All Saints Day.
- Use this observance to attend both to death itself and to the dead themselves.

THE DAY

To get our minds around November 2, we begin millennia ago, long before Christianity arose. One of the several roots of this observance is found in the northern European pagan autumnal rituals that focused on the dead. In pre-Christian times, with winter approaching, the people in the Northern Hemisphere wanted to be sure that the dead stayed dead and the living remained alive. Anticipating the approach of winter, all threats of death must be met and overcome. The space separating the dead from the living must be firmly maintained. So in a festival called Samhain, various rites were undertaken, such as feeding the spirits at their gravesites, to pacify the dead. Thus the practices that we associate with Hallowe'en, turned mostly now to children's play and costume parties, were originally serious communal rituals that gave the dead their due, so that the dead would be satisfied with their condition and leave the living alone.

Fast forward into Mediterranean Christianity: already in the second century, Christians were honoring their dead. Especially martyrs were venerated, any of the baptized who like Christ had been put to death for their faith. But increasingly any and all Christians who died in the faith came to be remembered in liturgical prayer. And when the medieval church encountered the autumn pagan rituals that honored the dead, it got busy with its continual efforts at enculturation. Always adept at christianizing non-Christian rituals that were important to the people, the church turned this pagan focus on the dead into the celebration of All Saints on November 1.

But as the centuries moved along, "saints" came to be a term applicable only to officially canonized saints. Thus, according to a proper keeping of the liturgical calendar, November 1 focused only on those dead Christians who had gone directly to heaven, those who were already with the angels in glory. So what of our grandmother? All the faithful departed who were not "saints," who were thought to be suffering now in purgatory—and that was nearly everyone who had died in the faith—were commemorated on the following day. The abbot of Cluny in the late tenth century is remembered as having set such an observance on November 2, and its popularity spread throughout Europe. November 2 came to be designated as the time to pray with intensity for all the souls in purgatory, for All Souls. It is likely that many people cared a great deal more about their grandmother than about some saint or other, and so it is not surprising that All Souls Day became a treasured observance in late medieval times.

> Spirit of Life, we remember the women, named and unnamed, who throughout time have used the gifts you gave them to change the world. We call upon these foremothers to help us discover within ourselves your power—and the ways to use it to bring about the reign of justice and peace.
> —Ann Heidkamp[1]

In the last century, many Roman Catholics are speaking far less about purgatory than about the church's confidence in God's gift of heaven. Thus among Roman Catholics in our society November 2 is the day to remember those in the parish or the family who have died over the last year. Prayers for the dead include the names of those who have recently died. Bells are tolled for all the faithful departed.

Most Protestants always rejected speculation about a state called purgatory, and so All Souls did not figure much throughout the history of the Protestant churches. However, an annual remembrance of the beloved dead has caught on also in many Protestant churches. For most Anglicans and Protestants, who were never inclined to designate only a few of the faithful departed as "saints," this memorial of the beloved dead coincides with the parish celebration of All Saints Day.

So in an American city, we might encounter any of the following: some churches stipulate November 1 as a single annual festival to remember the dead, combining the medieval All Saints with All Souls. Some Christians keep two observances, an annual celebration of All Saints Day with a second commemoration of all the beloved dead on November 2. Many churches are now moving this observance to an adjacent Sunday. Thus at the beginning of November God is thanked for the lives of all those who have gone before us in the faith. There may be specially chosen lectionary readings, or the names of the dead may be read out in a final petition of the intercessions without any alteration in the cycle of Sunday readings. One Roman Catholic source explained that the day links the whole church together: both the living and the dead together await the fullness of eternal life with God.

> All of us go down to dust,
> yet even at the grave we make our song:
> Alleluia, alleluia, alleluia!
> —*Evangelical Lutheran Worship*[2]

Mexican Christians are famous for their folk festival called *Los Dias de los Muertos*—the Day of the Dead. Their comic skeleton art and decorations of dancing bones mean to tease away our fears of death. Yes, we will all end up as skeletons, but the communal camaraderie means to cover terror with laughter, to smile in the face of death. Yes, we will die, but we can party along the way.

However, many commentators suggest that without anything like the Mexican Day of the Dead, most Americans are exceedingly poor at dealing with death. We isolate the dying out of our sight; we make up the corpse to look as if it were alive; we drive off to the post-funeral meal before the coffin is lowered, before the dirt is shoveled. We hear a great deal about mourners seeking "closure," which is precisely what a religious funeral ritual is meant to provide. The very verb *died* is being replaced by euphemisms. Yet biblical scholars tell us that the Gospels are passion narratives with a long preface. That the promise of the Messiah appeared to conclude with the execution of Jesus opened up to the hope that Christ was risen, and thus all death could be viewed in the light of Easter. For Christians, death is always there, but as the gate to life.

Thus it is appropriate that Christians work on accepting the reality of death. However our parishes decide to keep November 1–2, a worthy goal is to use this observance to attend both to death itself and to the dead themselves. Recalling our own departed family and friends may inspire happy memories, or it may hold before us the Christian obligation to forgive. It is wise if our liturgical celebration does not attempt to face death with a pretense that believers have only positive feelings about their own "faithful departed."

THE READINGS

Here we will focus on only several from a lengthy list of readings that are suggested as possible for the commemoration of the faithful departed. The diversity of readings reflects the several ways that the Scriptures speak of the destiny of the dead.

The Bible does not proclaim one specific doctrinal understanding about the state of the dead. The first reading from *Wisdom 3*, a late intertestamental writing, uses the language of "soul," a category that Jews adopted from their Greek neighbors. Such a soul, an immortal quality within each mortal human, goes after death to reside with God. That is, the soul returns to the immortal world from which it came. There is nothing particularly Jewish or Christian about this idea: college students encounter it when reading Plato. For the Jews, in the face of the undeserved suffering of the just, the believers can trust that at least at the end is peace in the protection of the Almighty.

On the other hand, the first reading from *Isaiah 25* is more explicitly Jewish. The promise of life is not to the individual dead soul, but to all the nations in a new turn to history, a final end of all tears, when the whole created order will enjoy a feast on the mountain of God. There is a Hebraic earthiness about the promise: there will be even really good wine poured out for us all.

These two readings present two of the classic pictures common in Christianity for the goal of the faithful: "immortality of the soul," that is, the reception of an immortal part of the dead into the presence of God, or the eschatological fulfillment of all things, when God will provide for an embodied universe a new life of justice and joy. The selections from *1 Thessalonians 4* and *1 Corinthians 15* add their particularly Christian way to understand the goal of life after death. In the early decades after the life and death of Jesus, Christians assumed that the second coming of Christ was imminent, and just as Christ's body has been raised from the dead, so at his return to earth all of those who are in Christ will rise from their graves. The Thessalonians

> Then John saw the river, and the multitude was there. And now they had undergone a change; their robes were ragged, and stained with the road they had traveled, and stained with unholy blood; the robes of some barely covered their nakedness; and some indeed were naked. . . . No power could hold this army back, no water disperse them, no fire consume them. No, the fire could not hurt them, and the grave was not their resting-place, the earth was not their home. They looked unto Jesus, the author and the finisher of their faith . . . . Jesus going to make up my dying bed!
> —James Baldwin[3]

passage is central to the beliefs of those Christians who anticipate the rapture, while the Corinthians passage relies on the oxymoron "an imperishable body" to describe what it is that will participate in the resurrected life.

Two psalms are suggested, each one, like the readings, presenting a different tone of the promise. *Psalm 130* assumes that we are in the depths. That is, the dead go down into Hades, into the darkness of death, and await the morning, a time of light at the end. *Psalm 116*, on the other hand, is more positive in tone. We know that death is coming, but we lift up the cup of salvation, throughout life and into death, praising God for all that we have received that is good.

The Gospel option from *John 5* presents yet a different angle on the query about eternal life. In what is sometimes termed "realized eschatology," Jesus is quoted as proclaiming that eternal life is already known and experienced by those who are in Christ. Believers have already "passed from death to life." Christian teaching has usually combined this sense of an eternal life that is already enjoyed with the promise of some kind of a life beyond our knowing.

The message of these diverse readings cannot easily be meshed together. We might think of the biblical statements about the destiny of the dead as if they are a patchwork quilt. Here is a patch of deep blue, here is a patch of light green, here is a swatch of paisley, here is a gingham pattern of flowers. If we stand too close to only one swatch, we will see only that one, but the effect of standing back and surveying the whole is to be gifted by the overall effect of several different pieces forming a fascinating pattern. Commemorating our dead ought not be turned into a simple catechetical dictum about the state of the dead. There is no scriptural basis for a simplistic solution to the mystery of death. What we are given instead is a variety of pictures, each of which depicts its own vision of God's gracious gift of unending life. The gospel proclaimed on this day, on every funeral, and indeed at every Sunday Eucharist, is that however we imagine our state after death, all that is certain is the mercy of God, and in that mercy is our hope and our joy.

FOR FURTHER COMMENT

Additional comments on the Scripture texts, in part or in full, may be found in the seasonal volumes of *New Proclamation* as follows:

- Isaiah 25:6-9—Year A, Proper 23; Year B, Easter Sunday, All Saints; Years ABC, Easter Evening
- Wisdom 3:1-9—Year B, All Saints
- Psalm 23— Year A, Lent 4, Proper 23; Year B, Proper 11; Years ABC, Easter 4

- Psalm 25—Year A, Proper 21, Year B, Lent 1; Year C, Advent 1, Proper 10
- Psalm 27—Year A, Epiphany 3; Year C, Lent 2
- Psalm 116:10-17—Year A, Easter 3, Proper 6; Years ABC, Holy Thursday
- Psalm 130—Year A, Lent 5; Year B, Proper 5, Proper 8, Proper 14
- 1 Thessalonians 4:13-18—Year A, Proper 27
- 1 Corinthians 15:50-58—Year C, Epiphany 8/Proper 3
- Romans 5:5-11—Year A, Lent 3, Proper 6
- Romans 5:17-21—Year A, Lent 1
- Romans 8:31b-35, 37-39—Year A, Proper 12
- Romans 14:7-9, 10c-12—Year A, Proper 19
- 1 Corinthians 15:20-28—Year C, Easter Sunday
- 2 Corinthians 4:14—5:1—Year B, Proper 5
- 2 Corinthians 5:1, 6-10—Year B, Proper 6
- Philippians 3:20-21—Year C, Lent 2
- 2 Timothy 2:8-13—Year C, Proper 23
- Matthew 5:1-12a—Year A, Epiphany 4
- Matthew 11:25-30— Year A, Proper 9
- Matthew 25:31-46—Year A, Reign of Christ; Years ABC, New Year's Day
- Luke 7:11-17—Year C, Proper 5
- Luke 23:44-46, 50, 52-53; 24:1-6a—Year C, Passion/Palm Sunday, Easter Vigil, Easter Sunday
- Luke 24:13-16, 28-35—Year A, Easter 3; Years ABC, Easter Evening
- John 6:51-59—Year B, Proper 15, Proper 16
- John 11:17-27—Year A, Lent 5
- John 11:32-45—Year A, Lent 5; Year B, All Saints
- John 14:1-6—Year A, Easter 5

Notes

1. Ann Heidkamp, "A Litany of Women's Power," in *No Longer Strangers: A Resource for Women and Worship*, ed. Iben Gjerding and Katherine Kinnamon (Geneva: WCC Publications, 1983), 24–25.

2. "All of us," acclamation for funeral rite, *Evangelical Lutheran Worship* (Minneapolis: Augsburg Fortress, 2006), no. 223.

3. James Baldwin, *Go Tell It on the Mountain* (New York: Dell, 1953), 203–05.

PART TWO
NATIONAL DAYS AND OTHER CELEBRATIONS

Jennifer L. Lord

INTRODUCTION

JENNIFER L. LORD

This section contains comments on ten national days and other occasions not part of the church year that are nevertheless frequently observed in congregations: New Year's Eve/Day; Martin Luther King Jr. Day; Christian Unity; Earth Day; Memorial Day; Independence Day; Labor Day; Veterans' Day; Harvest; and Peace. The comments for each of these occasions include a description of the day according to its historical development and theological meanings, commentary on the texts that are appointed or suggested for that day, identification of key themes, and a collection of illustrations that connect to different thematic aspects of the day's observance.

And yet there are other questions about these days. How do they fit in to Lord's Day worship? Some parishes and congregations expect, for instance, an Independence Day Sunday service and are disappointed (or worse) if the liturgy is not focused on American patriotism. Other local assemblies choose not to mention any national observance in the liturgy. Some assemblies may include intercessions pertinent to national observances in the Prayers of the Faithful but do not expect to hear about them in the sermon or homily. Different local assemblies will engage national observances to different degrees. Some of this will depend on political sensibilities. Some of this will depend on the national day: for instance, congregations with Native American members may have particular ways to observe Harvest Day or Independence Day that are distinct from congregations with mostly Euro-American members. And how might themes from Labor Day observances look different in an urban parish as compared to a beachfront resort-area congregation?

The issue at hand is not really about incorporating these observances into a liturgy. Rather, the issue is how a preacher understands these observances to be a part of the context of the preaching. These are different ways of thinking about the church and a Lord's Day assembly in relation to these national days. The first way simply becomes a way of dressing up the liturgy, if you will. It is a way of using national observances as decoration. Churches do this for different reasons, one being that the day holds broad cultural symbolic significance and simply referencing it, singing certain related hymns, or repeating particular words (like "freedom" or "equality") will fulfill expectations about church/world connections.

This commentary, however, attends to the second way of thinking about the church's relating to national observances. These national observations exist in our North American culture and are therefore a part of our cultural context. Yet they are interpreted in different ways just as our culture is not static but varied and dynamic. This means two things for the preacher on these days: (1) the preacher will question and thing about the normative words and ceremonies connected to these days—that is, the preacher will put on her/his theological thinking cap and scrutinize the convertional use of rhetoric and symbols for these days. (2) the preacher will understand that these observances are a part of the context, and context is not the same thing as gospel. They are linked, though, for the astute observation of context means preachers can bring a focused announcement of human despair and need and an equally focused announcement of the gospel of the triune God.

Preachers should work with the Sunday texts for the Sunday gathering. Let the work with texts appointed or suggested for the observance be a way to study context. Let those secondary texts guide the way the particular observance is exegeted for our time. The preacher may wish to use the suggested texts if the communal observance occurs midweek. But even midweek services point us to the Lord's Day gathering.

All of this work is a way of seeing that each Sunday is each of these days, each Sunday is the day of freedom, equality, earth care, and just labor. The purpose here is not to remake the Sunday assembly into a theme day or a teach-in for a national observance. Sunday is the Lord's Day and our gathering on the day of resurrection is the primary way of keeping time in Christ. The purpose of the comments on these special occasions is to enable the trinitarian meanings of the regular, ongoing Sunday gathering to scrutinize and interact with all of the words, symbols, and ceremonies of these cultural observances. All of this work is toward the end of proclaiming Christ for the sake of the world.

NEW YEAR'S EVE / DAY

DECEMBER 31 / JANUARY 1

JENNIFER L. LORD

REVISED COMMON (RCL)
Eccl. 3:1-3
Psalm 8
Rev. 21:1-6a
Matt. 25:31-46

KEY THEMES

- Keeping time with Christ: the life, death, and resurrection of Christ as the pattern for our days.
- God is the giver of new life.
- Resolutions as a practice of Christian baptismal discipleship.

The civil calendar cycles through a digit-change and people around the world celebrate the New Year. Some of us can recall watching television on December 31, 1999, when reporters told us about Pacific Islander people's celebrations: places like Tonga and Samoa being among the first to mark the new century. But even when we do not go through a century change or even a decade change, we are surrounded by merrymakers on this night. Some people eat lentil soup and look for the hidden penny. Many people in Europe and North America imbibe festive drink—champagne at midnight for a New Year's toast—and sing *Auld Lang Syne*. Noisemakers, firecrackers, food, and, in the United States, the crystal-ball countdown in Times Square are all favored traditions.

Some people emphasize the opportunity for a fresh start by declaring New Year's resolutions. I know one person who temporarily papers the walls of her house so that guests can create graffiti-art of gratitude for the year past and of their hopes for themselves and the world in the new year.

This is where Christians see tensions between church and cultural practices. And here is where Christians can practice admonitions and affirmations in adapting cultural practices. New Year in the church's calendar begins with the lighting of the fire at the Great Vigil of Easter. Easter—Pascha—is the annual event in the life of the church marking deliverance from death and from the powers of evil, of deliverance unto life, of life in the Spirit of God who makes all things new. Easter is our great and annual renewal liturgy. The festival nature of New Year's celebrations should beg us to ask how we truly keep the feast of Eastertide—the Triduum, the night, the octave, and the fifty days. How do parishioners know that this indeed is the great renewal of our year, of our lives? Do we too have festive song and food, all prepared with longing and careful intentions? Do we too have songs of new life, rituals of being born anew, and the assurance of being a part of something that is beyond our individual lives? The civic traditions of New Year and the human yearnings represented in them should admonish the church to reflect on its liturgical life—that our gatherings be rich in symbol, be memorable and intense, participatory, beautiful, strong in gathering us around God's gifts in Christ of word and table, font and prayer, for the good of the world.

O holy city, seen of John, where Christ, the Lamb, does reign, within whose four-square walls shall come no night, nor need, nor pain, and where the tears are wiped from eyes that shall not weep again. O shame to us who rest content while lust and greed for gain in street and shop and tenement wring gold from human pain, and bitter lips in blind despair cry, "Christ has died in vain."
—Walter Russell Bowie[1]

And, in another layer of complexity, Christians know that the First Sunday in Advent is the time when the church changes its calendar. While the main Christian annual feast is Pascha, the calendar change for the three main lectionary traditions—the RCL, the BCP, and the LFM—occurs with the first Sunday of Advent. We begin the cycle of readings with a focus on the second coming that gives way to remembering the nativity of Christ. Our New Year thus is about Alpha and Omega, the One who is our end and our beginning. Our New Year is not *deus ex machina*, but is born in the One who is fully human and fully divine. Though our calendars change with the foci of second coming and the holy birth, our great annual feast comes only as this life is fully lived.

Texts for the Day

What then of December 31 and January 1? Some Christians observe watch-night services. New Year's watch-night services were a way of seeing in the new year, marked by intercessions for the world. Some Christians observe Name of Jesus on January 1, recalling at the start of the civil calendar year that Jesus Christ is savior of the world (see the Christmas sections of *New Proclamation* for more on this observance). In all this we know that we humans yearn for newness, for fresh starts and new chances in life. Even in the church this is not only recognized once a year at Easter. Instead, because of our life in the crucified-risen One, the church gives us language year-round to recall our new life in Christ, the ongoing work of the Spirit, our life in God who knows all passages of time. The themes of the civil-calendared New Year are not anathema to the church. Instead, we can show how the yearnings for the new year correspond deeply to words of life given to us in the very actions we do each Sunday liturgy.

The reading from *Ecclesiastes 3* gives welcome contrast to traditional feelings around New Year traditions. While New Year's festivities often emphasize being part of a crowd, belonging to a beloved (the midnight kiss!), being upbeat and giddy, the reading from this text offers the viewpoint of someone who might have been an outsider and who most certainly is not willing to gloss over life with pretend levity. Written by a teacher (and an outsider to the royal court, see 3:16; 4:13-16; 8:1-6; 10:16-20), this writer speaks to the powerlessness of the individual and the power of fate. What makes this writing even more poignant is that this book is often dated between 450 and 330 B.C.E., a span of time that saw economic growth and national possibilities for Israel. The teacher refuses to get caught up in passing bear markets but looks to the larger picture and says human beings have no control over their lives. How interesting to hear the words from Ecclesiastes 3 read on New Year's Eve when many of us normally hear this passage read at funerals. Hopes for fresh possibilities in the new year are tempered by words that declaim human strategies for the future.

> Eternal God,
> You have placed us in a world of space and time,
> and through the events of our lives
> you bless us with your love.
> Grant that in the new year we may know your presence,
> see your love at work,
> and live in the light of the event which give us joy forever—
> the coming of your Son, Jesus Christ our lord,
> whom with you and the Holy Spirit we worship and praise,
> one God, now and forever. Amen.
> —Prayer of the Day, New Year's Eve[2]

Psalm 8 repeats this theme, stressing that it is God who has created human beings with any power for authority in life. And yet this psalm nuances the Ecclesiastes reading in that humans are given glory and dominion. It is so important to keep these readings in tension, lest we imagine a sort of biological supremacy that grants leeway to disregard the rest of God's creation. If we think too highly of our powers and dominions, we need only be reminded that in the end, we have no control over our days.

Ah, but the One who does have control over our days does so in this way: promising the gift of the holy city, a place of no more death and no more mourning, crying, or pain. The epistle reading from *Revelation 21* offers that this God who oversees all things is not cold and distant, but is the very One who will dwell with us, wiping away all tears, making all things new. This very text is read in Eastertide in the RCL. The theme of all things made new is emphasized, even against strong words about our not being in control. The preacher has the opportunity truly to truly proclaim grace—it is God who makes all things new. Our resolutions do not, in the end, have the power to make everything right.

The Gospel reading, *Matthew 25:31-46*, comes in beautiful contradistinction to these other texts. From the other readings we might get the idea that we simply sit back and leave everything up to God's design, God's appointment, God's power to make new. But here we are brought to Jesus' feet at the last judgment and questioned about our care of the needy and poor in the name of God. The ones with dominion and honor, created a little less than gods (Psalm 8) are to serve the hungry, the thirsty, the stranger, the naked, the sick and in prison. Royal status on our part and the sovereignty of God on God's part do not excuse us from action in God's name. Because of the promises of God to make all things new, we act on those promises now.

PREACHING ON NEW YEAR'S EVE/DAY

The preacher may incorporate these themes into a Sunday sermon. This can be done by mention of upcoming New Year's events in the cultural context, and adding to the sense of meaning-making by speaking of New Year in terms of what we know as Easter people: God makes us new. This occasion occurs in Christmastide so the preacher can make connections between the nativity of Christ and God's purposes in being born human. For preaching that occurs at a special occasion service on New Year's Eve or New Year's Day, the preacher can work specifically with the texts and set out the tensions of the readings: God is sovereign, yet creates us to have dominion. And more, God makes us new, but we are given dominion and new life in order to serve the needy and the poor. Our being made in the image of God is not for the purpose of individualism or distinction from the whole created order. Any New Year's resolutions, then, are not for the purpose of creating self-serving or self-aggrandizing agendas. Our resolutions are for our continued participation in the body of Christ for the needs of the world. While this day holds thematic foci of gratitude for past blessings and trust in new life, the preacher can certainly ground these themes textually and proclaim the particularities of the readings. Above all, the preacher can proclaim that it is God who makes all things new.

> One thing I wasn't waiting for was a miracle.
>
> I don't like to admit it. Shouldn't that be the last thing you release: the hope that the Lord God, touched in His heart by your particular impasse among all others, will reach down and do that work none else can accomplish—straighten the twist, clear the oozing sore, open the lungs? Who knew better than I that such holy stuff occurs? Who had more reason to hope?
>
> —Leif Enger[3]

FOR FURTHER COMMENT

229

NEW YEAR'S EVE
/ DAY

DECEMBER 31
/ JANUARY 1

Additional comments on the texts for the day, in full or in part, may be found in the seasonal volumes of *New Proclamation* as follows:

- Psalm 8—Years ABC, Holy Name; Years A & C, Trinity Sunday; Year B, Proper 22
- Revelation 21:1-6a—Year B, All Saints; Year C, Easter 5
- Matthew 25:31-46—Year A, Reign of Christ

Notes

1. "O Holy City, Seen of John" (text: Walter Russell Bowie, 1909), in *The Presbyterian Hymnal* (Louisville: Westminster John Knox, 1999), no. 453.

2. Prayer of the Day, New Year's Eve, *The Church's Year: Propers and Seasonal Rites, Renewing Worship 8* (Minneapolis: Augsburg Fortress, 2004), 233.

3. Reuben Land in Leif Enger's novel *Peace Like A River* (New York: Atlantic Monthly Press, 2001), 292.

MARTIN LUTHER KING DAY

Jennifer L. Lord

Year A	Year B	Year C
Isa. 49:1-7	1 Sam. 3:1-10 (11-20)	Isa. 62:1-5
Ps. 40:1-11	Ps. 139:1-6, 13-18	Ps. 36:5-10
1 Cor. 1:1-9	1 Cor. 6:12-20	1 Cor. 12:1-11
John 1:29-42	John 1:43-51	John 2:1-11

KEY THEMES

- Church and state.
- The manifestation of God in human agency for social change.
- The relationship of racism, poverty, and violence.

In the history of the Christian church the celebration of a saint occurs on their death-day. There are some Christians who think that Martin Luther King Jr. Day should be celebrated on April 4, the day of his death. This is not in order to celebrate that he died but instead to honor him because he is thought to be a Christian martyr. Throughout his life and in his life commitments that led to his death King exemplified discipleship in Jesus Christ on a grand scale that became a witness to the world. His witness brought about his death. King strategized, taught, and lived certain commitments that were commitments in the life of Christ, even unto death.

Martin Luther King Jr. was assassinated in 1968 in Memphis, Tennessee, while he was there to support the strike by sanitation workers. It was fifteen years later that a federal holiday was created to honor King. While legislation for a commemorative holiday was introduced a mere four days after his assassination, it took a petition (with six million names) to submit the bill to Congress. The legislation did not pass and was resubmitted in each session thereafter. It finally passed in 1983 and was signed into law. By 1989 the holiday was adopted in forty-four states, but not without difficulties. Some persons contested the date, arguing that fixing the federal holiday on his birthday (January 15) was too close to Christmas and New Year's celebrations. Others contended that many persons led the civil rights movement and it was too limiting to name a holiday after one leader. One governor, in Arizona, even rescinded the holiday, an action that was met with a tourist boycott and later with the location change of the Super Bowl from Arizona to California in 1991. Today Martin Luther King Jr. Day is held on the third Monday in January.

These are all contestations after King's death. During his life he met conflict and setbacks with steady commitment to nonviolence, civic activism for civil rights, and increasing commitment to the interdependence of all people and Christians' work in the making of justice in the world.

King was born in Atlanta, Georgia, in 1929, and held degrees from Morehouse College (B.A., 1948), Crozer Theological Seminary (B.D., 1951), and Boston University (Ph.D., 1955). He was ordained in the Baptist church in 1947 and took his first post as minister of Dexter Avenue Baptist Church in Montgomery, Alabama. There he was drawn into the bus dispute after the arrest of Rosa Parks, a church worker, activist, and secretary of the local NAACP. As the new local minister who was a well-educated person and a powerful orator he was elevated to a key leadership position in what became the 381-day nonviolent bus boycott (1955–1956). This resulted in the Montgomery buses operating on a desegregated basis and the Supreme Court ruling bus segregation illegal. As a newly recognized civil rights leader, King organized the Southern Christian Leadership Conference (SCLC), which provided a base for ongoing civil rights work. Today that nonprofit, nonsectarian, interfaith advocacy organization carries on King's work through national efforts to use conflict resolution to end violence in all communities.

> If we are to survive today, our moral and spiritual "lag" must be eliminated. Enlarged material powers spell enlarged peril if there is not proportionate growth of the soul. When the "without" of man's nature subjugates the "within," dark storm clouds begin to form in the world. This problem of spiritual and moral lag, which constitutes modern man's chief dilemma, expresses itself in three larger problems which grow out of man's ethical infantilism. Each of these problems, while appearing to be separate and isolated, is inextricably bound to the other. I refer to racial injustice, poverty, and war.
> —Martin Luther King Jr.[1]

King traveled nationally to speak, visited India to study Gandhi's philosophy of nonviolence, and in 1959 resigned from his pastorate to concentrate fully on civil rights work. The Kings moved to Atlanta where he became copastor of Ebenezer Baptist Church with his father. King continued to travel, speak, engage in nonviolent protests, and endure subsequent arrests and jail time. In 1963 the Birmingham campaign (peaceful demonstrations for desegregation of merchants) was launched, setting in motion a series of events (demonstrations, a violent police response, and the bombing of Ebenezer Church) that brought him worldwide attention and garnering some 250,000 persons for a march on Washington (site of the famous "I Have A Dream" speech). In 1964 Martin Luther King Jr., at age thirty-five, was awarded the Nobel Peace Prize. In his acceptance speech King spoke of the inextricably bound evils of racism, poverty, and violence.

Therefore, though the Civil Rights Act of 1964 brought a comprehensive ban on segregation, King was hard at work on further action, now for voting rights. It was decided that SCLC would launch this initiative in Selma, Alabama. The Selma campaign echoed that of Birmingham with its peaceful demonstrations that were met by police and illicit violence that was in turn reported nationally. In 1965 the Voting Rights Act was signed into law and King began to speak more pointedly about socioeconomic problems. In 1967 he announced the beginning of the Poor People's Campaign, which focused on freedom and jobs for the poor, regardless of race. A march was announced, but the plans for this march on Washington were interrupted by King's fateful decision to travel to Memphis to march in support of the sanitation workers' strike there.

The nation celebrates Martin Luther King Jr. Day in late January, which for the church is the season after the Epiphany. Themes of light, manifestation, and God's mission to the world come from the texts for these Sundays. Even with this sketch of some events in King's life the preacher can see evidence of the witness of this person that bears witness to the manifestation of God shining in our days.

We are reminded in many ways of the quiet ministry of the spirit of the living God in our lives and in life that abounds around us. The little healings of the silent breaches, the great redemptive acts when times are out of joint, the lifting of our horizons of hope when to have hope seems to be against all wisdom and against all judgment, the stirring of the will to forgive when for so long a time we have been buried under an avalanche of great hostilities—there are so many ways by which the ministry of the living God tutors the spirit, corrects the times, gives lift to the days.
—Howard Thurman[2]

Texts for the Day

The texts associated with this day are the texts from the Second Sunday after Epiphany (RCL; see the seasonal editions of New Proclamation on this date for further comment). The Gospel According to John is appointed for each year and each of the lections emphasizes who this Jesus is: he is the Lamb who will change our sinful condition; he is the One who makes disciples and beckons all to come and see what he will do; he is the One who, like at the wedding, is the revelation of God and is able to do all things. In this Gospel Jesus is the eternal Word and by his resurrection we live eternal life now.

Year A pairs Isaiah with the Johannine Lamb of God. God also calls the servant in this section of Isaiah before birth to bear God's prophecy to the nations. This servant with skills of speech and stealth is to speak God's salvation to the ends of the earth. The reading from 1 Corinthians announces the Corinthians' strength in God through Jesus Christ. All speech, knowledge, and spiritual gifts are gifts of God in the community.

Year B appoints the account of the call of Samuel to accompany the Gospel account of the call of Jesus' disciples. The epistle reading from 1 Corinthians speaks about food and fornication but is part of a larger argument by Paul concerning the church's ethic: what is beneficial to the whole community rather than beneficial to individuals. The call to discipleship is service as part of a body.

Year C includes a reading from a later chapter in the book, hence a portion of Third Isaiah. These verses speak of the future of Zion (in the face of exilic return from Babylon). The prophet will not keep silent until the world knows that the glory of the Lord is upon the nation Israel. This passage is set next to the account of the wedding at Cana and the manifestation of Jesus' identity through his miracle there. The epistle reading contains the familiar words about the multiple gifts of the Spirit, which are of the one Lord.

Martin Luther King Jr. committed his life to the civil rights movement. Many people simply think of King's Washington speech, "I Have a Dream." But in the later years, beginning with the Nobel Prize acceptance speech, King spoke repeatedly of the interrelationship of poverty and violence with racism. In the civil rights movement King dedicated himself to the eradication of racism, poverty, and violence. It will be helpful for the preacher to make these connections evident to parishioners. Additionally the preacher may work to show how racism, poverty, and violence are full-fledged systems of oppression in which we (wittingly and unwittingly) participate each day.

The preacher may move through the texts of these Sundays and find clear connections to the discipleship of Christ evidenced in Martin Luther King Jr. It is important to keep in mind the witness aspect of Dr. King's life and work. The sermon should not be a biography laced with Scriptures from the day. Rather, the witness of Dr. King helps us look for ways that ongoing witness to the justice of God is manifest now in our days: his life, even with human shortfallings, was full of good work and work that pointed out systemic sin. This is what the saints do: in their humanness they witness to the gospel of Jesus Christ.

Long after King himself began to doubt the goodness of the "white brother" and the tainted principles of civil religion, his expression of hope in the kinship of the races endures, as the Sermon on the Mount endures, as a mark to aim at in a sinfully divided society. The more pessimistic he grew with regard to humanity, the more optimistic he became about God. Even in the darkest period of his own discouragement, he continued to say to African Americans, "Go ahead! God can be trusted." The power of God still shapes the believer of individuals and institutions.

After King's death, his old mentor Pius Barbour said in a sermon, "Mike was a great believer in this, the attitude of Jesus: He believed spiritual power could down any power. Can it?"

It is a measure of the preacher's abiding influence in our lives that we still ask the question and want to answer, Yes.
—Richard Lischer[3]

Notes

1. Martin Luther King Jr., Nobel Prize Acceptance Speech from *Nobel Lectures, Peace 1951–1970*, ed. Frederick W. Haberman (Amsterdam: Elsevier, 1972), http://nobelprize.org/nobel_prizes/peace/laureates/1964/king-acceptance.html (accessed July 3, 2007).

2. Howard Thurman, in *A Reconciliation Sourcebook,* compiled by Kathleen Hughes and Joseph A. Favazza (Chicago: Liturgy Training Publications, 1997), 55.

3. Richard Lischer, *The Preacher King: Martin Luther King Jr. and the Word That Moved America* (New York: Oxford University Press, 1995), 269.

CHRISTIAN UNITY

JANUARY 18 (EARLIEST)–JANUARY 25 (LATEST)

JENNIFER L. LORD

LUTHERAN (ELW)
Isa. 2:2-4
Psalm 133
Eph. 4:3-6
John 17:15-23

KEY THEMES

• Unity in diversity.
• Gifts and challenges of Christian unity.
• Christian unity, multiculturalism, and religious pluralism.

In the twenty-first century two of the most recognized international structures for ecumenical Christian relations and action are the World Council of Churches (WCC) and the annual Week of Prayer for Christian Unity. The Week of Prayer for Christian Unity began as the Church Unity Octave, initiated in 1908 by a Franciscan friar. Now the Roman Catholic Church and the WCC organize this effort jointly and prepare resource materials for parishes and congregations to use during this annual week of prayer for Christian unity.

The history of the formation of the WCC begins in earlier centuries. Protestants were involved in efforts for interdenominational work in nineteenth-century missionary societies and in Christian organizations such as the YMCA, the YWCA, and the Student Volunteer Movement. In the early twentieth century these initiatives became part of two groups: the Life and Work movement and the Faith and Order movement. The Life and Work movement was an ecumenical effort by Protestants and Orthodox Christians that focused on practical actions of the church in society. The initial meeting was in Geneva in 1920. This movement later became a part of the WCC. The Faith and Order movement became a compliment to the Life and Faith movement in that it focused on diversities of belief, liturgical practices, polity, and ministry for the purpose of understanding differences between Christian churches and issues in possible reunions. The Faith and Order movement also was incorporated into the WCC. Two additional ecumenical tributaries also joined the WCC in later years, the International Missionary Council and the Council of Christian Education (with roots back to the eighteenth-century Sunday school movement).

Church leaders agreed to the establishment of the WCC in 1937 but the actual assembly happened after World War II, in 1948 in Amsterdam with 147 churches assembled. Though the Roman Catholic Church is not a member of the WCC it works closely with the Council and sends representatives to the major conferences and committee meetings. Members include most Orthodox churches, Anglican, Baptist, Lutheran, Methodist, Reformed, and independent church bodies. The goal is to deepen fellowship so that Christian church bodies may see in others the apostolic faith as expressed in the creedal language, "one holy, catholic and apostolic church." The goal of the WCC is not to form a world church but to be an instrument for bearing witness to Jesus Christ and to work for the unity that Christ wills for the church.

What are the ways that Christians can be different from each other and what should be held in common unity? It is difficult to differentiate between diversity and disunity. Some would say that Christians encounter disunity every day in many ways. If we pay attention to lobbyists and political news we will hear opinions by self-identified Christians who think differently than we do. Members of any local parish or congregation will have divergent understandings of the words sung in a hymn or prayed together. We may not be able to recognize those from different cultures as Christians. At many seminaries women will sit in classes alongside those whose church bodies do not ordain women for ministry. In small (and large) towns certain pastors will not join local ministerial groups because of theological tensions. Some members of denominations are weary of church battles over different causes and find it easier to form splinter groups. Local parishes and congregations know their own interchurch histories of conflict. Some of these differences merely make for high emotions. Some of these differences are the reason for ongoing wars in many countries. What are the distinctions between unity in diversity and disunity?

In addition, the issues of Christian unity are not only about how we diverge in practice and beliefs, but are also about how we do and do not consider others to be Christians. For instance, some churches identify themselves as the true church while other churches identify themselves as a part of the true church.

Long ago, Plotinus wrote, "If we are in unity with the Spirit, we are in unity with each other, and so we are all one." . . . When I have lost harmony with another, my whole life is thrown out of tune. God tends to be remote and far away; when a desert and sea appear between me and another. I draw close to God as I draw close to my fellows. The great incentive remains ever alert; I cannot be at peace without God, and I cannot be truly aware of God if I am not at peace with my fellows. For the sake of my unity with God, I keep working on my relations with my fellows. This is ever the insistence of all ethical religions.
—Howard Thurman[1]

In other words, some church bodies think that only their form of the Christian tradition is the real Christian church and all other forms need to convert to their tradition. Yet other church bodies think that the diversity of Christian traditions and denominations is an expression of the fullness of the body of Christ. These church bodies believe that they are one part of the greater church. This has been the historic tension with the Orthodox churches and this is a newer tension with Pentecostal churches: both groups have understood themselves to be the one true church to which others need to convert.

We also make these distinctions about who is and is not Christian based both on doctrines and based on actions. We are not even in agreement about how we are to discern our or another's fidelity to Christ. This tension often plays out between theological reality and praxis (as if the two are not related) with either one taking priority (theology is an abstraction to be set aside for real actions, or, our experiences and actions are minimized to fit the theological categories that are held to be preeminent). In other words, are our descriptions of Christian unity or division based on visible practices or on theologies? Is it right to perpetuate the disjunction between the two?

It is an irony that Christian soteriology presumably based on Paul's theology in Galatians and Romans generally has tended to claim a "universal validity" and become triumphalistic and exclusivist as a result, refusing to see authenticity in any form of "other"-ness. We have seen . . . that a holistic understanding of Paul's theology does not necessarily support such an exclusivist soteriology. Therefore, the conventional, exclusivist Christian soteriology will have to be revised through careful historical reconstruction as well as existentially meaningful theological appropriations.
—Eung Chun Park[2]

Texts for the Day

The Evangelical Lutheran Church in America appoints these texts for the Occasion of Christian Unity: Isa. 2:2-4; Psalm 133; Eph. 4:3-6; and John 17:15-23. These texts may bring other texts to mind, but let us begin here.

The passage from Isaiah dates from the eighth century B.C.E. and was written at a time of international tension. The Assyrian empire was expanding and beginning attacks on Syria, Israel, and Judah and even replaced the king of Judah (Ahaz) with a king more amenable to their causes. It is in the midst of this time of international wars, national unrest, and appointment of puppet kings that this passage about international relations was composed. This section along with 4:2-6 brackets a series of judgments against Israel. The words that bracket the judgments are words of future hope and the enduring centrality of Jerusalem as the house of God. Here is a picture of nations united, of universal disarmament, of settled disputes. The psalm echoes these ideas with depictions of how good it is to live in unity. God will bring unity to the nations.

The passage from Ephesians also speaks to a context of disunity but emphasizes the necessity of human actions to maintain unity. This letter was written sometime in the first century C.E., though most likely not by Paul. It is written to a Christian community of both Jews and Gentiles in the important city on the west coast of Asia Minor, Ephesus, a town on the Aegean Sea. There was tension between Jewish and Gentile believers and this book sets out theological teaching and ethical exhortation. Chapter four is part of this exhortation and this passage. Here we read that Christ makes unity possible but we must put human effort into maintaining this unity. This passage names seven ways that Christians are one.

Jesus' final prayer in the Gospel according to John includes a petition for all disciples and all who will believe. It is a petition for all to be one. This petition rests on Jesus' oneness with the Father. This Gospel, with its theological understanding that eternal life is upon us now, underscores the necessity for the unity of the disciples. This prayer reaches out to us: we are the future believers for whom Jesus prays. By these words, God gives us unity now and we are to continue in the unity of God as believers.

The preacher will need to select a focus for this day. Even the focus on unity is too large for one sermon. The preaching will be most powerful when it attends to the particular church context even as it teaches, expands

> Singing is the most human, most companionable of the arts. It joins us together in the whole realm of sound, forging a group identity where there were only individuals and making a communicative statement that far transcends what any one of us could do alone. It is a paradigm of union with the creator. It is what the words talk about. We *need* to sing well.
> —Alice Parker[3]

views, or reframes theological understandings. Perhaps a focal issue is that people understand Christianity as a gathering of individuals rather than a corporate entity. The preacher may wish to begin there and then expand our views to name all with whom we are joined when we are incorporated into the Body of Christ (the communion of saints, different nationalities, races, incomes, ages, and so forth). Or the preacher may identify that there are judgments between who is and who is not a Christian. The Ephesians passage is a helpful starting place as it speaks of both actions we share and systems of belief. The preacher may feel moved to give a rallying cry for unity—and all three passages depict the greatness of God's uniting work. The preacher can then move to address our human actions that flow from such a sense of corporate identity—how do our actions in Lord's Day worship depict our unity? The preacher may explore how efforts of Christian unity help us live faithfully in the even broader networks of religious pluralism and multiculturalism. Christian unity is a vast topic and the preacher will need to select a focus for the day.

For Further Comment

Additional comments on these Scripture texts, in part or in full, may be found in the seasonal volumes of *New Proclamation* as follows:

- Isaiah 2:2-4—Year A, Advent 1
- Psalm 133—Year A, Proper 15; Year B, Easter 2, Proper 7
- Ephesians 4:3-6—Year B, Proper 13
- John 17:15-23—Years B & C, Easter 7

Notes

1. Howard Thurman, *The Mood of Christmas* (New York: Harper and Row, 1973).

2. Eung Chun Park, *Either Jew or Gentile: Paul's Unfolding Theology of Inclusivity* (Louisville: Westminster John Knox, 2003), 80.

3. Alice Parker, in *Music: A Sourcebook about Music*, compiled by Alan J. Hommerding and Diana Kodner (Chicago: Liturgy Training, 1997), 1.

EARTH DAY

APRIL 22

JENNIFER L. LORD

SUGGESTED TEXTS
Gen. 1:28-31
Psalm 8
Rev. 7:1-3
John 6:1-14

KEY THEMES

- Theological understandings of human dominion and subjugation: How does our freedom in Christ call us to live?
- Interdependence of humans with each other, all species, and the cosmos.
- Stewardship for coming generations.

In 1962 Senator Gaylord Nelson began strategizing ways to bring environmental concerns to the forefront of United States political agendas. He requested that President Kennedy go on a national conservation tour. Yet repeated efforts to introduce legislation proved unsuccessful. Finally Senator Nelson decided to tap into the antiwar energy of the late 1960s. At a 1969 conference in Seattle it was announced that April 22, 1970, would be a day of national grassroots demonstrations on behalf of environmental concerns. On that day millions of persons demonstrated, including many local schools and communities.

In our century the Earth Day Network (for one) continues to promote "environmental citizenship and year round progressive action world wide." This Network coordinates the efforts of 15,000 organizations in 174 countries for any environmental-focused work ranging from work for clean air to better public schools and transportation means for all people (http://www.earthday.net/). Christians of different nations and denominations have made environmental efforts. Many of us remember early initiatives to stop the use of styrofoam cups for coffee hour. Youth groups planted trees and collected trash. Sunday school curriculum for all ages began to emphasize care for environment. Seminaries of the church now contract with companies using wind-generated electricity.

Here is one way the church speaks of environmental citizenship: the Litany of Penitence for Ash Wednesday from *The Book of Common Prayer* includes this petition: "For our waste and pollution of your creation, and our lack of concern for those who come after us, Accept our repentance, Lord." In other words, the Christian church has long prayed for the very concerns now voiced by those who participate in Earth Day events.

This is key. The interest in environmental concerns is not new to the church. It is not a social cause spearheaded by idealists. It is a theological, biblical, historical, and ecumenical claim: the church is to pray and care for the earth. And while some Christians want to read cosmological passages like Genesis 1 and Psalm 8 to assert humanity's dominion over the earth, the sacramental center of the church's practice says otherwise. In the very gifts of God in the earth's provision of grain, fruit, and water, the church encounters the One who came not to dominate but to serve. In Jesus' name we care for all creation as stewards of God's gift of land, water, air, and space. At our annual Paschal feast we tell time according to our planet's relationship to sun and moon, we light the new fire (like other ancient cultures' fires of new year) and proclaim Christ is our light, we hear the bees extolled for making the wax of our candles, we call upon heavenly powers to rejoice, the readings are full of accounts of creation and new creation, we are baptized or sprinkled again with living water and fed from the abundance of God's good earth at the table. Year-round our Sunday assemblies shape us for caring for all life, including that of the earth.

The world is charged with the grandeur of God.
It will flame out, like shining from shook foil;
It gathers to a greatness, like the ooze of oil
Crushed. Why do men then now not reck his rod?
Generations have trod, have trod, have trod;
And all is seared with trade; bleared, smeared with toil;
And wears man's smudge and shares man's smell: the soil
Is bare now, nor can foot feel, being shod.
And for all this, nature is never spent;
There lives the dearest freshness deep down things;
And though the last lights off the black West went
Oh, morning, at the brown brink eastward, springs—
Because the Holy Ghost over the bent
World broods with warm breast and with ah! bright wings.
—Gerard Manley Hopkins[1]

Yet this is true: in our time we see only increasing complexities in environmental issues. In the United States we could begin by thinking about land and land rights—whose land is American soil, historically? And now, in many areas, land purchase does not necessarily include the water, mineral, or even air rights of that land area. What does it mean that we have the concept of owning and dividing land, air, water, and mineral? What does ownership mean in discussions of shared and dwindling resources? A look through a telescope at the rings of Saturn or at the clouds and gases of a Nebula can remind us of the precariousness of such perceived ownership: the universe and its environments are vast and are beyond our control. Our attempts to own, divide, and use natural resources thoughtlessly are causing damage.

The preacher's task in all of this is to study deeper issues of environmentalism such as interdependence between humans, between humans and environment, and, as the litany says, our responsibility to others of future generations. At the same time let the preacher balance information that seems to present overwhelming odds of deteriorating natural resources and civilities of stewardship with announcement of what our hope and our work is as the body of Christ. In all of this, how can a sermon on Earth Day be more than a teaching sermon (which often teach but lack proclamation of gospel) or, worse, a lecture (we must, ought, should) that poses as a sermon because Scripture is quoted?

Texts for the Day

Genesis 1:28-31 is a portion of the larger creation account of Genesis 1 and shows the emphasis on God as all-knowing, all-powerful, and distinct from human beings. It could be important to include this passage in preaching because it contains the imperative for human dominion over other aspects of creation and it describes a food chain. This is the imperative often misconstrued as sanction for human disregard of earth and space. But the preacher can set this alongside the good intent of God's creating work and the twisted distortions that come to all relationships because of human sin (see Genesis 2, 3).

Likewise the preacher may want to include *Psalm 8*, again as a way of naming clearly how these words are often spoken with human hubris. This psalm has been used to assert human dominion over the rest of the created order. Instead the words themselves set out the very perspective of seeing ourselves in relation to the moon and the stars, indeed of seeing ourselves in relation to the Sovereign One, God's very self.

> Merciful Creator,
> Your hand is open wide
> to satisfy the needs of every living creature.
> Make us always thankful for your loving providence;
> and grant that we,
> remembering the account that we must one day give,
> may be faithful stewards of your good gifts,
> through Jesus Christ our Savior and Lord,
> whom with you and the Holy Spirit we worship and praise,
> one God, now and forever. Amen.
> —Prayer of the Day, Stewardship of Creation[2]

And these texts could be set against the verses of *Revelation 7:1-3*, part of the great vision of John at the end time. Here the imperative is the opposite: do not harm tree, land, or air. These verses were part of the letter written to a community under great oppression and the visions urge faithfulness to God over against the world's emperor. In this passage the four angels stand at the four corners of the earth and hold back the destructive forces of the four winds, protecting the sea, land, and trees. These are the trees whose leaves will be used for the healing of the nations. The force of God is in our surroundings; the force of God cries out protection for sea, land, and trees. The protection of these is until all humans are sealed in God's own protection. And we wait for that day.

The preacher could set alongside these passages the Johannine account of the feeding of the five thousand, *John 6:1-14*. The portrayal of Jesus by this Gospel writer is that this One is the eternal Word, with God and of God from the beginning. Jesus, then, is the new creation. And here, in the midst of a "great deal of grass" (6:10), the people sit and are fed. Out of five loaves and two fishes there is enough for five thousand. After the feeding, there are twelve baskets of leftovers remaining. There is instruction to feed all. There is right use of resources, according to the imperative of Jesus. And there is abundance in the feeding and in the fragments that remain.

> The Christian faith trusts that God has joined us amid the damage. The center of the cosmos, by the biblical account, is not just the "throne." It is also the wounded Lamb. In the cross-death, Jesus shares the lot of the little, powerless, and persecuted ones. But he also comes among trees torn down to become execution posts, seas overfished by starving people, and the earth desperately farmed for the sake of absentee landlords and unjust taxes.
> —Gordon W. Lathrop[3]

There is no set list of readings for this day; these are suggested texts. April 22 will always be during Lent, the Great Three Days, or the fifty days of Easter. The themes of new creation, of God's abundance and forgiveness, and of our resurrection life are constant. These are true foci for each Lord's Day assembly, but we immerse ourselves in them during the baptismal preparations for Easter and the fifty days of Eastertide. An Earth Day observance would not trump our time in Lent or Easter. But this observance can tug at sleeves and remind us that the whole earth cries out in longing for redemption.

Earth Day Preaching

If the preacher approaches sermon preparation with the law/gospel tension in mind, then the law that convicts us is how we have not lived out a dominion of stewardship. Evidence abounds with the statistics of rising temperatures, dying species, and animals dislocated by destruction of natural habitats. There will be no leaves left to heal the nations; we have not gathered the loaves and fishes for others. Yet the texts tell us that creation is not ours to control and God is powerful to perpetuate abundance. There is gift upon gift of sea, land, air, animals, plant, trees, loaves, and fishes in these passages. The preacher could also prepare to preach by reflecting on the elements of liturgy; we are shaped weekly in our assemblies to care beyond ourselves, beyond our little territories of home, family, and work. We gather and by our words say we are not gathered in our own name but in the name of the triune God, creator of all things. We confess our sins. We listen to readings and proclamation that reorients us. We pray for all needs of the world. We offer our first fruits. We are sent as Christ's own body into the world Christ loves. The preacher can help us see that our dying and rising in Christ, enacted each Sunday, is deeply a dominion of stewardship, of care, of interdependence. Here are two ways to think about preaching on this occasion that are not agenda driven, but that look at the ways we are formed to see the world, the cosmos, even the great expanse of grass where Jesus feeds us too.

For Further Comment

Additional comments on the suggested texts for the day, in full or in part, may be found in the seasonal volumes of *New Proclamation* as follows:

- Genesis 1:28-31—Year A, Trinity Sunday; Years ABC, Easter Vigil
- Psalm 8—Years ABC, New Year's Day, Holy Name; Years A & C, Trinity Sunday; Year B, Proper 22
- John 6:1-14—Year B, Proper 12

Notes

1. Gerard Manley Hopkins, *God's Grandeur,* in *Poems of Gerard Manley Hopkins,* 3d ed. (New York: Oxford University Press, 1948).

2. Prayer of the Day, "Stewardship of Creation," *The Church's Year: Propers and Seasonal Rites, Renewing Worship 8* (Minneapolis: Augsburg Fortress, 2004), 232.

3. Gordon W. Lathrop, *Holy Ground: A Liturgical Cosmology* (Minneapolis: Fortress Press, 2003), 211.

MEMORIAL DAY

Last Monday in May:
May 25 (earliest)–May 31 (latest)

Jennifer L. Lord

Suggested Texts
Job 38:22-25, 27-38
Ps. 104:1-9
Eph. 6:10-20
Mark 10:35-45

KEY THEMES

- A theology of remembering.
- Patriotism for country and/versus God's kingdom.
- Military service and Christian discipleship.

Memorial Day was first known as Decoration Day. It was established nationally in 1868, three years after the Civil War ended. It was perhaps first observed at the end of May (May 30) because it was thought that flowers for grave decorations would be available nationwide. In the early years speeches were given at the Arlington mansion near Washington, D.C., and children from the Soldiers' and Sailors' Orphan Home and members of the organization of Union veterans (the Grand Army of the Republic, or the GAR) walked through the National Cemetery dispersing flowers, singing hymns, and reciting prayers for those who had died in the Civil War. Many towns in both the North and South claim to be the birthplace of Decoration Day observances. After World War I the day was expanded to honor all who had died in American wars. In 1966 President Lyndon Johnson declared Waterloo, New York, to be the birthplace of Memorial Day. A ceremony there one hundred years prior had honored those who had died in the Civil War; businesses were closed, flags were flown at half-staff. Memorial Day was declared a national holiday in 1971 and appointed for the last Monday in May.

In December 2000, The National Moment of Remembrance Act was signed into law. This act encourages all U.S. citizens to observe commemorations, specifically to keep a moment of silence at 3 P.M. local time on Memorial Day.

One grassroots tradition is the distribution of red poppies to veterans on Memorial Day. In the early twentieth century a World War I Canadian colonel, John McCrae, had written a poem, "In Flanders Fields," about the Flanders' battlefield (western Belgium and northern France), which dwelt upon the image of the red poppies among rows of white crosses. The recital of this poem has become a standard part of community Memorial Day observances.

In the year I write this, as with many years, Memorial Day weekend coincides with the fiftieth day of Easter, Pentecost. Memorial Day will always fall either within the great fifty days of Easter or in the days close after Pentecost. Those persons preparing liturgies and sermons may make mention of remembrances for those who have died in American wars. Most often such remembrances occur in the form of prayers as a part of the intercessions of the day. Yet great numbers of parishioners will visit graves of loved ones and many still will attend a local commemorative service to honor those who have died.

Memorial Day reflections in civil speeches and in sermons can often bear the same sense as some eulogies: a remembrance of the dead that dwells on all the good, right, and honorable characteristics of the person or the deed. Those in attendance are right to sense a falsity in this because certain realities are not named. The preacher will do well to keep in mind the focus of funeral sermons and (even) eulogies: namely a truthful remembrance that names the shortfalls as well as the good of the person, all in the light of God's gift of life. In Memorial Day remembrances there is a great sense of grief for the deceased themselves as well as for their great numbers. And there is grief for the absence of peace and the necessity of the history of wars. The preacher will do well to work to enable persons to hear both things: honoring of lives but lament for any bloodthirst and the necessity of military service. These days, as we live with division of opinion about the ongoing Iraq War, we can all be helped by deeper discussions of patriotism and love of country. Some persons would have us think that the only way to be a patriot is to say all manner of positive things about all American wars and veterans. Theologically this is untenable since all human decisions and actions are not yet lived out in the full righteousness of God's intending.

Thus it is helpful to think about the place and function of memory. The ultimate point of memory for Christians is the paschal mystery, the life, death, and resurrection of Christ Jesus. In life, in death, and in life beyond death we belong

> In Flanders fields the poppies blow
> Between the crosses, row on row,
> That mark our place; and in the sky
> The larks, still bravely singing, fly.
> Scarce heard amid the guns below.
>
> We are the dead. Short days ago
> We lived, felt dawn, saw sunset glow,
> Loved, and were loved, and now we lie
> In Flanders fields.
>
> Take up our quarrel with the foe:
> To you from failing hands we throw
> The torch; be yours to hold it high.
> If you break faith with us who die
> We shall not sleep, though poppies grow
> In Flanders fields.—John McCrae[1]

to this One and no other. Many Christians participate each Sunday in this ultimate remembering through the Eucharist. This remembering is God's gift to us, making us participants in Christ. In the meal we are claimed freshly in Christ as his body, for each other, for the world. Memory at Eucharist means identity making: we are who we are in the life of the triune God. Our identities are sealed in our baptisms and each week at table we partake of this truth.

Memorial Day remembrances, then, are at best penultimate. They are about humans remembering humans and human actions. And we are off the mark if we permit these remembrances to give definitive identity. And yet many will need help to discover an identity beyond such descriptions of heroism, beyond events of magnitude (wars) that through their trauma create deep connections. The deaths need a reason, otherwise they seem so senseless, violent, wrenching, distant, and costly. The preacher can do this work in sermons all through the year so that when such things are heard on Memorial Day they are not a surprise: all human decisions and efforts do sometimes serve the glory of God but still fall short of the fullness of God's desires. In other words, patriotism writ large is a falsity because it assumes that we, our nation, know and act with the mind of God. Instead, we need help to think about the nobility of patriotism in small and large acts as we seek good for all, safety for all, and freedom for all. We remember those who died in service for this country. We give thanks for everything in them that was good and kind and faithful. And by the power of the Spirit of Christ we trust God to bring new life from all of our human works.

> O Trinity of love and power,
> All travelers guard in danger's hour;
> From rock and tempest, fire and foe,
> Protect them where-soe'er they go;
> Thus evermore shall rise to Thee
> Glad praise from air and land and sea.
> —William Whiting[2]

TEXTS FOR THE DAY

A parish may hold a Memorial Day liturgy or the preacher may wish to focus more on the themes of this day for a particular occasion. Suggested texts include Job 38:22-25, 27-38; Psalm 104:1-9; Ephesians 6:10-20; and Mark 10:35-45.

This passage from Job reflects the nature of Wisdom literature and its focus on human concerns. It is not a book about particular historical events, but a book about a human being (innocent) enduring suffering. Scholars, not knowing an author or date for this writing, heighten this universal theme, though it is supposed to have been collected in final form between the seventh and fourth centuries B.C.E. The suggested text is a portion of what is known as the whirlwind speech. Here God finally responds to Job and there is no answer given to Job's questions about righteousness and suffering. Instead, in this whirlwind speech

God is portrayed as the great creator and deliberator who has made and oversees all things. This passage is surely set beside questions of suffering for our time. But it can also be set beside our contemporary human propensity for saying that various national actions are part of the purpose of God. To our unwavering certitude these whirlwind words bring perspective. The psalm continues this train of thought with its recital of God's oversight and control of created order.

Set next to this grand reminder of our smallness in God's order is the text from Ephesians with its battle imagery. The preacher can remind hearers that these words about putting on armor were intended for Christians' battle with the enduring evil powers. The emphasis is that evil is a great power and that the baptized community must bear witness against those powers. It is so easy to literalize such passages. It is also easy to avoid this battle imagery. Yet it may be helpful in some contexts to use this battle imagery in a way that does not easily equate it with national wars but instead with our ongoing baptismal posture as those in Christ who belong first to Christ and therefore question every other power that might dissuade the church from its purpose. Throughout this epistle there is a contrast of the old life with new life in Christ as the church endeavors to live as Christ's body for the world.

> Lord of all worlds, guide this nation by your Spirit to go forward in justice and freedom. Give to all our people the blessings of well-being and harmony, but above all things give us faith in you, that our nation may bring glory to your name and blessings to all peoples, through Jesus Christ, our Savior and Lord.
> —*Evangelical Lutheran Worship*[3]

The Gospel reading continues this theme of reoriented power in the contrast between the disciples' question about being great and Jesus' response about the cup of suffering. This passage is surrounded by continuous teachings about being a servant in order to be great. The power structures of the time are upended in Jesus' description of glory that includes suffering. This passage is surrounded by the sense of threat from local and empirical powers and yet Jesus continues to reference his own condemnation, death, and rising. It is this path that he sets out as the path of glory for his followers. In the face of the disciples' ambition Jesus says that to share his cup is to be a servant in the kingdom of God. And God's kingdom judges all earthly kingdoms.

The preacher's context will make a difference for how Memorial Day is observed. Nonetheless, preachers can ultimately help deepen conversations around these issues even if not all of it happens in one sermon or specifically on this day. It is also important to note that in practice Memorial Day observations blend both with Veterans' Day (honoring all who have served, living or dead) and All Saints Day (remembering all the dead, even those who did not die in an American war).

FOR FURTHER COMMENT

Additional comments on the suggested texts, in part or in full, may be found in the seasonal volumes of *New Proclamation* as follows:

- Job 38:22-25, 27-38—Year B, Proper 24
- Psalm 104:1-9—Year B, Proper 24
- Ephesians 6:10-20—Year B, Proper 16
- Mark 10:35-45—Year B, Proper 24

Notes

1. John McCrae, "In Flanders Fields;" http://www1.va.gov/opa/speceven/memday/history.asp#hist (accessed June 5, 2007).

2. William Whiting, "Eternal Father, Strong To Save," in *The Presbyterian Hymnal* (Louisville: Westminster John Knox, 1990), no. 562.

3. Prayer of the Day, National Holiday, in *Evangelical Lutheran Worship* (Minneapolis: Augsburg Fortress, 2006), 136.

INDEPENDENCE DAY

July 4

Jennifer L. Lord

Episcopal (BCP)
Deut. 10:17–21
Psalm 145 or 145:1–9
Heb. 11:8–16
Matt. 5:43–48

KEY THEMES

- All nations under God.
- Our baptismal identity and the command to love our enemies.
- Public debate and the processes of democracy.

Independence Day (The Fourth of July) is a national holiday in the United States that marks the official adoption of the Declaration of Independence by the Second Continental Congress on July 4, 1776. By this act the Congress declared that the American colonies were free from all allegiance to the British Crown. Earlier that spring several of the thirteen colonies had taken steps toward declaring independence from Great Britain. One of the most notable efforts was the resolution proposing independence brought to Congress on May 15, 1776, by Richard Henry Lee of the Virginia delegation. In addition to this governmental activity historians note the influence that Thomas Paine's pamphlet, *Common Sense,* had on public attitudes about the inevitability of independence from Britain. The date July 4 represents national independence and all of the civil strife, political debates, rebellion, heroism, treachery, and risk that were a part of the formation of a new nation.

The Declaration of Independence is the document that was adopted that day. Eight days later that Congress was presented with a draft of "Articles of confederation and perpetual union," written by John Dickinson, chair of a committee representing the colonies. Appointed members of the Congress had been developing a new form of government for the confederated colonies at the same time that Thomas Jefferson was writing a draft of the Declaration of Independence.

After Dickinson's draft was read at Congress on July 12, 1776, it was resolved that copies would be printed and brought to each member of the Congress. Debates then continued, especially around issues of taxation, congressional representation, and western borders. Debates were postponed while Congress was relocated from Philadelphia to Baltimore and elsewhere later due to continuing threats of British occupation. Even subsequent debates and ratification were delayed due to shortage of printed copies. The Articles of Confederation were not approved until March 1, 1781 (after they had been engrossed in 1778).

In September 1786 a number of delegates met in Annapolis, Maryland, to discuss lacuna in the Articles. These delegates passed a resolution calling for all delegates to meet to discuss how the government could address certain exigencies (such as lack of trade regulation). Resolutions that came to be known as the Virginia Plan and the New Jersey plan were presented to Congress, outlining the power and structure of the three branches of government. After many debates and amendments a draft was handed to each delegate on August 6, 1787. The Constitution was signed on September 20, 1787. Not too much later amendments to the Constitution were proposed (through efforts of the so-called anti-Federalists) and ten of them were ratified, becoming the ten amendments that we today know as the Bill of Rights.

Though July 4 marks the date of only one of these four documents it is the pivotal date in national identity, giving cause for the subsequent congressional meetings, actions, and official documents for the newly united states. The Fourth of July, then, is a day to celebrate our political processes. It is a day to celebrate that we are continuing to be a country that strives to uphold the ideals set out in the Declaration of Independence, including equality, life, liberty, safety, and happiness.

Independence Day is traditionally a day for picnics, parades, and civic speeches. In many small villages and towns these traditions are still alive. Some communities hear speeches given by junior high students who have competed to write the best civic speech essay for the July 4 celebration. In a way these speeches by children and local politicians recall great orators who also spoke of the ideals of the Declaration. One may think of Abraham Lincoln's Gettysburg Address and Martin Luther King Jr.'s speech, "I Have A Dream."

Justo L. González derives the title of his book *Mañana: Christian Theology From a Hispanic Perspective*, from the word *mañana*, which in Spanish means "tomorrow." According to González, some people interpret the expression *mañana* used by many Latinos as to be a sign of laziness or procrastination, leaving for tomorrow what can be done today. While this may be the case in some instances, González argues that for a people who live in bondage, suffering, and poverty, *mañana* can also be taken as a sign of hope. . . . Such a reading of *mañana* leads to two conclusions. First, *mañana* manifests the hope that the future can be radically different from the present, that tomorrow can be radically different from the present, that tomorrow might be a better day than today. Second, it implies that this future places a demand on the present and upon us by asking why it is not so.
—Luis G. Pedraja[1]

The ideals named in the Declaration are worthy of ongoing attention, engagement, and mutual admonition. And so is the process. The civic and congressional events leading up to July 4 and those events that shaped the writing of the other subsequent official documents are all examples of public work, public debate, and public decision making. It is good and right to celebrate the content of this day and crucial to remember the public actions surrounding this day. Along with this we recall that the colonists were not the first inhabitants of this land, it was a nation of indigenous peoples' nations. In our continued efforts at public work and public decision making we do well to watch for those who are marginalized from the debates. These aspects of Independence Day can remind churches to evaluate our place in the public sphere and the way we, all the baptized, are civic theologians.

TEXTS FOR THE DAY

The Episcopal Church, in *The Book of Common Prayer*, appoints lections for July 4: Deut. 10:17–21; Psalm 145 (or 145:1–9); Heb. 11:8–16; and Matt. 5:43–48. The Old Testament reading is from Deuteronomy and is concerned with the marginalized. In this text we are told that the Lord our God is God of all gods and makes justice for the marginalized, the orphan, widow, stranger. This declaration is followed by creedal language reminding the hearers of the mighty acts of God that they have seen, reminding the hearers of their ancestors who were freed from Egypt by this God. In this passage the Israelites are instructed in obedience to God, which means following the commandments. Obedience means being in God's image and loving neighbor in a way that reaches across boundaries of nationality, ethnicity, or station in life. Taken literally, these verses speak clearly of God above any other gods (including ways we fashion state and nation as gods) and the social ethic of care for the other. Understood in historical context, the verses still underscore these ideals. The book of Deuteronomy originated in the seventh century B.C.E. during the increasing threat of imperial domination by Assyria and Babylon. The writers make use of ancient Near Eastern state treaties in the description of Israel's covenant with God. But whereas other nations used these treaty forms to show national allegiance to a state or ruler, the oath called for here is to the divine sovereign, not a human overlord. The psalm appointed for the day repeats the ideas of God as the divine king who oversees all generations and all creation.

> With malice toward none, with charity for all, with firmness in the right as God give us to see the right, let us strive on to finish the work we are in, to bind up the nation's wounds, to care for him who shall have borne the battle and for his widow and his orphan, to do all which may achieve and cherish a just and lasting peace among ourselves and with all nations.
> —Abraham Lincoln, "Second Inaugural Address," March 4, 1865

The text from Hebrews cites models of faith as seen in Abraham, Isaac, and Jacob. They are examples because they possessed a way of seeing God's reality, trusting beyond that which could be seen by other humans. And yet this text names them as strangers to the land, foreigners who sought a different homeland. It is the city of God that is prepared for them. This passage continues the theme of human allegiance to God in a way that understands all earthly homelands; states and nations are at best penultimate. This text also continues the theme of strangers and foreigners and here, in a reversal, the stranger Abraham is the father of all nations.

The text from the Gospel according to Matthew is an account of Jesus' reinterpretation of the law. Here Jesus expands the commandment to love neighbor to be a commandment to love enemies. This human work is far beyond loving those who love us. Instead, perfect obedience now includes loving the enemy. With this text set next to the other texts it is not just that Israel cares for the stranger and orphan and widow or that God rules over all rulers. This commandment purports that even if we recognize the enemy in strangers or in strange nations that we are to love. God is sovereign in holiness and justice and we are to be perfect as God is perfect.

If preaching a midweek observance of Independence Day, the preacher may choose to use these texts. Or the preacher may choose to follow the appointed Sunday texts of a particular lectionary system. If preaching in the Sunday assembly, the Sunday texts are the preaching texts. Either way, the preacher may refer to Independence Day themes. July 4 will always occur during the time after Pentecost and therefore in that time of the liturgical year when the readings focus on the work of the church as the body of Christ in the world. It may not be far off, then, to work with particular themes of this day alongside the focus of the Sunday texts. Some general ideas about Independence Day have already been named: celebration of independence from tyrannical powers; celebration of the civic and political privileges and duties of all citizens; all nations under God; scriptural injunctions to care for stranger and enemy; God alone is sovereign, judging even earthly rulers. The preacher cannot work with all of these themes but perhaps one or more may fit with the focus of the Sunday texts. If the preacher uses the lections mentioned here it will be important to find a word of good news. But the news is there: God alone is our ruler (Deuteronomy); God gives us homeland (Hebrews); though we are all strangers (Gentiles), God makes us a nation (Matthew alongside the other readings). In all

> There is not one of us, individually, racially, socially, who is fully complete in the sense of having in himself all the excellence of all humanity. And this excellence, this totality is built up out of the contributions of the particular parts of it that we all can share with one another. I am therefore not completely human until I have found myself in my African and Asian and Indonesian brother because he has the part of humanity which I lack.
> —Thomas Merton[2]

of this the preacher will need to consider the context and in particular the prevailing attitudes about the national holiday.

FOR FURTHER COMMENT

Additional comments on these Scripture texts, in part or in full, may be found in the seasonal volumes of *New Proclamation* as follows:

- Psalm 145 or 145:1-9—Year A, Propers 9, 13, 20; Year B, Proper 12; Year C, Proper 27
- Hebrews 11:8-16—Year C, Proper 14
- Matthew 5:43-48—Year A, Epiphany 7

Notes

1. "Eschatology," Luis G. Pedraja, in *Handbook of Latina/o Theologies*, ed. Edwin David Aponte and Miguel A. De La Torre (St. Louis: Chalice, 2006), 116–17.

2. Thomas Merton, *A Eucharist Sourcebook,* compiled by J. Robert Baker and Barbara Budde (Chicago: Liturgy Training, 1999), 18.

LABOR DAY

First Monday in September:
September 1 (earliest)–September 7 (latest)

Jennifer L. Lord

Suggested Texts
Gen. 3:14-19
Psalm 127
Rev. 21:22-27
John 15:1-8

KEY THEMES

- The relationship between new life in Christ and human work.
- The relationship between local and global economies.
- The economy of the Trinity.

Preachers know that there are aspects of sermons that are for the whole human condition. And there are ways that our sermons are shaped so that they speak to particular congregations and particular needs. One preacher said that a sermon is biblical not because of how much Scripture it quotes but because it is dialogical: it speaks to the particular context just as Scripture is the account of God's ongoing conversation with humanity.

Being dialogical will strengthen a sermon that attends to the civil occasion of Labor Day. For instance, the preaching context of churches along the southern border of the United States begs that preachers attend to issues of legal and illegal immigration that are lived out each day. The preaching that occurs in the context in a dying mill town or an economically depressed coal town will address different dynamics. And sermons preached in churches near Wall Street will be different than all of these. And yet sermons will be this particular in a way that focuses on immediate context while still connecting the assembly to contexts beyond their own.

While Labor Day for many marks the end of summer, it was an occasion created to honor the achievements of American workers for the well-being of the country. In the early 1880s a New York Union committee organized a day off from work for parades and family picnics. By 1885 this occurred in many industrial centers and gained government recognition as many states adopted the holiday. Craft guilds with trained laborers and other unions of skilled and unskilled laborers formed and reformed, institutionalizing the complexities of American work in historical movements.

The early Labor Day celebrations were to laud the social and economic achievements of these workers. Some of the issues in the early days were fair wages, decent working conditions and management-worker relationships, and training for unskilled workers. In our time we have this same list. We want to value workers and good work. We want the opportunity for all to be employed and no one to be underemployed. We want to value the worker above the profit. We want all work to be for the health and welfare of a good and just society and for a good and just global society.

> One paradox of the Eucharist is this: in breaking, we are made whole. As bread is fragmented, the body of Christ draws together. Work that is broken open no longer belongs to itself or to a single worker, but to the whole world. Our work becomes whole, too, as it is broken for others, as the work of one draws on the work of many.
> —David H. Jensen[1]

What is our work in God, in this lifetime we have? Some of us do not have the work we want; it is drudgery and we are demeaned. Yet some of us use language of blessing and calling to describe our work. Some of us work too hard by choice—an addiction that impinges on leisure and rest. Some of us cannot find the work we want, or need for survival. Some of us have good relations in our places of work. Some of us endure work situations that demean, cause pain, and even endanger us. Some of us are isolated from others by our work. Some of us only know ourselves by our work.

A sermon that attends to the occasion of Labor Day cannot take on all the complexities of the American work situation. However, all of these intricacies cannot be ignored for the purpose of generalized statements about working too hard or paying attention to our calling in our life's work. What are the dynamics about the congregation's context that shape their attitudes toward work? What are the dynamics of individuals' occupations that will give the preacher insights about work situations and values about work? It is not that these things show up in a sermon (it is rare that there is a reason for the preacher to announce someone's work situation from the pulpit). These are ways of describing the operative theology of work in our context. What is it and what could it be? Labor Day is one time to think about these questions.

TEXTS FOR THE DAY

Labor Day occurs on the first Monday of September. For the church, Labor Day will always fall during Ordinary Time when our readings proclaim the life of the church in the life of Jesus Christ. The readings during this time emphasize faith, belief, and community—giving pictures of what community in Christ looks like. The preacher will often work with the passages of the RCL (or BCP or LFM) and look to make connections between the occasion of Labor Day and the set texts. A way to think about these connections is to identify the claims that these texts make on our lives and consider what these claims mean for our time with work. In doing this, the preacher should take care to think through all the possible work situations represented in the congregation as well as all the possible work situations that may not be represented but that Christians should not ignore. For instance, the preacher may identify lives burdened with work schedules and lack of Sabbath rest but the preacher will also need to call us beyond a sense of taking care of ourselves to the bigger picture of other workers' needs (employment? decent conditions? fair wages?). Again, the preacher can ask what these texts say about a theology of work for all people. What follows are suggestions for readings related to the occasion of Labor Day.

Almighty God, you have so linked our lives one with another that all we do affects, for good or ill, all the other lives: So guide us in the work we do, that we may do it not for self alone, but for the common good; and, as we seek a proper return for our own labor, make us mindful of the rightful aspirations of other workers, and arouse our concern for those who are out of work; through Jesus Christ our Lord, who lives and reigns with you and the Holy Spirit, one God, for ever and ever. Amen
—Collect for Labor Day, *The Book of Common Prayer*

Genesis 3:14-19 is an account of God's punishment for human sin. This particular punishment is about the original connections being broken down. Now the connections between woman and man and between humans and the rest of the created order are in disrepair. The economy is not as it was created to be. The inclusion of this passage provides the truth told in mythic form: interdependence degrades to personal toil and connections with all others are disregarded. Through the images of this text we are able to name the way things are in our world. *Psalm 127* could be the accompanying responsive reading, with its emphasis on God's activity in human work and in human households.

Revelation 21:22-27 tells of a different order. Here, in the new heaven and the new earth, is a holy city. It is where God has wiped away all tears and has announced that all things are being made new. There is no temple there, for the temple is God Almighty and the Lamb. But there is a city. There is a city with commerce—the nations come and the kings come and the people bring the glory of the nations to this city. In this end-time vision there is a city, a city made new by the glory of God. And this city remakes us. It is a safe place (its gates are always open) and it is a place of glory. Here, as opposed to the first reading, there is sense of all things working together, all people working in the city with joy and all things giving God glory.

John 15:1-8 gives us yet another way to focus on issues raised by the occasion of Labor Day. Here is language to talk about living in God's household. To abide in God is to make our home in God. We are at home in community; we make our home with others as we live in God. The holy center is no longer the temple (as in Revelation) but is the triune God and our abiding in God. In this relationship there is abiding, pruning, flourishing, bearing fruit, and giving glory to God. There is an economy of activity in taking nourishment and bearing the fruit of discipleship. It is an image for the world community: like our life in God, like life in the economy of the Trinity, we participate in the relationship of giving and taking that is a good, just, and productive exchange.

LABOR DAY PREACHING

The reading from Genesis 3 may function as a way of naming people's attitudes and experiences of work: sometimes (or often) painful and demeaning. It is crucial to set out gospel claims next to this passage: there is no condemnation in Christ and even our work is redeemed in God. The preacher will take care not to equivocate poor working conditions (or unemployment) with God's present judgment. Instead, let Genesis 3 stand as a judgment on the ways that our worldly economies perpetuate sin as we disregard the needs and rights of workers worldwide in favor of product and profit. The preacher will also need to reflect on the balance between global and local community. In Christ we are members of both and always attending to the relationships of both communities. The preacher does not need to be an economic specialist but will do well to think about justice issues of work and workers and the interrelatedness of local and global economies. The preacher can practice empathic imagination and consider different working scenarios around the world as a way to gain perspective on a local community. In all of this the preacher will strive not to preach in a manner that alienates a congregation but, by setting out our hope in Christ alongside human brokenness, call us to a more truthful and faithful way of life in the city of God, which in Christ Jesus is now.

Come, labor on!
Who dares stand idle, on the harvest plain
While all around us waves the golden grain?
And to each servant does the Master say,
"Go work today."

Come, labor on!
No time for rest, till glows the western sky,
Till the long shadows o'er our pathway lie,
And a glad sound comes with the setting sun,
"Well done, well done."
–Jane Laurie Borthwick[2]

For Further Comment

Additional comments on these suggested texts, in full or in part, may be found in the seasonal volumes of *New Proclamation* as follows:

- Psalm 127—Year B, Proper 27
- Revelation 21:22-27—Year C, Easter 6
- John 15:1-8—Year B, Easter 5

Notes

1. David H. Jensen, *Responsive Labor: A Theology of Work* (Louisville: Westminster John Knox, 2006).

2. "Come, Labor On" (text: Jane Laurie Borthwick, 1859), in *The Presbyterian Hymnal* (Louisville: Westminster John Knox, 1990), no. 415.

VETERANS' DAY / REMEMBRANCE DAY

NOVEMBER 11

JENNIFER L. LORD

SUGGESTED TEXTS
Deut. 10:12-13, 17-
21 or Amos 5:11-15
Psalm 2 or 117
Gal. 5:13-26
John 8:31-36

KEY THEMES

• Nationalism.
• Justice for the marginalized.
• Freedom in Christ.

Veterans' Day is a legal holiday appointed by the President of the United States to honor veterans of American wars for their patriotism, their love of country, and their willingness to serve and sacrifice for the common good. Since 1918 this day has been observed on November 11th (with the brief exception of moving the commemoration to a Monday in 1971, a decision that was overturned in 1978), regardless of the day of the week.

Veterans' Day historically has a broader purpose than patriotism and heroism. Many may recall the earlier designation of the day as Armistice Day. Though the official treaty ending World War I was signed on June 28 of 1919, the armistice between Allied forces and Germany occurred seven months earlier on November 11, 1918. The following year President Wilson declared November 11th Armistice Day and that its purpose was to recognize the heroism of those who had died in the war to end all wars and to show that America had sympathies for peace and justice with all nations. The theme of international peace continued with a declaration by Congress in 1926 that spoke of thanksgiving and prayer to perpetuate peace and mutual understanding between nations. In 1938 Armistice Day was declared a legal holiday for the purpose of honoring the veterans of World War I and for the cause of world peace. Yet World War I had not ended all wars.

Attention to the great mobilization of forces for World War II and the war in Korea necessitated a means of honoring these veterans as well. With this, the emphasis on international peace and understanding gave way to a focus on American veterans, their heroism and service to country. In 1954 Congress amended the title and description of the day: thus Armistice Day was changed to Veterans' Day and the focus was to honor veterans of all American wars.

There are strong emotions associated with honoring veterans. Some Christians oppose all war and view this honoring as vainglory, a misdirected effort. Others oppose war but still wish to honor the persons who have protected this nation and who have voluntarily put themselves in positions of danger. There are veterans who disagree with military mind-set and who criticize military power and decision making. There are civilians and military personnel who understand military service to be the highest calling for a human life. Gulf War veterans received an intentional heroes' welcome, which is in contradistinction to the way the American public spurned Vietnam War veterans. These political positions do not describe the variety of personal experiences around war. In our time Cindy Sheehan represents parents of military personnel who have been killed in action; parents who do not support the war in Iraq. Other parents of military personnel support the United States' sacrifices in this war. Many people in a congregation will know someone who is currently on active duty in the Middle East or elsewhere in the world and concern for this person's safe homecoming is the preeminent focus of their prayers. Add to this list the dynamic of the elderly, mostly men, who have served in past wars but who are ignored because of the dynamics of American culture that favors youth. I write this during months when there has been a great amount of news coverage about the shortage of medical and psychiatric care for veterans of the Iraq War. One recent radio interview with a mental health counselor for the Department Of Veteran's Affairs talked about his work to get traumatized veterans into care.

These are too many issues for one sermon. But even this beginning list indicates that the preacher should never think that one approach to Veterans' Day represents the mind-set of the entire congregation. Rather, like preaching in

> Righteous God, you rule the nations.
> Guard brave men and women
>   who risk themselves in battle for their county.
> Give them compassion for enemies
>   who also fight for patriotic causes.
> Keep our sons and daughters from hate that hardens,
>   or from scorekeeping with human lives.
> Though they be at war,
>   let them live for peace,
>   as eager for agreement as for victory.
> Encourage them as they encourage one another,
>   and never let hard duty separate them
>   from loyalty to your Son, our Lord, Jesus Christ. Amen.
> —Prayer for Those in the Military, *Book of Common Worship*, PC(USA)

times of crisis, the preacher does well to briefly acknowledge many attitudes and emotions before moving to focus on one particular aspect of this commemoration. Also, as with crisis sermons, there is a good deal of theological groundwork that can be laid ahead of time. The preacher can be thinking of the theological ramifications of these different attitudes toward war and Veterans' Day celebrations throughout the year. Theological groundwork could include: Does Christian faith and witness mean nationalism trumps international relationships? What are theological ways to talk about patriotism? How are Christians supposed to treat persons different from ourselves? How do Christians understand other world religions? What are theological ways to talk about violence? What are the differences between honoring a person and supporting (or not) a larger movement?

Texts for the Day

Although none of the lectionary traditions give official selections of texts for Veterans' Days services, an Internet search may help you locate appropriate pericopes used by different traditions. For instance, the General Board of Discipleship of the United Methodist Church, in its worship Web site (http://www.gbod.org/worship/) suggests a number of texts and other resources. The Web site suggests a choice between *Deuteronomy 10* and *Amos 5* for the first reading. In Deuteronomy the reader must pay attention to the way 10:12-13 redefines obedience to God as obedience of fixed law as it has been expounded in chapters 8–10. The rest of this lection emphasizes that God is mighty and just and cares for all the marginalized of society; specifically that God renders justice both for Israel and for the stranger (resident alien). A key focus in this passage is that this justice work is normally the prerogative of the monarch and here God Almighty does this work in human history. Here *hesed*, steadfast love, goes across ethnic and national lines. The Amos reading reiterates the theme of treatment of the poor and marginalized. What is key is that Amos is prophesying in the early eighth century, a time of Israel's prosperity but also a time when the wealthy took advantage of the poor. Throughout the book Amos stresses Israel's responsibility toward other nations and the marginalized within Israel.

Psalms 2 and 117 are suggested responsive readings. While *Psalm 2* is an enthronement psalm, asserting Israel's divinely appointed king over kings of other nations, and *Psalm 117* calls all nations to praise Israel's God,

I am entitled to despair over the likelihood of further atrocities. Indolence and cowardice do not drive me—despair drives me. I remade my war one word at a time, a foolish, desperate act. When I despair, I am alone, and I am often alone. In crowded rooms and walking the streets of our cities, I am alone and full of despair, and while sitting and writing, I am alone and full of despair—the same despair that impelled me to write this book, a quiet scream from within a buried coffin. Dead, dead, my scream.

What did I hope to gain? More bombs are coming. Dig your holes with the hands God gave you.

—Anthony Swafford[1]

the preacher is wise to recall that these are chosen as responses to the first reading. Perhaps Israel's God is to be praised because Israel's God also demands just action for all people of all nations.

The proposed second reading from *Galatians 5* stresses freedom from the law yet emphasizes mutual submission by asserting that those in Christ are slaves to one another. The list describing works of the flesh is contrasted with the list describing fruit of the Spirit. Though free from the law, this fruit of the Spirit is indeed the sum of the law, loving others as we love self. The suggested Gospel reading from *John 8* contains an encounter between Jesus and religious authorities (and those who follow them). Jesus claims to be the way to know truth yet his listeners balk at being slave to him. Jesus counters that he is able to make them free.

None of the suggested texts give a foothold for a type of honoring of persons apart from life in Christ. Instead there are words of judgment against a nation that pursues its own supremacy without concern for other nations. There are prophetic words against any national practices that would eschew care for the poor and marginalized. People who do not follow the law of loving God and neighbor are not in obedience to God. The national themes of patriotism and heroism are tempered by this aspect: the corporate nature of our life with God and the command to ethical actions in our life together toward each other, stranger, and marginalized. Only in the triune God are we free. The preacher cannot, then, lightly cite themes of Veterans' Day akin to what one will hear on the evening news. The preacher must listen to the texts, and with the sensitivity of a pastoral caregiver who attends to where people are yet calls them to more in Christ, set out the gospel of God for us in these texts. It may well be that the preacher calls us to see how we break the commandments as we pursue national supremacy in lieu of care for others, but the preacher will do this in a way that not only echoes the strength of the prophets but also in a manner clothed with love.

For Further Comment

Additional comments on the suggested texts, in full or in part, may be found in the seasonal volumes of *New Proclamation* as follows:

- Amos 5:11-15—Year B, Proper 23
- Psalm 2—Year A, Last Epiphany/Transfiguration
- Galatians 5:13-26—Year C, Proper 8
- John 8:31-36—Year A, Proper 12

Notes

1. Anthony Swafford, *Jarhead: A Marine's Chronicle of the Gulf War and Other Battles* (New York: Scribner, 2003), 254.

HARVEST DAY

Jennifer L. Lord

Suggested Texts
Isa. 25:6-9
Psalm 23
2 Cor. 9:6-15
Matt. 9:35—10:8

KEY THEMES

- The relationship between abundance and benevolence.
- The global dynamics of food production and availability.
- Theological understandings of church as both laborer and as harvest.

The church uses agricultural language. As disciples we plant, water, and sow. And we are those whom the triune God plants, waters, and sows. This language appears throughout Scripture and Harvest Day is an occasion to live in these images. Churches have the option of celebrating the occasion of Harvest Day at any time, though in the Northern Hemisphere it is commonly associated with fall harvest times. Both Scripture and Christian tradition speak to the foci of this occasion.

Israel was once nomadic but became agrarian. The Scriptures connect Israel's agricultural practices to Israel's relationship with God: God is the landowner; Israel is God's vineyard; God desires plentiful harvests; poor harvests are God's punishment for sin; God is praised for good harvests. The annual religious festivals of the covenant people were layered onto the agricultural cycles of their livelihood. In the Old Testament, Pentecost is the harvest festival of first fruits and Tabernacles is the festival of ingathering from threshing floor and wine press. Passover occurred at the time of the barley festival. In the New Testament this agrarian language is adopted and turned toward christological meanings. Paul speaks about the resurrection of Christ in terms of first fruits. And in the Christian life we give our best and first to God and God's work in the world: our first-fruit offerings. Both Christ and we are harvests of God.

In medieval times the church in many places observed what were known as Ember days, a Christian observance layered on pagan agricultural festivals. Ember days were those series of days, three or four times a year, that were singled out for the purposes of spiritual renewal through prayer, fasting, and almsgiving. The times of the year corresponded with sowing and harvest times. The general Roman calendar no longer includes these days, but it is important to note that both Ember days and Rogation days (days of intercessory prayer) were marked by remembrance of God's providence over crops and seasons.

Observances of Harvest Day do well to acknowledge contemporary complexities that are a part of the human–food source relationship. For instance, some Christians live in urban centers and are distant from a sense of dependence on seasons and crop productivity. For many of us, everything is always available; our grocery stores have multiple suppliers. A 2006 disruption of the U.S. supply of a favorite leafy green vegetable (due to food borne illness) lasted only for a month. Yet other Christians live close to the cycle of the seasons and drought, heavy rains, unseasonable cold or heat are a daily concern. A few years ago many Amish farmers in Lancaster County, Pennsylvania, were working to bring in the corn crop but a series of heavy storms made the harvest impossible. The news headlines told the rest of us that the area's bishop had finally granted a dispensation to those farmers, permitting them to use mechanical means to harvest the crop. In a dire case, the community's traditional reliance on horse and human muscle was honorably set aside for the importance of the harvest and its livelihood.

Industrial agriculture has supplanted a complete reliance on the sun for our calories with something new under the sun: a food chain that draws much of its energy from fossil fuels instead. (Of course, even that energy originally came from the sun, but unlike sunlight it is finite and irreplaceable.) The result of this innovation has been a vast increase in the amount of food energy available to our species; this has been a boon to humanity (allowing us to multiply our numbers), but not an unalloyed one. We've discovered that an abundance of food does not render the omnivore's dilemma obsolete. To the contrary, abundance seems only to deepen it, giving us all sorts of new problems and things to worry about.—Michael Pollan[1]

Yet harvest is not available to all. Many people participate in or sponsor others in C.R.O.P. (Communities Responding to Overcome Poverty) walks. Over two thousand communities in the United States provide funds through these walks so that the agency can partner with eighty countries in life-giving projects. Since 1985 Farm Aid concerts have provided emergency relief to thousands of family farmers across the United States when they have faced foreclosure due to bad harvests, low crop prices, or predatory lending practices that favor big agribusiness operations.

And other complexities include how we relate to food personally and communally: we have eating disorders; we overeat transfats; we eat organic and fair trade foods; food is manipulated to meet our desires (low fat, no sugar, low carbohydrates); we eat foods with high "food miles" (that is, how far our food travels to be on the plate in front of us and how much energy is used for that travel); we must forsake the feast days of the church because of health problems; we neglect the interrelatedness of harvest, global economy, and climate crisis. And Harvest is beyond food: we harvest wind energy, natural gas, ocean currents, and oil. And perhaps we even harvest persons for low wage labor. Perhaps theologically we, the laborers, are all immigrant workers: in the end the land is not our own. All harvests are about global connections, individuals, labor, and justice.

Texts for the Day

Harvest Day observations often occur at the end of the season of Pentecost and as we look forward to Advent. Both liturgical times bear the images and themes of harvest: the church is God's harvest—the body of Christ as life of plenty for the world; the church and world as the great and final harvest. Congregations may consider harvest themes in Thanksgiving Day observances. If a community wants to hold a harvest observation midweek the Scripture selections might include Isa. 25:6-9; Psalm 23; 2 Cor. 9:6-15; and Matt. 9:35—10:8.

The imagery in Isaiah brings us to the top of a mountain and the feast of fat things—food and wine that is for sustenance and joy. In this portion of First Isaiah we hear this prophecy of restoration and plenty. An unnamed city is destroyed (24:10-13) and in its place God vindicates the poor and the needy. Now all nations have their tears wiped away and all peoples are brought to this mountain for a feast. Isaiah sets out this eschatological mountaintop scene in contrast to the invasions and wars that tore apart eighth-century Judah. There is a difference between God's people and the empires of the world.

In the psalm a table is set before us, too. There is plenty given in pastureland, in water, in anointing, at the table. Instead of being brought to a mountain for this sustenance and abundance, we are accompanied, guided, and brought to safe dwelling.

With Paul's words to the church at Corinth the notion of abundance is not only available but becomes that which is to be shared. Here it is not that we are invited to abundance or shepherded with abundance. Rather, our abundance in the life of God is factual and we are to share out of that richness. Paul writes to a church that exists in the Hellenistic culture of a large city, asking them to share (a collection for the Jerusalem church) because what is shared is from God's

Harvest is a commonplace liturgical metaphor that can draw us, not only to our own full dinner table, but in two other directions as well. One is to the triune God, the Bread who is God, the firstfruit who is the resurrected Christ, the fields of mown grain that is the Spirit in the community. The second direction is toward all who suffer from lack of harvest we tend to take for granted. We do well to add a second couplet to the traditional table prayer:

Come, Lord Jesus, be our guest,
and let these gifts to us be blest.
Blest be God, who is our Bread.
May all the world be clothed and fed.

—Gail Ramshaw[2]

sufficiency. It is to be shared with those in another city that is far away from them as a cross-cultural, connectional church offering. Here our benevolence is harvested for use now that may not be in our physical presence.

In the Gospel According to Matthew Jesus is the one who proclaims and fulfills God's plan. This Gospel was written following the destruction of the Temple. It was a time when the church struggled for leadership and clarity of purpose: What laws would govern? In this time of instability, here is a passage that presents a summary of Jesus' healing, teaching, and proclamation of the good news of God's kingdom. Using harvest language, it says that the harvest is made up of all those who are like sheep without a shepherd. The harvest is all the sick and diseased and harassed ones. Here are words about the purpose of the church: laborers for the harvest of the sick, harassed, and needy ones. We are to be laborers for the harvest.

Come, you all: enter into the joy of your Lord. You the first and you the last, receive alike your reward; you rich and you poor, dance together; you sober and you weaklings, celebrate the day; you who have kept the fast and you who have not, rejoice today. The table is richly loaded: enjoy its royal banquet. The calf is a fatted one: let no one go away hungry. All of you enjoy the banquet of faith; all of you receive the riches of his goodness.
—St. John Chrysostom[3]

Harvest celebrations are ancient festivals of abundance and sustenance. God has once again provided for human need. The stockpiles are high and the foreseeable future includes the base provision of food. Yet harvest celebrations are also about human connections with the natural seasons and with all cycles of supply and demand. The suggested texts bring to our attention these additional dynamics of harvest: Who has plenty and who has nothing? What are other types of harvests? How are cycles of demand and supply connected? The preacher may choose to balance harvest/thanksgiving themes with the realities of global connections and universal needs: we cultivate awareness of plenty and thanksgiving in our lives and yet we labor for provision for all people. There are too many themes here to be mentioned in any one sermon. Yet these themes could be a lens for other texts during the time after Pentecost (with its many harvest themes). On this day the preacher will want to focus on one guiding idea or image that speaks to our sin: our complacency, our ignorance, our participation in cycles that hurt others. And the preacher will find gospel news that brings another way to live. As the preacher works to raise our awareness or to call us to action, it is on the foundation of gospel news. God gives harvest.

Additional comments on the suggested texts, in part or in full, may be found in the seasonal volumes of *New Proclamation* as follows:

- Isaiah 25:6-9—Year A, Proper 23; Year B, Easter Morning, All Saints; Years ABC, Easter Evening
- Psalm 23—Year A, Lent 4, Proper 23; Year B, Proper 11; Years ABC, Easter 4
- Matthew 9:35—10:8—Year A, Proper 6

Notes

1. Michael Pollan, *The Omnivore's Dilemma* (New York: Penguin, 2006), 7.

2. Gail Ramshaw, *Treasures Old and New: Images in the Lectionary* (Minneapolis: Fortress Press, 2002), 207.

3. John Chrysostom, "The Paschal Homily," in *A Triduum Sourcebook* (Chicago: Liturgy Training Publications, 1988), 111–12.

PEACE

JENNIFER L. LORD

SUGGESTED TEXTS
Jer. 6:13–15
Psalm 85
Rom. 16:17–20
Matt. 5:21–26

KEY THEMES

- The task and duty of peace.
- The relationship between interpersonal actions and global peace.
- Peace manifest in the Lord's Day gathering.

In order to speak about a Peace Sunday let us begin with what happens in our gatherings on Sunday mornings. Throughout the world each Sunday many Christians greet other Christians in their assembly with the peace of Christ. In most places this is done with a handshake. In some places it is done with a kiss. In other locations there may be a bow. The words accompanying these gestures echo the words Jesus speaks to the disciples in the locked room, "Peace be with you" (John 20:21).

It is an old greeting. In the Old Testament the word used is *shalom,* which carries with it a sense of wholeness, well-being, and prosperity. YHWH is *shalom.* Peace is God's gift of God's self and it is for the present and the future (see Ps. 29:11; Isa. 26:12; Ezek. 34:25–31). The Messiah himself will be the Prince of Peace (Isa. 9:6). This *shalom,* this peace, is relational rather than individual. It is for the whole community, for the nations, and between people and God.

All of this is layered into our Sunday greeting of peace. And these meanings help us to see our actions for what they are—a covenanting of sorts to be rooted in Christ's peace. It is a way of seeing that in our Sunday assemblies we do not simply greet one another with cheery salutations or innocuous inquiries as to our health. We speak Christ's peace to one another. This ritual greeting says something about what it is to be a part of Christ's body, the church, dwelling in the

Holy Spirit that Christ himself has breathed upon us. It forms us in a way that is distinct from the segregations of the rest of our lives. We greet all those around us and this may include the rich, the homeless, the working poor, those of different nationalities, races, and ethnicities, the physically and developmentally disabled, children, women, men. We are one body with all Christians; we keep Christ's peace with all peoples.

This peace occurs in the midst of the assembly and in the middle-time of the liturgy itself. Historically it has been understood in different ways: as the bridge between the service of Word and Eucharist; in relation to the offering; in direct relation to Eucharist. As an element of the liturgy it is *adiaphora*, a secondary (indifferent) thing but secondary only in the sense that it is to be caught up with and serve the central actions of Sunday. This is to say that the small act of passing the peace is integrally related to the meaning of Word and Sacrament, to the paschal mystery.

What then of Peace Sunday? If we understand that our repeated actions each Sunday are always about the triune God's peace and our being formed in that peace, what do we add to that? A place to start is to remember that our liturgies do not present a theme but instead welcome us into Christ and, through the texts of the day, speak a particular aspect of the gospel to us in that gathering. But each Sunday we are formed in the image of Christ who is our reconciliation, our *shalom*, the very wholeness of the world.

The history of Christianity shows the continuous tension between war and peace. Some understand Christ's peace to be peace that is brought about by human conquest. Others believe it means a lifestyle of nonviolence. We question whether or not peace is for the individual or the community. Scripture speaks communally but is replete with warrior and battle imagery alongside injunctions to peace. Jesus' name is that of the Old Testament warrior leader Joshua and the title *Christ* means "anointed one." Jesus Christ's own dying and rising is explained as a victorious battle over death and the powers of sin, and many Christians speak and affirm baptismal vows that include renunciations of these powers. The baptismal life itself is described by daily victories. And yet our life in Christ's dying and rising puts us in that locked upper room where the Spirit of peace is breathed upon us and we are sent out to the world in this peace.

"When are we going to get some peace liturgies?". . . [These] questioners I began with do not need "new liturgies" (a semantic barbarism) or different rites to bring their public worship into harmony with their social conscience. What has happened is that their social conscience has finally caught up with (in ways appropriate to our particular moment in space and time) the vision celebrated symbolically in the liturgy for thousands of years. . . . Like the phrase "institutional church," the phrase "peace liturgies" is a tautology. There ain't no other kind of church . . . and their ain't no other kind of liturgy.
–Robert W. Hovda[1]

A peace celebration speaks, then, to these matters that are intrinsically Christian. It is not a day that surprises parishioners with the notion that Christians think about matters of justice and righteousness for all peoples as a part of the peace of Christ. It is a day when preachers can point to the deep ways that we are formed by our ritual actions of peace in Word and Sacrament, in our prayers and offerings, in the passing of the peace. Peace celebration is a time to proclaim the gospel in its complexity and through the preacher's honest wrestling it is a time to see again the eschatological vision of the kingdom of God (already encountered in baptism) alongside our present realities of war and violence. It is a time for us to be taken more deeply into patterning our lives in Christ and questioning what this means for self, community, nation, and world.

Texts for the Day

Given this, the preacher will see the deep ways that each Sunday with its texts is a Peace Sunday. For the purpose of an additional midweek celebration the suggested texts are Jer. 6:13-15; Psalm 85; Rom. 16:17-20; and Matt. 5:21-26.

> The Lord has fed us with his own sacred flesh. . . . What excuse shall we have, if eating of the lamb we become wolves? If, led like sheep into the pasture, we behave as though we were ravening lions? This mystery requires that we should be innocent not only of violence, but of all enmity, however slight, for it is the mystery of peace. —St. John Chrysostom[2]

The prophet Jeremiah brings the cry of God to the world and in this cry we recognize when there is peace and when there is not. In this passage the leaders of the people cry out peace when there is none. These false words stand as an indictment of the leaders and of the people who have been seduced into thinking all is right in the world. Jeremiah speaks of the wound of the people; these false cries of peace only deepen the wound. Jeremiah speaks to the people of Judah under the threat of the Babylonian invasion and just before the ensuing destruction of the city and the Temple. Psalm 85 sets a petition for divine favor and blessing alongside Jeremiah. It presents a vision of the world awash in God's favor: the land is fertile and virtues are given human traits. It is the fullness of *shalom*.

Paul writes, near the very end of his letter to the church at Rome, a warning about those who cause dissensions. What is striking are his words in verse 20: "The God of peace will shortly crush Satan under your feet. The grace of our Lord Jesus Christ be with you." Here is battle imagery, Satan is the enemy and God is the warrior. But the defeat is for us and this warrior God is named here the God of peace. And this action of God is on a grand scale—this is not nation against nation or neighbor against neighbor but God against the personification of the powers of death and hell. Those powers, Paul says, back in Romans 8, will not hurt or overcome us.

The Gospel reading from Matthew brings this cosmic victory of peace to a communal level, even to a one-to-one level within the community. Here we are given Jesus' words just after the Sermon on the Mount. Jesus expands traditional understandings of the law: now anger and insult will receive the same recompense as murder. This is the text that finds its echo in 1 Corinthians: we are to be a community at peace with one another before bringing our offerings to the altar (or coming to the Eucharist). In this Gospel account, Jesus and his followers fulfill the law as taught by Jesus. This section of the Gospel (along with verses 38-42) is cited as key to understanding the nonviolence of Jesus' teaching and actions.

Peace Sunday is not a theme Sunday but is every Sunday when, through attention to the gospel and work with the texts, the preacher points us again to our peace in Christ. It is too much for one Sunday. But over time the preacher will help us faithfully engage with the ways that peace is more than the absence of war, that peace is more than inner clam, and that our local Sunday gathering forms us to be citizens of the world.

> A pacifist who is willing to endure the scorn of the unthinking mob, the ignominy of jail, the pain of stripes and the threat of death cannot be lightly dismissed as a coward afraid of physical pain . . . . A pacifist even now must be prepared for the opposition of the mob who think violence is bravery. A pacifist in the next war must be ready for martyrdom.
> —Dorothy Day[3]

FOR FURTHER COMMENT

Additional comments on the suggested texts, in part or in full, may be found in the seasonal volumes of *New Proclamation* as follows:

- Psalm 85—Year A, Proper 14; Year B, Advent 2, Proper 10; Year C, Proper 12
- Matthew 5:21-26—Year A, Epiphany 6

Notes

1. Robert W. Hovda, "Where Have You Been? 'Peace Liturgies' Are the Only Kind We Have!" in *Robert Hovda: The Amen Corner*, ed. John F. Baldovin (Collegeville, Minn.: Liturgical Press, 1994), viii.

2. St. John Chrysostom, *Homilies*, sermon 33, in *Short Breviary*, ed. Monks of St. John's (Collegeville, Minn.: St. John's Abbey Press, 1975), 220–21.

3. Dorothy Day, *The Catholic Worker* (May 1936), 8.

CONTRIBUTORS

William F. Brosend II is associate professor of homiletics at the School of Theology at Sewanee: The University of the South. Previously associate director of the Louisville Institute, he is an ordained Episcopal priest. His publications include a volume in the New Cambridge Bible Commentary Series, *James and Jude* (2004); *Conversations with Scripture: The Parables* (Morehouse, 2007); and the section on Advent and Christmas for *New Proclamation, Year B* (Fortress Press, 2005).

Bill Doggett is Associate Rector of Christ Episcopal Church on Capitol Hill in Washington, D.C., and holds a Ph.D. in liturgical studies from the Graduate Theological Union in Berkeley. A specialist in children's hymnody, he teaches and consults in worship and liturgical matters, including work for Wesley Theological Seminary and Washington National Cathedral.

Gordon W. Lathrop is Charles A. Schieren Professor of Liturgy, Emeritus, at the Lutheran Theological Seminary, Philadelphia. His many Fortress Press publications include *Holy Things: A Liturgical Theology* (1993); *Holy People: A Liturgical Ecclesiology* (1999); *Holy Ground: A Liturgical Cosmology* (2003); *The Pastor: A Spirituality* (2006); and, with Timothy Wengert, *Christian Assembly: Marks of the Church in a Pluralistic Age* (2004).

Jennifer L. Lord is associate professor of homiletics and dean of the chapel at Austin Presbyterian Theological Seminary, Austin. Ordained in the Presbyterian Church (U.S.A.), she has served churches in New York state and has taught previously at Lancaster Theological Seminary and the Graduate Theological Union, Berkeley, where she also earned her Ph.D.

David B. Lott is an editorial consultant who serves as series editor for *New Proclamation* and as online host for its companion Web site www.NewProclamation .com. His twenty years of experience in religious book publishing includes work for Augsburg Books, Fortress Press, the Alban Institute, and Cowley Publications. A resident of Washington, D.C., he is editor also of *Conflict Management in Congregations* (Alban Institute, 2000).

Ruth A. Meyers is professor of liturgics and academic dean at Seabury-Western Theological Seminary, Evanston, Illinois. A past president of the North American Academy of Liturgy, she is the author of *Continuing the Reformation: Re-visioning Baptism in the Episcopal Church* (Church, 1997), and coeditor, with Phoebe Pettingell, of *Gleanings: Essays on Expansive Language with Prayers for Various Occasions* (Church, 2001).

Gail Ramshaw is professor of religion at LaSalle University in Philadelphia and a scholar of liturgical language. A past president of the North American Academy of Liturgy and The Liturgical Conference, she served on the Revised Common Lectionary design committee and on the Church's Year task force for the Renewing Worship project of the ELCA. Her many publications include the Fortress Press books *Treasures Old and New: Images in the Lectionary* (2002), and *God Beyond Gender: Feminist Christian God-Language* (1995).

Craig A. Satterlee is associate professor at the Lutheran School of Theology at Chicago, where he holds the Axel Jacob and Gerda Maria (Swanson) Carlson Chair in Homiletics. His publications include *Ambrose of Milan's Method of Mystagogical Preaching* (Liturgical, 2002); *Presiding in the Assembly* (Augsburg Fortress, 2003); *When God Speaks through Change: Preaching in Times of Congregational Transition* (Alban, 2005); *The Christian Life: Holy Baptism and Life Passages* (Augsburg Fortress, 2007); and *When God Speaks through You; How Faith Convictions Shape Preaching and Mission* (Alban, 2007).

Gerard S. Sloyan is a priest of the Roman Catholic Diocese of Trenton, professor emeritus of religion at Temple University, and visiting professor of religion and religious education at Catholic University of America, Washington, D.C. His numerous books include the Fortress Press titles *The Crucifixion of Jesus* (1995); *Why Jesus Died* (2004); and *Preaching from the Lectionary: An Exegetical Commentary with CD-ROM* (2004).

About the Cover Artist:

Los Angeles artist John August Swanson is noted for his finely detailed, brilliantly colored Biblical pieces. His words are found in the Smithsonian Institution's National Museum of American History, London's Tate Gallery, the Vatican Museum's Collection of Modern Religious Art, and the Bibliothéque Nationale, Paris.

Full-color posters and cards of Mr. Swanson's work are available from the National Association for Hispanic Elderly. Proceeds benefit its programs of employment and housing for low-income seniors. For information, contact: National Association of Hispanic Elderly, 234 East Colorado Blvd., Suite 300, Pasadena, CA 91101, (626) 564-1988.